SOFIA COPPOLA

FOREVER YOUNG

SOFIA COPPOLA

FOREVER YOUNG

HANNAH STRONG

Little White Lies

Abrams, New York

Sofia taking a break on the grip truck while
filming *The Bling Ring*. Los Angeles, 2012.

CONTENTS

Sofia sampling Sofia Champagne on the
set of *Marie Antoinette*. Paris, 2005.

SOFIA COPPOLA: FOREVER YOUNG

Il Giardino di Sofia

ALICE ROHRWACHER

UN GIARDINO È il luogo misterioso dove molte storie hanno inizio. Forse, ancor più di un giardino, è la memoria di un giardino in cui non possiamo tornare ciò che ci spinge a raccontare.

Il rigoglioso giardino dell'Eden, il giardino selvaggio delle Esperidi, gli stupefacenti giardini pensili di Babilonia. . . . Oh, se potessimo entrarci! Oh, se potessimo stenderci all'ombra dei loro alberi, cogliere quei frutti, odorare quei fiori! Eppure, ne siamo stati esclusi. Sono ormai luoghi mitologici, pietre di paragone della nostra vita, nostalgia incolmabile e suadente di un altrove.

Tra tutti i giardini, per me che sono nata negli anni ottanta, ce ne è uno che i nostri antenati ancora non conoscevano, ma è uno dei primi che mi appare quando chiudo gli occhi. È il giardino di una villetta americana.

Si accede dalla porta sul retro, una porta chiara, luminosa. Abbraccia tutta la casa e la protegge, oltre le sue siepi si ripetono altri giardini all'infinito, come onde del mare. Lì erano ambientati gran parte dei film e delle serie che vedevamo. Era un luogo dei sogni, in cui sbocciavano amori, si costruivano case sugli alberi, si accendevano i primi baci, il luogo in cui gli amati ancora si arrampicavano di notte dalle finestre e i figli a turno dovevano tagliare l'erba. Io che crescevo tra campi brulli pieni di spine, tra paesi invasi dal cemento, sognavo quell'erba soffice, quelle storie avventurose come la cosa più deliziosa del mondo. E mi struggevo al pensiero che la mia casa era sbattuta ai venti, non era protetta da un giardino, e in più non aveva nessuna porta chiara sul retro.

Ma anche da questo giardino, dolce memoria d'infanzia, sono stata cacciata. La maga che mi ha svelato il suo mistero etereo e spietato è una delle più grandi registe che conosco, Sofia Coppola. Ricordo bene il giorno in cui, sul limite del millennio che stava per finire, sono andata a vedere "*il giardino delle Vergini Suicide.*" Quel giorno il mio sguardo si è trasformato. Sofia, come una Calipso dei nostri giorni, tesse una gabbia dorata, una bellissima prigione assolata da cui si può uscire solo attraverso la porta più buia e segreta, quella della morte.

Da allora ho sempre rincorso i suoi film come si rincorre un rito arcano, cercando le sue storie come si cercano le formule magiche per aprire nuove porte dell'anima.

Il suo sguardo fiorito e ironico, quanto spietato e affilato come una lama, mi ha accompagnato e trasformato. Il suo cinema è per me come l'isola di Ogigia in cui abitava la dea Calipso: è sempre *da qualche parte.*

Da qualche parte, sarebbe a dire in un luogo che tutti conosciamo ma non possiamo tracciare con sicurezza sulla mappa. Spesso sentiamo di riconoscerlo, ma mai fino in fondo. È un luogo dell'anima. E verso questo "*da qualche parte*" si muovono i suoi personaggi, che non sanno bene dove andare perché quello che importa è lo *stare,* che accolgono il loro destino come un vecchio amico ubriaco, con gioia mista a rassegnazione. Che siano diafane adolescenti spiate dalle finestre della memoria, che siano ragazzine perdute in un albergo che assomiglia a tutti gli alberghi del mondo, o uomini soli in cerca di una cura, che siano donne rese insolenti dalla solitudine o adolescenti bizzarre, su tutti è piombato addosso un destino senza che loro potessero farci niente. E nei suoi film Sofia traccia l'educazione di un'anima, l'educazione di un'attenzione, affinché anche un piccolo gesto possa produrre una eco poderosa. Si entra in un film di Sofia proprio come si entra in un giardino: all'inizio si è frastornati dai colori delle foglie, dei fiori, dai profumi e dai canti degli uccelli, ed è bello stare lì. Ci viene voglia di esplorare i viottoli segreti, di giocare con l'acqua di una fontana. Ma dopo poco lo sguardo viene condotto su un unico piccolo insetto che succhia il nettare di un unico fiore. E come d'incanto sparisce il giardino, sparisce l'abbondanza, per trovarsi di fronte a qualcosa di piccolo ed essenziale. Penso ad una delle mie scene preferite di *Lost in Translation*, la scena in cui Bob e Charlotte finiscono a letto non per fare l'amore, ma per parlare. Si raccontano il passato, il futuro, sogni e aspirazioni. E alla fine, tutto il loro intenso quanto vago rapporto si riassume in quel piccolo gesto con cui Bob sfiora il piede di Charlotte, e che racchiude in sé con precisione tutto l'amore non visto, le parole non dette.

Ecco, i personaggi di Sofia sanno tutti che non si finisce mai di crescere, e che crescere è sempre un mistero, un baratro che attrae e respinge. E che per crescere c'è sempre qualcosa a cui dobbiamo rinunciare, l'isola di Ogigia che dobbiamo, marinai nell'alba, abbandonare.

I personaggi di suoi film continuano ad accompagnarmi nel mio viaggio e sembrano guardarmi negli occhi e dirmi "non c'è niente che possiamo fare, è andata così", mentre sorridono e piano piano scompaiono portandosi nel buio il loro segreto.

Mentre penso ai suoi film, ai suoi personaggi, penso a una discesa, vertiginosa. Una scalinata che si scende di corsa, col cuore in subbuglio, tra il riso e il pianto, verso il mare. ✿

Sofia and *Somewhere* production designer
Anne Ross. Chateau Marmont, Los Angeles, 2009.

SOFIA COPPOLA: FOREVER YOUNG

Sofia's Garden

ALICE ROHRWACHER

A GARDEN IS a mysterious place, where many stories have their beginnings. Perhaps, even more than a garden, it is the memory of a garden we cannot return to that compels us to tell a story.

The verdant Garden of Eden, the wild Garden of the Hesperides, the stunning Hanging Gardens of Babylon. . . . If we could only enter them! Oh, to lie in the shade of their trees, pick those fruits, smell those flowers! And yet, we have been excluded from them. They are now mythological places, touchstones of our lives, the unbridgeable and persuasive nostalgia for an elsewhere.

Of all the gardens, there is one that our ancestors weren't aware of but is the first one I see, as someone born in the 1980s, when I close my eyes. It is the garden of a small American home.

It is accessed via the back door, a bright, light-colored door. It embraces the whole home and protects it; beyond its hedgerows are other gardens, repeated, stretching out infinitely like waves in the sea. This is where a large part of the films and series we watched were set. It was a place of dreams, where love blossomed, treehouses were built, first kisses were experienced, a place where lovers still climbed from windows at night and children took turns cutting the grass. Growing up among barren fields, overgrown with thorns, among villages invaded by cement, I would dream of that soft grass, those adventurous tales, as if they were the most delicious thing in the world. I was tormented by the thought that my house was beaten by the winds, unprotected by a garden and, what's more, lacked a bright back door.

But even from this garden, my sweet childhood memory, I was banished. The sorceress who revealed its ethereal and unforgiving mystery to me is one of the greatest directors I know, Sofia Coppola. I can easily recall the day when, on the verge of the new millennium, I went to see *The Virgin Suicides*. My gaze was transformed that day. Sofia, like a modern-day Calypso, weaved a golden cage, a beautiful, sun-kissed prison from which one can only exit through the darkest, most secret door, that of death.

From then on, I've always sought her films like one seeks an arcane ritual, searching for her stories like one searches for a magic formula to open new doors to the soul. Her ornate and ironic gaze, as ruthless and sharp as a blade, accompanied and transformed me. Her films are for me like the Island of Ogygia, home of the goddess Calypso: they are always *somewhere*.

Somewhere, is to say a place that we all know but cannot pinpoint with any certainty on a map. We often feel like we recognize it but never completely. It is a place of the soul. It is towards this somewhere that her characters travel, unsure of where to go because what matters is staying; they welcome their destiny like an old, drunken friend, with a mix of joy and resignation. Whether they are ethereal adolescents, spied through the windows of memory, young girls lost in a hotel that resembles every other hotel in the world, or lonely men in search of a cure; whether they are women turned insolent from solitude or bizarre adolescents; a fate has befallen all of them without them being able to do anything about it. In her films, Sofia traces the education of a soul, the education of attention so that even a small gesture can produce a thundering echo.

You enter one of Sofia's films just as you would enter a garden: initially, you are dazed by the colors of the leaves, by the smells and the birdsong, and you are content in being there. You want to explore secret pathways, to play with the water in a fountain. But shortly after, your gaze is drawn to a small insect that is sucking the nectar of a single flower. And, as if by magic, the garden disappears, abundance disappears, and you find yourself in front of something small and significant. I think back to one of my favorite scenes from *Lost in Translation*, the scene in which Bob and Charlotte end up in bed, not to make love but to talk. They talk about the past, the future, dreams and aspirations. In the end, the entirety of their relationship, as intense as it is indistinct, is summarized in that small gesture, where Bob brushes Charlotte's foot, which perfectly encapsulates all their unseen love, their unspoken words.

Sofia's characters all know that you never stop growing and that growing up will always be a mystery, a chasm that attracts and repels. And in order to grow up there is always something that you have to give up, the island of Ogygia that, as sailors at dawn, we must abandon.

The characters from her films continue to accompany me on my journey and seem to look me in the eyes with a smile, saying "there's nothing we can do, this is how it is," whilst slowly fading away, taking their secrets into the darkness.

When I think of her films, her characters, I think about a vertiginous descent. A staircase that you descend at great speed, your heart in turmoil, between laughter and tears, towards the sea. ✿

An Introduction

The first time I wanted to kill myself I was thirteen years old. I would stay up all night obsessing over everything and nothing, trying to work out how feasible it would be to hang from the high-sleeper bed in my room. After being referred to an adolescent psychiatric unit, I developed an obsession with art that reflected my own psychosis back at me. Susanna Kaysen's *Girl, Interrupted* and Sylvia Plath's *The Bell Jar* were seminal texts, but it was Sofia Coppola's *The Virgin Suicides*—discovered during my endless apathetic internet exploits brought on by insomnia and a desire for intimacy, or at least a synthetic approximation of it—that jolted me from the melancholia I had come to accept as inevitable.

WHAT WAS IT about those willowy teenage girls in suburban, seventies Michigan that called out to me from an ocean and a decade away? There was very little physical resemblance, as much as I might have wanted to look like a movie star and longed to live in the country I regarded as being at the vanguard of pop culture. But *The Virgin Suicides* was responding to a silent shout I had expressed into the void. It was the first film I saw that understood a condition I did not, and certainly one I couldn't articulate to my parents, friends, teachers, or doctors: the audacity of wanting to end your life before it's even begun.

After *The Virgin Suicides*, I threw myself wholeheartedly into Sofia's work. At the time she had made three films; I eagerly rented *Marie Antoinette* from my local library, and recall being somewhat disappointed at how frivolous it seemed. I was a self-serious adolescent who wanted to read history at Oxford University and didn't quite comprehend the concept of historical fiction as I would in years to come. Now, I take comfort in my initial misjudgement: the cinema of Sofia Coppola is the cinema of growing up.

I didn't read history at Oxford. I became more unwell, spending week after week in bed, and was eventually diagnosed with clinical depression and chronic fatigue syndrome. A long time after that, my depression was reassessed as borderline personality disorder. It's strange to come to terms with these truths, and even stranger to write them down for the whole world to see, but I believe these formative experiences are integral to my understanding of the world around me—in particular the films that have stayed with me and the influence they have had on my life.

The defining characteristic of Sofia's filmography is honesty. Across seven features and various other creative endeavors, she appears to be always in search of something real, from the teenage grief of her pastel debut to the marital strife in 2020's *On the Rocks*. While her privilege as the daughter of one of Hollywood's most renowned filmmakers is considerable, it also allows Sofia a sense of creative freedom; she has never tried to be her father, and her films are undoubtedly better for it, striking in their intimacy and vulnerability, drawing from fine art, fashion, pop music, and celebrity to create something both familiar and abstract at once.

Sofia Carmina Coppola was born on May 17, 1971, the youngest child and only daughter of Francis Ford and Eleanor Coppola. In her published diary *Notes on a Life*, Eleanor recalls an evening in New York City that spring, while Francis was shooting *The Godfather*. George Lucas and his then-wife Marcia Griffin were visiting for dinner, and Eleanor was heavily pregnant with Sofia. "You could have it on my birthday, you know, it's tomorrow," Lucas joked. At 9 p.m. Eleanor went into labor. She called her doctor who said, "Well, come in after midnight. If you come in before, you'll have to pay for a full day today." "It sounded right; we didn't have much money," Coppola writes. "Sofia was born at 2 a.m., on George's birthday."

Sofia's first acting role came when she was only a few months old, playing the infant Michael Francis Rizzi in the baptism scene in *The Godfather*, and Eleanor recalls watching how Marlon Brando interacted with her. "He lifted her out of my arms so tenderly, holding her with an ease that only comes from experience. He looked at her with intense interest, examining her long fingers and tiny toes. A few days later a little gold bracelet arrived. The card said, 'Dear Sofia, Welcome to the world. Love, Marlon.'"

Sofia would frequently appear in smaller roles within her father's films throughout her childhood, counting *The Godfather Part II*, *The Outsiders*, *The Cotton Club*, *Rumble Fish*, and *Peggy Sue Got Married* (in which she played Kathleen Turner's younger sister, years before casting her in *The Virgin Suicides*) among her early filmography. But if you look in the credits of these films—with the exception of *Peggy Sue Got Married*—Sofia is credited by the mononym "Domino," having decided at the age of ten to change her name to something more glamorous. It's charming to think that even the daughter of a lauded filmmaker could yearn for a more interesting moniker.

Eleanor's memoir provides an intimate look inside the Coppola family; a rarity given their taciturn nature. Sofia has always allowed her art to do the talking, and for the most part has led a very private life, but glimpses appear within her mother's selected diary entries. In her November 11, 1979 entry, Eleanor reflects on leaving eight-year-old Sofia at the family home in Napa, California, while she travels to Tokyo with Francis to visit the set of Akira Kurosawa's *Kagemusha*: "When I put her to bed she said 'Why are you gone so much? Why aren't you home more? I wish we could just be normal.'" But as Eleanor reflects some twenty-two years later, watching Sofia on the set of *Lost in Translation*, "Moviemaking, which as I grew up seemed so exotic, was now a way my family spent an evening together."

Sofia's first acting role independent of her father came in 1984, when she starred alongside Barrett Oliver and Shelley Duvall in Tim Burton's short film *Frankenweenie*, playing the role of Victor Frankenstein's classmate and neighbor Anne Chambers, who suffers a fright when the precocious young scientist brings his dead dog back to life. It's not a particularly demanding role; in her scene, Sofia appears in a blonde wig practicing aerobics with her Barbie doll in her bedroom, when the shadow of Sparky appears at her window. Mistaking the dog for a monster, Anne and her father confront the Frankensteins. Sofia only has one line (she berates Barbie for not working hard enough on her callisthenics) but her appearance does precede a body of work that both revels in and challenges stereotypes of girlhood.

A few years later, Sofia went to Paris for a summer to intern for—who else?—Chanel. "It was so exciting to go to Paris in the eighties at the height of Chanel," she later recalled. "I was in the design studio, so I got to see Karl Lagerfeld doing haute couture sketches for the final shows. It was incredible—he is so creative. I was getting coffee and doing intern stuff, but just to be around him was amazing." Fashion would remain an enduring interest for Sofia, but before that came the acting role which would live in infamy: Mary Corleone in *The Godfather Part III*.

On the morning of December 28, 1989, Eleanor Coppola received a phone call from Francis's assistant director on the set of *The Godfather Part III*. Winona Ryder, who had been cast as Michael Corleone's daughter Mary, was diagnosed with exhaustion and sent home from the production. Francis wanted to cast Sofia in her place. She had read for the role originally but Paramount insisted on a more famous name. Francis himself said, "I wanted her all along. I was fashioning Winona in her image." The part was plagued by a series of difficulties. Julia Roberts was interested, but scheduling conflicts with *Flatliners* prevented her involvement. Madonna had wanted the part, but at thirty-six was too old to play Diane Keaton's daughter. Rebecca Schaeffer had been set to audition but was tragically murdered by her stalker that morning.

Sofia stepped in at the last minute as a favor to her father, despite her reservations about taking on such an important part. Eleanor's memoir reflects the difficulties of the production; Francis and Sofia's relationship came under strain, and both were acutely aware of the pressure on each other. "Well-meaning people tell me I am permitting a form of child abuse, that she is not ready, not trained for what is being asked of her and that in the end she will be fodder for critics' bad reviews that could scar her for years." Eleanor writes, in an unfortunate case of foreshadowing, "I am told that Francis can't afford to take a chance on a choice that could weaken his work at this point in his career."

The press were not kind to the final installment in the Godfather trilogy, but reserved the majority of their contempt for Sofia's performance. Cries of nepotism were rife (seemingly forgetting Francis's sister, Talia Shire, had played Connie Corleone in the previous two films) and *Time* magazine scathingly declared that her "gosling gracelessness comes close to wrecking the movie" while Todd McCarthy judged "she can't act on a level with the other people in the film." Pauline Kael, writing for *The New Yorker*, was kinder: "It's obvious that this teenage girl is not a trained actress; she seems uncomfortable at times, and her voice lacks expressiveness—which is a serious flaw in her last scene. But she has a lovely and unusual presence; she gives the film a breath of life, and I grew to like her."

When Coppola released his preferred cut of the final Godfather film in 2020, under his original title *The Godfather Coda: The Death of Michael Corleone*, he reflected on the reception at the time of the original film's release, in particular the reaction to his daughter's performance. "It must have hurt her terribly," he said. "The daughter took the bullet for Michael Corleone—my daughter took the bullet for me." In his re-edited version, Coppola's most significant changes impact the beginning and the end of the film—chiefly, the scene of Michael Corleone's death as a lonely old man is removed. The final shot of the film sees him screaming silently as he cradles the body of Mary, who is caught in the crossfire during an attempt on her father's life.

Comparisons between *King Lear* and *The Godfather* have been made time and time again, but in opting to end Michael's story on the death of his beloved daughter, Coppola makes this connection in his third installment more explicit. Just as Lear, wracked by madness, held the dead body of his daughter Cordelia, Michael finally understands the consequences of his crooked ways—albeit too late to save her. He has to live with the knowledge he was responsible for his daughter's death. This is made all the more poignant by Sofia's performance, which lacks refinement, yes, but has no shortage of warmth and charm. She plays Mary as a naive teenager with a crush on her handsome cousin Vincent, played by Andy Garcia, desperately attempting to appear more grown-up than she really is. When she is shot on the steps of the Teatro Massimo, there's a childlike look of shock and fear on her face. Her death is the final straw for her father; the culmination of an epic familial saga about the lasting pain of grief and guilt. Michael tried to shield his daughter from his world, and even convinced his nephew to give up their romance in an attempt to protect her. But atonement always eludes the guilty man.

In the years since, Sofia has maintained a sense of humor about her critical mauling—undoubtedly it helps that her filmmaking efforts have proven so richly rewarding in the interim. "It was embarrassing to be thrown out to the public in that kind of way," she said in 2020. "But it wasn't my dream to be an actress, so I wasn't crushed. I had other interests. It didn't destroy me."

♛

After *The Godfather III*, Sofia shied away from appearing in front of the camera, taking a small role in Jefery Levy's 1992 indie comedy *Inside Monkey Zetterland* and another seven years later as one of Padmé Amidala's handmaidens in *Star Wars: Episode I – The Phantom Menace*, directed by family friend George Lucas. In the Coppola spirit of keeping things in the family, she also appeared in her brother Roman's directorial debut, *CQ*, in 2001 as the unnamed mistress of flashy movie producer Enzo, played by Giancarlo Giannini.

Instead, Sofia explored various other artistic endeavors. She studied at the liberal arts university Mills College and then joined the Fine Arts program at the California Institute of the Arts. "I wanted to be a painter, then my painting teacher told me that I wasn't a painter and I was really upset. I'm so glad he said that so I didn't waste more time," she told Lynn Hirschberg in April 2021. She then studied photography at the Art Center College of the Design under Paul

Jasmin, who encouraged her to explore her point of view, and would contribute street style and fashion photography to Japanese cult magazine *Dune*.

Inspired by her love of fashion, in 1994, Sofia launched a clothing line called Milk Fed with her friend Linda Meltzer, which became particularly popular in Japan, sparking an ongoing relationship with Tokyo that would later inspire the script for *Lost in Translation*. A profile in the January 1994 issue of *W* chronicled this endeavor. "I always wanted to be a designer," Sofia mused, "but I didn't think I knew enough. When I helped Kim Gordon and Daisy von Furth put on the X-Girl show in SoHo, I discovered they didn't know how to sew, either. I realized I admire people who just jump into things and do it."

Advertisements for the brand's cutesy baby tees feature Sofia alongside her friends Lisa Ann, Zoe Cassavetes, Amanda de Cadenet, and Stephen Dorff, future star of *Somewhere*. The girly, slogan-heavy styles feature the likenesses of Steve McQueen and Che Guevara printed on oversize garments; in the *W* article Sofia credits fashion designers Marc Jacobs and Anna Sui with guiding her through the process. Some twenty-six years later, Sofia's teenage daughter Romy Croquet would become the face of Jacobs's fashion line Heaven, directly inspired by the slogan tees and grunge fashion of the nineties that Sofia had helped to popularize.

The filmmaking came later, first with music videos and a short lived dalliance in television featuring plenty of Sofia's famous friends. It was the experience of creating her first short film that crystallized Sofia's interest

1
Sofia Coppola with her mother and father.

2
Sofia as a teenager.

3
Sofia on the set of *Peggy Sue Got Married* with Kathleen Turner, Don Murray, and Barbara Harris.

1

2

3

in filmmaking. "I had so many interests—design, photography, music—but I just couldn't find one medium that really clicked for me," she reflected in 2018. "Then I made a short film, *Lick the Star* in 1998, and it brought together all the things I loved."

◆

As I admire the piercing honesty of Sofia's work, I hope you might find a similar candidness in this book. It's strange to owe so much of your development as a person to someone you have never met—such is the nature of loving art in any form. Countless authors, musicians, artists, and filmmakers have left an indelible mark on people around the world, and will only ever comprehend a minute number of them. I have never met Sofia, never interviewed her about her work, but the process of writing this book has served as a sort of open letter to her as much as an exploration of her work.

Rather than opting for a chronological structure, I have chosen to match each of Sofia's feature films (and her 2015 holiday special) with a chapter heading that I feel best encapsulates its spirit: Innocence & Violence, Celebrity & Excess, Fathers & Daughters, and finally, Love & Loneliness. While certain titles could easily fit into multiple chapters, I found this approach enabled me to take a more granular look at each film, as well as placing it within the context of her career, life, and creative pursuits. Furthermore—in the spirit of Sofia, who starts every project with a cinematic reference of her own—I have included some notes on "further viewing," either directly or tangentially related to her body of work. These sections could have easily spanned

a book of their own, as every Sofia Coppola film is a marvel of artistic and pop culture references, lovingly spun together into something quite unique.

Sofia's influence on popular culture since her filmmaking debut has been substantial. In 2007, Marc Jacobs's Daisy perfume campaign lovingly borrowed the iconography of *The Virgin Suicides*, while the gleefully anachronistic *Marie Antoinette* (which so frustrated me as a teenager) has inspired fashion designers as well as informing a particular brand of historical pop fiction, notably Yorgos Lanthimos's *The Favourite*, Tony McNamara's *The Great*, and Chris Van Dusen's *Bridgerton*. *The Bling Ring* lives on in memes of Emma Watson's bratty line reading, "I wanna rob," while *Somewhere* remains my favorite cautionary tale of how having everything is never enough. Lonely teenagers are still discovering *The Virgin Suicides* and *Lost in Translation*, yearning for closeness at a time when it feels like you're still waiting for your life to begin.

My aim with this book is to provide something I've always thought was hard to find when it came to Sofia Coppola: A critical appraisal from her target audience. While her privilege as part of a Hollywood dynasty and subsequent financial freedom to make artful independent films about rich (or at least middle class) white people are often the focus of much criticism surrounding her work, I believe there is—and always has been—more to her than that, while still recognizing that to some extent, her films feel like fairy tales. But isn't there some truth at the heart of every fable?

★

I still can't really explain why, at thirteen, I wanted to die, or why the thought still plagues me now and then, a treacherous little voice in the back of my head I'm yet to drown out completely. Depression has no blueprint, and perhaps out of self-preservation my memory doesn't recall much beyond the way desperation was something I understood deep in my bones. Everything about me was mundane, yet I was crippled by the sensation of feeling nothing at all one moment and everything too deeply the next. Sofia's vision of the agony and the ecstasy of being a teenage girl is the closest anyone has come to articulating that excruciating feeling—the curious, foggy sensation of watching the world go by from behind a pane of glass. With *The Virgin Suicides*, the foundation was laid for a career observing how women are seen, but her elegical debut is still as crisp as ever, immortalizing "teenage angst" with a tenderness I have appreciated since the very first time I heard the opening notes of Air's "Playground Love." ☁

Music Videos

"I NEVER THOUGHT I would be a filmmaker. It wasn't something I ever planned," Sofia Coppola told the *Guardian* in 2018. While her brother Roman had followed their father into the world of directing, and prior to his tragic death in 1986, eldest sibling Gian-Carlo had been forging a similar path, she had resisted the possibility of "joining the family business" despite—or perhaps because of— her childhood and adolescent years spent on and around film sets. Nevertheless, Sofia still moved in the same circles as plenty of budding filmmakers, and in 1992, on the set for Sonic Youth's "100%" music video, met young director/skateboarding enthusiast Spike Jonze.

Spike was already working as a videographer within the skateboarding world, and his promotional short *Video Days* brought him to the attention of Kim Gordon. The subsequent video for "100%" featured Sonic Youth performing at a house party intercut with footage of Jason Lee skateboarding. Sofia had previously appeared in the video for Sonic Youth's "Mildred Pierce" and was good friends with Thurston Moore. A year later, she would direct a music video of her own for alt rock outfit Walt Mink; filmed at the Coppola estate, "Shine" features now-familiar Sofia trademarks such as a group of young girls reclining on a lawn in the sunshine, and underwater footage of them swimming in a pool. The inclusion of these stylistic elements so early in Sofia's career shows her aesthetic sensibilities had already begun to develop, and she would later incorporate them into *The Virgin Suicides* and *Somewhere*.

♫

Sofia's interest in filmmaking continued throughout the nineties, even as she pursued other interests. Perhaps the most curious of these formative experiences was *Hi Octane*, a short-lived Comedy Central series which

aired in 1994. Created by Sofia and her friend Zoe Cassavetes (daughter of John Cassavetes and Gena Rowlands), the magazine-style show featured monster trucks, musicians, and Martin Scorsese among its esoteric segments; "kind of like *Baywatch* but with cars" Sofia quipped to talk show host Jon Stewart in 1995. As critic Charles Bramesco observed when looking back on *Hi Octane* in 2020, "Comedy Central executives built the show around the idea that these two women were so synonymous with Gen-X-er cool that anything acting as an extension of their taste would be, too." Four twenty-minute episodes were produced, but only three were ever broadcast.

With a combined runtime of just over an hour, the available episodes of *Hi Octane* make for a delightful study in nineties pop culture, as well as reflecting the celebrity cache of Coppola, who enlists all manner of pals to appear. Her cousin Nicolas Cage gives a memorable performance as a fan who enthuses about appearing on the show, while Thurston Moore's interview segment Thurston's Alley (with a theme song reminiscent of *Wayne's World*, another sign of the time) sees the Sonic Youth star sit down for a chat with Johnny Ramone. Sofia picks up a stranded Keanu Reeves from the roadside; backstage at Paris Fashion Week, It Girls Naomi Campbell and Jenny Shimizu play up to their model personas.

Despite its stagey nature, *Hi Octane* feels charmingly candid, offering rare glimpses of humor in usually austere figures such as fashion designer Karl Lagerfeld and *Vogue*'s famously icy editor in chief Anna Wintour. Sofia's insider status is undoubtedly integral to this—it's obvious that there's a relationship between her subjects outside of *Hi Octane*. These are her real-life friends and colleagues, and their ease on camera comes from a camaraderie that's hard to fake between

television hosts and their guests. Parlaying her friends in high places for creative purposes would serve Sofia well in future, albeit with more polished results.

♫

Sofia's interest in the intersection of film and music continued throughout the decade with appearances in the Black Crowes's video for "Sometimes Salvation" and Madonna's "Deeper and Deeper," as well as a further directing stint on the Flaming Lips' "This Here Giraffe" in 1996 (the video starred Leslie Hayman, who Sofia would go on to cast as Therese Lisbon in *The Virgin Suicides*). Yet the most famous of Sofia's music video appearances would come courtesy of Spike Jonze, for the Chemical Brothers' "Elektrobank." Preceding his iconic and similarly bizarre video for Fatboy Slim's "Weapon of Choice" by three years, "Elektrobank" sees Sofia play a young gymnast performing an energetic floor routine to the song. Though there's some noticeable CGI at play to give the star the moves of a seasoned athlete, Coppola gives a spirited performance and it's a memorable addition to the Jonze music video canon, despite its relative simplicity compared to, say, "Da Funk" by Daft Punk, in which a vaguely terrifying anthropomorphic dog with an injured leg seeks help in New York City.

While shooting *The Virgin Suicides*, Sofia also directed the music video for the film's theme, "Playground Love" by Air, alongside her brother Roman. Integrating several key scenes from the film into the video, the strange narrative follows a sentient used wad of chewing gum crooning the song's lyrics. (Gordon Tracks, the lyricist and singer, is actually a pseudonym for Thomas Mars of Phoenix.) It might seem tonally disparate from the bleak air about *The Virgin Suicides*, but perhaps it also offers a little comic relief (as well as forming a fun sentient food stuffs double bill with the video for Blur's "Coffee & TV," in which a milk carton leaves home to find the missing Graham Coxon). In a short video discussing the video, Sofia explains that the gum's dejected expression fits the melancholic tone of the song, but also its abandonment—something that seems particularly fitting for a film reflecting on the unwitting isolation and loneliness of adolescence.

In 2003, Sofia would create a further two videos: one for "City Girl," Kevin Shields's contribution to the *Lost in Translation* soundtrack; the other for the White Stripes' cover of Burt Bacharach's "I Just Don't Know What to Do With Myself." While the "City Bank" video primarily comprises footage from *Lost in Translation* and B-roll from their shoot in Japan, the provocative White Stripes miniature couldn't be more different. Shot in sultry black-and-white by Lance Acord (who also worked on *The Virgin Suicides* and *Lost in Translation*), it features supermodel Kate Moss pole dancing in black underwear. *New York Times* journalist Lynn Hirschberg reported from the video's set in her 2003 profile of Sofia, "The Coppola Smart Mob"; when asked how she pitched her concept for the video to Jack White, Sofia replied "I said, 'I don't know—how about Kate Moss doing a pole dance?' I said that because I would like to see it. That's the way I work: I try to imagine what I would like to see."

The video combines Broadway-style choreography (Sofia references American dance legend Bob Fosse) with the grainy, lo-fi aesthetic of Andy Warhol's *Factory* films, creating something feminine and alluring that doesn't stray into pornographic territory. In the early 2000s pole dancing was still largely associated with strip clubs and seen as distasteful despite the physical and mental skills required to successfully

choreograph and perform routines. Sofia's video positions it as the artform it truly is, lingering on Moss's physicality to create a hypnotic, alluring performance. The grungy aesthetic is different from any of the imagery in Sofia's previous films, though she would revisit pole dancing in *Somewhere* with two scenes featuring Playboy Playmates Karissa and Kristina Shannon.

Both Coppola and Moss had moved in the same fashionable circles since their teenage years, and Hirschberg notes that they're drinking Sofia champagne on the set, produced at the family vineyard in California. It paints a privileged portrait of Coppola, but Hirschberg also denotes a key difference between Sofia and her father: "He, like most directors, has a god complex. Sofia Coppola is much less dictatorial: soft-spoken, a listener, an encourager of those around her." It's an assessment Sofia herself seems to agree with: "He came on the set of *The Virgin Suicides* and told me, 'You should say "Action" louder, more from your diaphragm.' I thought, 'okay, you can go now.' [. . .] When you direct is the only time you get to have the world exactly how you want it. My movies are very close to what I set out to do. And I'm super opinionated about what I do and don't like. I may say it differently, but I still get what I want."

Although Sofia hasn't done as much music video work in recent years, it would be remiss to ignore her collaborations with the band Phoenix, first in Roman Coppola's quirky meta-video for 2000's "Funky Squaredance" (he points out Thomas Mars' cameo in *The Virgin Suicides*) and again in 2013, when she created a video for the song "Chloroform." Recording in slow-motion black-and-white, it shows the band performing and the emotional reactions of the crowd of teenage girls watching them. In an interview with the Museum of Modern Art, Sofia revealed that

the video was inspired by a Joseph Sterling photograph from his book *The Age of Adolescence*, a gift from her sister-in-law's boyfriend the previous Christmas. The video also marked a return to shooting in monochrome for the first time since the White Stripes video, the only previous example of this coming in her debut short film *Lick the Star*.

Given Sofia's thematic fascination with adolescence, the "Chloroform" video fits neatly into her body of work—but it also feels refreshingly stripped-back, with a simple, poignant concept executed in her signature dreamy style. As an artist she has always gone to lengths to explore and reclaim teenage indulgence, treating the intense emotions of youth with a respect that still feels relatively uncommon in popular culture. By lingering on the naked emotion of Phoenix's adoring fanbase, she connects the music to its material influence; the viewer gains a real sense for what it means to love something so purely. Equally, it feels in keeping with the tone of the song, which feels romantic, enigmatic, and aching at the same time. "Love is cruel," Mars croons in the chorus. It looks as though his teenage fans agree. ♫

Commercial Work

WHEN SOFIA MET fashion designer Marc Jacobs backstage at a Perry Ellis show in the 1990s, the pair hit it off immediately, discovering common ground in music and art. Over the course of the next two decades their respective careers would go from strength to strength, with Jacobs serving as Louis Vuitton's creative director for sixteen years while simultaneously creating his own iconic fashion house, and Sofia establishing herself as a major filmmaker. Their first collaboration came in 2001, when Sofia was cast as the face of Jacobs's eponymous perfume. Juergen Teller shot the campaign at the Coppola residence in Napa Valley, showing Sofia posing topless in a swimming pool—sometimes with a giant bottle of perfume. In terms of the weird world of perfume advertisements, they're definitely at the less bizarre end of the scale, and in keeping with Sofia's natural aesthetic.

Sofia created her first TV advert for Dior's Miss Cherie Rose in 2008, in which model Maryna Linchuk enjoys a day in Paris, taking in the sights on her bicycle and browsing pastries at a boulangerie. It feels more in keeping with Sofia's opulent aesthetic from *Marie Antoinette*, maintaining a sense of youth and mischief that fits the brand's target demographic for their perfume. Two years later she would reteam with Dior for a Miss Dior Cherie commercial starring Natalie Portman and Alden Ehrenreich (who had starred in her father's film *Tetro* the previous year). This second collaboration focused more on a romantic storyline, set to Serge Gainsbourg's "Je T'aime . . . Moi Non Plus" and featuring instantly recognizable Sofia signifiers: soft light, handheld camerawork, pastel colors. She would work with Portman and Dior again in 2013 on the La Vie En Rose perfume campaign, which features a reference to Federico Fellini's *La Dolce Vita* (a clip of the same moment had appeared in *Lost in Translation*).

Such is Sofia's standing in the fashion world, Jacobs would borrow from her debut feature in 2007 for the supporting imagery for his Daisy campaign: blonde models in simple white dresses lounging in the woods. She would direct an ad for the perfume line in 2013 with similar iconography, namely a group of young women frolicking in fields and by a creek while electronic music plays in the background. It is at once vibrant and low-key, reminiscent of Peter Weir's 1975 mystery drama *Picnic at Hanging Rock*, albeit more playful in tone. It captures the spirit of long, hot summers spent with friends, free from the pressures of home or school, a mood Sofia has always been so adept at conveying.

In addition to her work with Dior and Marc Jacobs, Sofia has also directed for various clothing brands, including a Marni for H&M collection filmed in Marrakech with Imogen Poots, a series of four amusing Christmas ads for Gap, and a Calvin Klein underwear campaign starring Kirsten Dunst and Rashida Jones. Despite their inherent differences, each of these works maintains an air of "the Sofia factor," be it through Roxy Music's "Avalon" in the H&M ad (she previously featured "More Than This" as a karaoke track in *Lost in Translation* and Bryan Ferry's cover of "Smoke Gets in Your Eyes" in *Somewhere*) or references to the iconic Calvin Klein ads of the nineties.

Oftentimes when a director collaborates with a brand it can be seen as "lesser" work somehow, perhaps because such commercial assignments typically afford less creative freedom. Yet Sofia has always nurtured these relationships, and in return they have given her more than a handsome paycheck; in 2008, a Louis Vuitton bag was named after her (an honor usually bestowed by a luxury fashion designer on their creative muses) and in October 2021, Marc Jacobs launched a capsule collection for his Heaven brand featuring images from *The Virgin Suicides* emblazoned on skirts, bags, and T-shirts, with a portion of sales going to New York's The Lesbian, Gay, Bisexual & Transgender Community Center.

In 2016, Coppola partnered with another fashion house, Valentino, to stage an ambitious production of Giuseppe Verdi's opera *La Traviata*. The fifteen-performance run at Teatro dell'Opera di Roma was a sell-out, and Christopher Nolan's go-to production designer Nathan Crowley worked on the opulent sets. Given Sofia's interest in troubled female protagonists it seemed like a perfect fit; a feature in *W* magazine took readers behind the scenes at the Valentino atelier in Rome, showing off the beautiful hand-crafted costumes that were created for Violetta and the cast of characters that comprise Verdi's most famous work.

It was Valentino who brought Sofia to the production, seeking a modern edge for a traditional story. It was a smart move: before the run had even begun almost a million dollars had been made in ticket sales, and Coppola's attachment was a draw for audiences who might ordinarily not have an interest in the opera. The production was later filmed by Philippe Le Sourd and broadcast in cinemas around the world, allowing a wider audience to experience the production. It may not differ radically from past stagings, but it's as beautiful and tragic as one would expect from Verdi's tale of the fallen woman, and it's hard to fault Sofia's willingness to explore new mediums and undertake ambitious projects. ☻

4
Audrey Kelly as Chloe
in *Lick the Star* (1998).

5
A still from Sofia's commercial
for Marc Jacobs's Daisy
fragrance (2014).

6
A still from Sofia's film for
the New York Ballet (2021).

4

5

6

Short Films

IN 1998, SOFIA directed and cowrote, with her friend Stephanie Hayman, a fourteen-minute black-and-white short entitled *Lick the Star*. It even features the first instance of "The Coppola Shot," as seventh-grader Kate (Christina Turley) returns to school after being absent for a week due to a broken foot. Her voiceover narration positions us squarely in Kate's mind as she frets about returning to class because of what she might have missed. Queen bee Chloe (who appears in a slow-motion musical sequence not dissimilar to Trip Fontaine's entrance in *The Virgin Suicides*) has developed a catchphrase during Kate's absence, "lick the star," and the students draw matching stars on their ankles to accompany it.

Kate doesn't understand the significance of the phrase and feels isolated from the group, until they reveal their plan to poison the boys at their school who harass them using arsenic, inspired by Chloe's obsession with V. C. Andrews's novel *Flowers in the Attic*. Kate is suspended by the principal (a cameo from Peter Bogdanovich) after she's caught smoking under the bleachers and misses school again; in her absence, a misunderstanding leads to Chloe being labeled a racist by her classmates, and she attempts suicide. This only encourages further gossip, and her friends turn on her, revealing the Lick the Star plot to the school.

By the time Kate returns to school, the social hierarchy has completely changed. Chloe is now an outcast and her fellow students openly mock her. Her former friends are thinking about starting a band, and she abandons Chloe out of concern for her own social standing. Now the school's resident loner, Chloe composes a poem about her feelings of isolation and clutches a biography of Factory It Girl Edie Sedgwick, whose estrangement from Andy Warhol and his inner circle contributed to her untimely death at the age of twenty-eight.

Sofia enlisted the services of Lance Acord as the film's director of photography, her brother Roman as second unit director, Zoe Cassavetes as second assistant director, and cast Cassavetes and her cousin Robert Schwartzman as a P.E. teacher and student respectively. Beyond these familiar names, it's clear that Sofia was already in possession of a strong artistic sensibility and in pursuing themes that would become prominent later in her career.

It's easy to see how this tale of girlish growing pains connects to Sofia's feature film work, from the role gossip plays in the court of *Marie Antoinette* to Johnny Marco's broken arm in *Somewhere*. There are some harder-hitting elements to the story, such as the students laughing off Chloe's attempted suicide, showing no concern for her well-being—the idea that teenage girls would feel so harassed by their male peers that they might attempt to harm them is equally disturbing. There are shades of *The Beguiled* here, too, particularly in how Martha Farnsworth resolves to deal with John McBurney once she perceives him to be a threat to the women at her seminary school.

High school itself is a recurring nightmare in Sofia's work, particularly in *The Virgin Suicides* and *The Bling Ring*. Her wry observation of the cruelty of teenage girls—and the hierarchy that exists in institutions the world over—is augmented by the film's short runtime, conveying the feeling that life comes at you all-too quickly when you're young. She coaxes dynamic performances out of a young cast (not always the easiest thing to do) and incorporates visual flourishes which lend themselves nicely to the dramatic nature of adolescence.

Given that Sofia would begin production on *The Virgin Suicides* later the same year, it is unsurprising that *Lick the Star* is often overlooked—although it was included as an extra on the Criterion Blu-ray release of *The Virgin Suicides* in 2018. It might be rough around the edges, but as an indication of things to come it's a fascinating piece of Sofia Coppola history.

⧖

In 2020, with the world in lockdown due to the COVID-19 pandemic, the art world found itself under threat. While film production went on pause, countless theater and performance groups also found themselves unable to perform, among them the world-renowned New York City Ballet. A year later, in 2021, Sofia—in partnership with Chanel—directed a twenty-six-minute short film for the ballet's Spring Gala, highlighting their return to work through a series of five different works.

With choreography from Justin Peck and featuring the music of Brahms and Chopin, Philippe Le Sourd lenses the majority of the film in stark black-and-white as the dancers move through various spaces within Lincoln Center, from the stage to training halls and narrow hallways. There's a poignant intimacy to the film, which often only features a handful of dancers at a time, and presents them in rehearsal as well as performing to an empty auditorium.

The arts are constantly under threat due to lack of public funding and lack of engagement from the public (though it's also possible to argue most audiences are shut out of "high arts" such as ballet and opera due to ticket prices) and the global pandemic did nothing to improve the situation. Despite the fact that many people throughout lockdowns and isolation needed art more than ever, the prospect of bankruptcies and layoffs loomed large; for many performers and artists the ramifications are likely to still be felt for years to come. Sofia's film reminds audiences what they have missed while at home, while also highlighting the isolation and frustration of the dancers who have longed to return to their craft.

Making use of the imposing setting and the contrast between the public and private spaces, Sofia's film creates a sense of watching the ballet from a unique vantage point, being able to study the intricate choreography and physicality of the dancers in a way that simply isn't possible when sitting in an auditorium. It's a compelling argument for returning to the theater, but also showcases her filmmaking talent for capturing emotion even without words. Famously Sofia doesn't love to write dialogue, so matching her with the ballet feels natural, allowing her to experiment with wide shots and close angles to create as intimate a portrait of life at the very top of the ballet world as many will ever witness.

As with *La Traviata*, Sofia's cultural cache worked wonders for the New York City Ballet, bringing a whole new audience to the elitist world of traditional ballet. The film neither feels like a commercial nor a plea for fundraising. Rather, it is a heartfelt celebration of the fine art of movement, and a testament to the commitment and craft of the dancers who have spent a year of their lives longing for a return to the spotlight. ⧖

THE

SUICIDES

VIRGIN

1
Cecilia is found in the bathtub clutching a card which bears an image of the Virgin Mary and a phone number. The same image is later used by her sisters when they begin to secretly communicate with the neighborhood boys; a reminder of Cecilia's spectral presence.

2
Cecilia lies in the bathtub after slashing her wrists. Although the reference to Millais's *Ophelia* is a given, the scene also mimics Juliet's introduction in Baz Luhrman's *Romeo + Juliet*, where the heroine is seen with her head underwater. It might also remind some viewers of Frankie Pentangeli's suicide in *The Godfather Part II*—directed, of course, by Francis Ford Coppola.

3

In this medium shot
we're introduced to the
neighborhood boys as they
admire the Lisbon girls
from across the street. The
orderly composition makes
them seem younger than the
Lisbons, but also positions
their introduction as a
spectacle, with the boys
as a rapt audience.

4–6

Cecilia undergoes a therapy
session in the aftermath of her
suicide attempt, counseled
by Dr. E. M. Horniker (Danny
DeVito) who encourages
her parents to host a party
for her, so she can socialize
with her peers and perhaps
make some friends. One of
DeVito's earliest roles came as
a psychiatric patient in Miloš
Forman's *One Flew Over the
Cuckoo's Nest*; perhaps his
cameo is a little nod to that.

7

Lux is told to cover up at the dinner table by her mother when fellow student Peter Sissen visits their house. Mrs. Lisbon's puritanical attitude towards the girls' appearance is interesting; they are permitted to wear make-up, but their clothes are loose and modest. This speaks to her desire to keep them girls forever, and fear regarding her daughters' transition into womanhood because of the severity of the adult world.

8–9

Peter takes the opportunity to snoop in the girls' bathroom, admiring nail polish and sniffing a lipstick. The adolescent fantasy the boys conjure is more compelling to them than the reality, but it's not necessarily malicious; teenage boys are often casual in their cruelty.

10
Lux—Latin for "light"—is
the most prominent of
the Lisbon sisters, in part
due to her more outgoing
nature. This particular shot
has inspired Marc Jacobs's
Daisy perfume commercials
and typifies the dreamy,
mysterious nature the girls
possess, at least according
to their young admirers.

11–12

A journalist reports on
Cecilia's suicide, which
occurs during a party held by
the family in her honor. One
of the most violent images
in the film is of her parents,
sisters and the neighborhood
boys discovering Cecilia's
body after she jumps from the
bedroom window, particularly
juxtaposed with the joviality
of the gathering in the
basement. Cecilia's death is
the catalyst that sends the
whole Lisbon family into a
downward spiral; later the
unnamed narrator remarks
on the time that has passed
since "Cecilia had slit her
wrists, spreading the poison
in the air" mirroring the felling
of the diseased trees.

13
Mrs. Lisbon is visited by
the family's priest, Father
Moody, played by Scott
Glenn. Glenn previously
appeared as Lt. Richard
M. Colby in *Apocalypse Now*,
who abandons his mission
to join Kurtz's command—
so there's some irony in
him playing a man of God
in his second Coppola film.
This shot of Kathleen Turner
in her bedroom, grieving
after Cecilia's death, evokes
the melancholy realism of
American artist Edward Hopper.

14
The surviving Lisbon sisters
in their bedroom. While their
mother's room is kept dark
even in the daylight, the girls'
is bright and colorful, despite
their clear pain at Cecilia's
death. This suggests a
pressure to remain desirable
even in the most dire
circumstances that is familiar
to many women.

15
Trip Fontaine, played by Josh
Hartnett, in the swimming
pool, from his introductory
montage. Coppola's interest
and experience in music videos
is perhaps most obvious here;
the use of slow motion and
Heart's classic rock anthem
"Magic Man" position him as
the high school heartthrob,
while this shot of him reclining
in a pool is reminiscent of
the photoshoots common
in magazines aimed at
teenage girls.

16
An animated Mr. Lisbon
photographs the girls for
prom. Mr. Lisbon, played by
James Woods, is the more
sympathetic parental figure,
but is content to live under
his wife's thumb and does
not challenge her parenting.
He becomes more visibly
unstable after the incident
at the prom.

17
Lux Lisbon as Trip sees
her; with a twinkle in her eye.
These little visual flourishes
add a playfulness to the film,
but also highlight how young
the girls are, as much as
the boys view them as
worldly creatures.

18–19
Disco ball and balloons
at the high school prom.

20
Lux awakens alone on the
football field after losing
her virginity to Trip, who then
leaves her. Her positioning
in this wide shot emphasizes
her fragility; the world is cruel
to girls.

21
Following Lux's broken
curfew, the girls are confined
to the house. Here they gaze
into the street as Cecilia's
beloved tree is cut down; the
shot evokes the earlier one
of the neighborhood boys
watching the sisters from
across the street.

SOFIA COPPOLA: FOREVER YOUNG

22
The neighborhood boys see
the Lisbon girls for a final
time before the girls die by
suicide in their family home.
Lux smokes a cigarette—
the smoke a visual metaphor
for the "poison" their deaths
create in the local community.

23
The debutante party where
the rest of the Grosse Pointe
neighborhood gathers
to socialize, embracing
the environmental smog
as a theme. The violence
associated with gas masks
paired with suits and delicate
dresses is unnerving, and
suggests a disassociation
among the partygoers
between their own lives and
those of the Lisbon girls,
who died months earlier.

The Virgin Suicides

1999
97 minutes

Budget $6 million
Box Office $10 million

24

24
Lux belatedly travels home
from the prom in a taxi; the
first instance of the "Coppola
Shot," demonstrating a
yearning for freedom
through transition.

25
Portrait of Ophelia by Millais.
Coincidentally the painting
would later inspire a scene in
Lars von Trier's *Melancholia*,
in which Kirsten Dunst plays
a depressed bride facing the
imminent end of the world.

26
The Bell Jar by Sylvia Plath.
For several years Kirsten
Dunst was attached to an
adaptation of Plath's book
into a film, starring
Dakota Fanning.

"I WANTED TO make something that was artful for girls," Sofia Coppola explained in a 2018 interview with Criterion, ahead of *The Virgin Suicides*'s rerelease in a plush special edition with a 4K restoration and a raft of special features. Her own experience as a film-loving teenager in the 1980s had left her disillusioned: "Movies made for teenagers didn't respect the audience. The cinematography was bad [. . .] and it would always be thirty-year-olds cast as teenagers. Besides John Hughes, there wasn't anyone portraying them in a way I could relate to. I felt like it was part of the culture that wasn't being dealt with." Indeed, Coppola's list of her favorite films, published in 2020 by Rotten Tomatoes, makes evident her fascination with youth on-screen. There's *Sixteen Candles*, but also Peter Bogdanovich's *The Last Picture Show*, Stanley Kubrick's *Lolita*, Jean-Luc Godard's *Breathless* and her own father's *Rumble Fish*.

It makes perfect sense, then, that Coppola would choose to channel this interest into her own art—out of an impasse in her young life after dabbling in acting, fashion design and photography came *The Virgin Suicides*. Her source material, the 1993 debut novel of Michigan-born author Jeffrey Eugenides, was inspired by a conversation he'd had with his nephew's babysitter, who told him that she and her sisters had tried to commit suicide. When he asked why, she said only, "We were under a lot of pressure." Coppola was recommended the novel by her friend Thurston Moore, founding member of Sonic Youth, and was instantly struck by a close-up photograph of long blonde hair on its cover—a detail that would become integral to her own vision of the Lisbon sisters, some six years later.

In both the book and film, a group of men (represented in dialogue by Giovanni Ribisi's unnamed narrator) from Grosse Pointe,

Michigan, reflect on the mystery surrounding the five Lisbon sisters (Cecilia, Lux, Bonnie, Mary, and Therese), who all committed suicide over the course of one year in the seventies. While the boys don't know the girls particularly well in reality, through meticulous observation and endless theorizing they form a unilateral connection with them, unable to understand what drove them to such an unspeakable end, they remain fixated on the sisters' story.

25

Coppola connected instantly: "It felt like Jeffrey Eugenides really understood the experience of being a teenager: the longing, the melancholy, the mystery between boys and girls," she explained. Yet the idea of adapting the novel for the screen—or entering the filmmaking field at all—didn't come about until later, when Coppola became aware that a film was in preproduction, with a male director and script written by Nick Gomez. "I really didn't know I wanted to be a director until I read *The Virgin Suicides* and saw so clearly how it had to be done," she said in the film's production notes. So despite warnings from her parents, she did the one thing a screenwriter should never do: adapted a novel she didn't have the rights to. Initially her script was intended purely as a thought exercise for her own development as a writer, but after catching wind that the Gomez production had fallen through, she sent her draft to Chris and Roberta Hanley of Muse Productions, who owned the film rights—and would coincidentally also oversee Mary Harron's blistering adaptation of *American Psycho*, released the same year—hoping they would consider her vision.

Undoubtedly Sofia's surname played a role in their decision to read this unsolicited script, as well as to take a chance on a first-time female director whose behind-the-camera experience was limited to assisting her father on his productions and creating one fourteen-minute short film (1998's *Lick the Star*.) It's important to recognize the impact that the Coppola name had on Sofia's debut: not only did the family production company American Zoetrope work alongside Paramount, Muse, and Eternity Pictures, but Kathleen Turner, who played the Lisbon matriarch in the film, was the first actor cast after having worked with Francis Ford Coppola on 1986's *Peggy Sue Got Married*—and he personally sent his daughter's script to his friend James Woods, who would sign on to play the girls' father, Ronald Lisbon.

Principal photography took place in Toronto in July of 1998, and lasted about a month. A documentary shot by Eleanor Coppola on set captures Sofia and her team at work, with Eugenides and her family spending some time behind the scenes. Francis Ford Coppola, wearing a selection of vivid Hawaiian shirts, is credited as "Proud Father/Filmmaker" and Sofia laughs about her father telling her to be more authoritative on set. But the young cast remain most beguiling to watch.

Kirsten Dunst—just sixteen at the time of shooting—remarks, "I think it's important that a female writes the script, because it's all about these five girls." If only Hollywood had her conviction when it came to crafting female-driven narratives. At the time *The Virgin Suicides* was released, it was still relatively novel to see a female filmmaker given the resources to write and direct her own feature; Coppola's access to resources was undoubtedly invaluable, but no substitute for the sharp eye and intuition which she brought to production.

So this is how it starts: with the ambient summer chorus of cicadas and children yelling, on a yellow-green tree-lined suburban street in Grosse Pointe, 1974. There, in the middle of the street, is Dunst's Lux Lisbon, squinting into the distance as she finishes a bright red popsicle. A woman waters her lawn, a couple walk a yellow labrador, and two workmen nail a gaudy orange "Notice for Removal" to an impressive elm tree, while the opening bars of Air's dreamy piano and saxophone "Playground Love" play. In an instant, the world goes quiet, save a dripping tap, as the scene cuts to the cool blue of the Lisbon bathroom: a cluttered shelf full of cosmetics; a crucifix. Then, the shriek of sirens, as Ribisi, in his flat, almost disaffected voice, tells us: "Cecilia was the first to go." A petite thirteen-year-old descendant of Millais's *Ophelia*, Cecilia lies supine in the pink water of a bathtub clouded with her blood, just for a moment—before the sunlight and music return, the world spinning madly on.

"What are you doing here, honey?" A doctor asks Cecilia (Hanna R. Hall, present for only twenty minutes of screentime but utilizing every second to portray a teenage girl on the brink of annihilation) as she recovers in hospital. "You're not even old enough to know how bad life gets." Despondent, Cecilia utters a line cemented in popular culture, word-for-word as it appeared in Eugenides's novel: "Obviously, doctor, you've never been a thirteen-year-old girl." These opening two minutes of *The Virgin Suicides* pose a question to the audience: are you the teenage boys and neighbors curiously watching the commotion from outside, or are you Cecilia Lisbon, glassy-eyed, waiting for oblivion? I knew instantly which one I was. To be a teenage girl is to exist in a seemingly endless state of limbo. Caught between innocence and experience, it's the first time young women become aware of so many strange, devastating things: the power and grotesqueness which simultaneously exists within our bodies; the magical, terrifying differences between girls and boys; the expectations suddenly thrust upon us regarding how to dress, act and temper our ambitions; our lack of control over any of these forces; and—perhaps most devastating of all—how difficult it is to articulate all of the above.

In Eugenides's novel, the Lisbon sisters are ethereal, faceless entities. Told from multiple perspectives, the story offers a male-given oral history of the unthinkable rather than a straightforward account, and in an interview with *Dazed*, the author said he wished each sister had been played by multiple actors, to reflect the shifting, inconsistent gaze of their admirers. Coppola cast a quintet of lithe, pretty blondes instead: Hall and Dunst as Cecilia and Lux, and Chelse Swain, A.J. Cook, and Leslie Hayman as their elder sisters, Bonnie, Mary, and Therese. Their introduction in the film imbues the girls with a rockstar quality, as they emerge from the family car to the sounds of Sloan's aptly-named rock bop "On the Horizon," each sister presented in freeze-frame with a different handwritten title card bearing their name, giving them individuality they are scarcely afforded for the rest of the film. The boys watch them, enthralled, before they begin to speculate about the details of Cecilia's suicide attempt. Gossip—traditionally associated with women and especially teenage girls—is the boys' main way of getting to know the Lisbon sisters, who are always just beyond their reach. It's a far cry from the traditional teen comedies Coppola cites as influences, where the guy always gets the girl, and the girl is happy with that.

Coppola's Lisbon girls are also unfailingly human, in stark contrast from their shape-shifting literary counterparts. While the

27

novel is preoccupied with visions of the sisters as perceived by their admirers, Eugenides remarks that Coppola was more interested in the women than the male narrators. But he adds that her version is closer to how he felt about the girls personally—an inherent sympathy, for both what they undergo and how their lives are vigorously dissected by a group of near strangers. This gaggle of observers realize in the aftermath of the Lisbons' deaths, over the course of years, that they never really saw them at all.

That's not for lack of trying. While visiting the house, neighborhood boy Peter enters Cecilia's cluttered bedroom, where he observes religious paraphernalia scattered alongside teddy bears and tea cups, a single flip flop and a ceramic tortoise. Snooping around their bathroom, Peter awkwardly notices boxes of Tampax in a cupboard, and impulsively sniffs a stray lipstick—the first instance in which the film shows the local boys attempting to understand the Lisbons through objects they collect. The minutiae of the sisters' lives is rendered in the kind of exquisite detail that has since become a trademark of Coppola's work: kitschy stickers, postcards, records, cosmetics. Like magpies, the girls collect trinkets which fill their pastel bedrooms, defying the drab, regimented decor of the rest of the house. Such overt femininity is fascinating and mysterious to the boys, and they're unable to stop themselves from trying to unpack it, searching everywhere for meaning.

Ribisi's nameless narrator refers to the objects they procure from the Lisbons as "our collection of souvenirs," as if the girls are a tourist attraction. This unwitting selfishness leads them to read Cecilia's diary, stolen from the Lisbon house after she successfully kills herself by jumping from a window onto a spiked railing. The boys read it with the intention of understanding her death, digesting her most private thoughts and observations about the world around her. Tim Weiner, one of the boys, "decodes" it, noting her "emotional instability," and claiming, "What we have here is a dreamer, someone completely out of touch with reality. When she jumped, she probably thought she would fly."

It's human nature to seek order within chaos. We try to infer meaning where there is none, or at least where meaning is hard to grasp. In attempting to understand the unfathomable act of teen suicide in suburbia, where problems appear few and far between (particularly for teenage girls), the boys of Grosse Pointe experience a form of apophenia, assigning great meaning to Cecilia's private journal—not uncommon for teenagers in the throes of romantic infatuation—though, it offers no insights into why she decided to end her life. Coppola instead hints at other potential causes for her malaise: before her death, Cecilia expresses concern to her mother over the number of animals being added to the endangered species list. Reading her journal, the boys, slightly irritated, note how preoccupied Cecilia is by the blight of Dutch Elm Disease in the neighborhood. At the party her parents throw in an effort to raise Cecilia's spirits, she seems uncomfortable when the guests urge a boy with learning difficulties to perform like a circus animal. A dissatisfaction with the ugliness of the world—being hyper sensitive to reality, rather than out of touch with it—seems more likely an explanation for Cecilia's desire to die than the delusion Tim Weiner points to. But teenage boys, for all their bravado (and there is so much of it, as they compete to win the affections of the Lisbon girls) do not make for convincing psychoanalysts.

The boy who comes closest to truly understanding any of the girls is Trip (Harnett), a teenage dream introduced to us standing before a shiny red convertible. In a wry sequence that shows his arrival at school set to Heart's electrifying power ballad "Magic Man," every female student and staff member turns to look his way, and Trip, aware of the power he wields, exploits it. Subverting the male gaze that has sexualized young women on screen for decades, Coppola positions Trip as the epitome of suburban cool—the kind of boy that girls get giddy over, writing his name in felt-tip on their notebooks. Even the use of such a breathy, confessional pop anthem echoes the way as a teenage girl you listen for hours to a single tune, just because it reminds you of the boy you have a crush on.

But when Trip encounters the one girl who isn't interested in him—Lux Lisbon—an inversion of this obsession begins. An older Trip, in rehab, reflects in the film's only interview-style segment: "She was the still point of the turning world, man. I never got over that girl. Never." In his mind, Lux is eternally that pristine fourteen-year-

28

old who coolly rebuffed him. When he confidently tells her during a geography class video presentation that he's going to ask her out, Lux snorts: "Fat chance." In the background, the video's narrator seems clairvoyant when he says, "The hurricane, one of the most awe-inspiring and truly spectacular storms nature has to offer."

After convincing Mr. Lisbon to let him come over and spend a fairly tame evening watching television with the family, Trip sits in his car, disappointed—perhaps having misread Lux's mischievous rebuff incorrectly. Another Heart guitar riff kicks in. Lux emerges from the darkness like a monster in a *Mystery Science Theatre 3000* movie—the ones where teenagers making out in cars would inevitably meet a sticky end when a giant centipede or hobgoblins took advantage of their distraction. Framing a teenage girl as a monster (even for a split second) points to Sofia's sense of humor, but also the way that women have been considered monstrous in the past for displaying any sexual desire at all. Lux jumps into Trip's car and kisses him frantically before leaving just as quickly as she arrived. Dazed, Trip catches his breath, removing Lux's gum from his mouth, while Ann Wilson sings exactly his sentiment: "I go crazy on you." Lux repeatedly demonstrates an agency uncommon for a seventies Catholic schoolgirl, much less one under the strict eye of her domineering (but undoubtedly loving, a point many of the film's critics seem to miss) mother. For so much of the film, Lux seems in control of herself and her desires, but Trip, clueless as he may be, eventually proves her undoing.

True to his word, Trip eventually asks Lux out—or rather, asks her father if he can take her to the Homecoming dance. Mr. Lisbon agrees on the proviso that Trip finds dates for her three sisters. This sends the neighborhood boys into a tizzy, each vying for one of the spots by highlighting their individual selling points (access to a Cadillac, good marujiana, good grades). Therese makes an astute observation when their father seems unconcerned with which boy is taking which girl: "They're just going to raffle us off." Because it doesn't really matter to the boys—a Lisbon sister is a Lisbon sister, and they can only tell them apart by sight anyway, as much as they profess to know the girls.

Trip and his selected companions arrive at the house, and the girls descend their staircase—Lux first, regally reminiscent of Scarlett O'Hara waiting for Rhett Butler in *Gone With the Wind* or Rose Calvert in *Titanic* (a similar scene would occur in teen rom-com *She's All That*, released the year before *The Virgin Suicides*). Trip stands in quiet awe, but it doesn't last, despite a short burst of adolescent euphoria at the dance as the gang bops around to Styx's

27
Sofia as Mary Corleone in
The Godfather Part III.

28
Sofia on the set of
The Virgin Suicides.

"Come Sail Away." Trip convinces Lux to sneak away to the football field, where they have sex. It's difficult to parse this moment, in which Lux seems giddy with the novelty of escaping from under her mother's thumb, but has also been drinking and does display initial hesitation when Trip asks her to come away. As mature as she seems, Lux is still a fourteen-year-old girl, desperate to seem older and more worldly.

By the time Lux awakens in the morning, bathed in the cool blue light reminiscent of Cecilia's bathroom scene, she is all alone, and the question of whether she gave her virginity to Trip or whether it was taken from her lingers.

In a shot that has become a signature of Coppola's films, reflecting the imprisonment of girl- and womanhood, Lux stares despondently out of a taxi cab window, chewing on the end of her Homecoming tiara. When she arrives at the Lisbon house, in a shot mirroring the departing ambulance that took Cecilia to the hospital, her parents confront her. While Mr. Lisbon's first question is "Are you okay?" an enraged Mrs. Lisbon immediately asks "Where have you been?!" A present-day Trip explains he didn't care how she got home, and that he doesn't know why he left her. "I liked her, I liked her a lot. But out there on the field . . . it was just different then." With a wistful smile he says, "You know, most people never taste that kind of love. But at least I tasted it once, right?" It's hard for him to understand why he left her, and perhaps even that he did love her, but so much teenage behavior—callous, reckless, selfish as it may be—has little explanation. It could be that he was only ever interested in sleeping with the most desired girl in school, and had no desire to get to know her (another disappointment amid so many the Lisbons experience) but Coppola knows there's little use in trying to present one, because it doesn't matter to Lux.

Things fall apart. Following Lux's missed curfew Mrs. Lisbon withdraws the girls from school and visitors are no longer permitted to the house. It's possible she knows what Lux

29

did with Trip and her decision is an extreme reaction to this, but it could equally be a misguided attempt at protecting her remaining daughters after the death of the youngest. Ronald Lisbon—unravelling enough that he can be seen talking to himself, and then the plants, in the school hallway—leaves his job at the high school. In a particular act of cruelty, Mrs. Lisbon, inspired by a church sermon, forces a sobbing Lux to burn her rock records. A moment of relief sees them coughing due to the acrid vinyl fumes, but the poison is metaphorical as well as literal. In the next scene, the Lisbon girls watch from the window as the neighborhood elm trees are felled and emerge in their nightdresses to protect the one in their front yard, with Cecilia's palm print in it. "If I leave that tree there, they'll all be gone by next year," the frustrated workman says. "They will be anyway," Mr. Lisbon jokes ominously. "The way things are going."

The boys, no longer able to watch the girls at school, begin spying on Lux, as she has sex with random men on the roof of the Lisbon home. They make jokes together about the men she sleeps with, oblivious to the deep loneliness that is settling into the Lisbon girls. Their souvenir collection grows, and they obsess over the travel brochures the sisters order to the house to feel connected to the world they are cut off from. The boys, equally desperate for connection, insert themselves into these fantasies, until eventually the Lisbons make a final attempt to reach out, and the teenagers play records down the phone line to one another in a tender expression of melancholy. But while the boys can be seen smiling in their room, the girls are unhappy. "We're suffocating," Lux tells her mother in a desperate whisper. "I can't breathe in here."

She means it. When the boys arrive to rescue the girls under

30

the cover of darkness, Lux is found, cigarette still in hand, asphyxiated in the garage. Her sisters are gone, too: Bonnie, hanging in the basement, Mary, with her head in the oven, and Therese overdosed on sleeping pills. After that, Mr. and Mrs. Lisbon leave Grosse Pointe, and the boys take their final

31

souvenirs: the family photos, left out with the trash. Who they really are is lost as they are converted into symbols, forever the epitome of teenage fantasies, unspoiled in the minds of the men who outlived them. The sensation that your life is not your own is familiar to me; I could understand the appeal of suicide to the Lisbon girls. Without the help I found, I'm certain I would have sought a more permanent solution.

The world spins madly on, as the narrator recalls how later that summer a green smog submerged the town, creeping like noxious gas released into the air when Cecilia cut her wrists. A disturbing green-tinged epilogue at a debutante ball shows guests in bejeweled gas masks, happily laughing and chatting, disaffected. But standing outside the Lisbon house a final time, the narrator offers a devastated final assessment: "We had loved them, and they hadn't heard us calling, still do not hear us calling them out of those rooms, where they went to be alone for all time, and where we will never find the pieces to put them back together."

When *The Virgin Suicides* premiered at the 1999 Cannes Film Festival, it was received well by critics, with *Variety*'s Emanuel Levy describing the film as "deeply disturbing" (a compliment!). But the response to its theatrical release in April 2000 was more muted. "Paramount Classics didn't really know what to do with it," Coppola explained, reflecting on the film in 2018. "They were afraid that girls were going to commit suicide if they saw it." It's interesting that this was the studio's big takeaway—that young women might mimic what they saw, rather than feel understood by it—and hints at the same moral panic within the film.

In subsequent years, the film found a new life online, where stills from it became popular among the (predominantly female) teenage users of social networking websites such as Livejournal, Pinterest, and Tumblr. Indeed, Coppola's hyper-feminine aesthetic (featuring frilly, flowy fabrics, stuffed animals, jewelry and trinkets) and pastel color palette have gone on to inspire fashion, perfumes, photography, and countless teenage girls around the world, as well as those who came of age when the film was released.

Air's effortlessly cool soundtrack—composed so it could be enjoyed separately from the film—stands as still one of the greatest musical embodiments of depression and summer inertia.

Distinct from the diegetic music cues, the score is more reminiscent of a requiem mass, with melancholy piano melodies and a creeping pace that takes cues from Air's electronic sensibilities but presents something slower and more ethereal. The vocals for "Playground Love" which bookends the film, were performed by "Gordon Tracks"— a pseudonym for Thomas Mars, frontman of the band Phoenix, who was originally brought in to lay down test vocals (David Bowie was supposed to perform the song). Coppola was so pleased with Mars's version, they never did record one with Bowie, and she used another song by Phoenix on the soundtrack for *Lost In Translation*. Years later, Mars and Coppola would marry and have two daughters, and Phoenix would create the scores for *Somewhere, The Beguiled,* and *On the Rocks*.

Of course the film wasn't without its detractors. Besides claims that *The Virgin Suicides* was only notable due to Sofia's surname, some critics complained about the subject matter; that it was not as interesting or endemic as the film suggests, or that—and this would be a repeated criticism throughout Coppola's career—it was in some way a shallow depiction of a serious matter. But this seems like a misreading of Coppola's film, which is more interested in the banality of depression and suicide, and concerned with the often dismissed interiority of teenage girls, than how the Lisbon sisters' deaths might be a metaphor for the great American rot.

There are whispers within the film of how Cecilia's suicide attempt spread "the poison in the air"—and maybe her death did wake the Lisbon sisters from catatonia. They reached outward to the world after Cecilia's death, finding brief fascination with the neighborhood boys, but ultimately were forced to retreat inward. Even so, we only know part of the story; we're constantly looking in, as bewildered as the neighborhood by what happened that summer. What drove the Lisbon girls to kill themselves can only be guessed at as their voices are silenced by death, and they leave no explanation behind.

Yet as Coppola always knew, and as the boys of *The Virgin Suicides* come to realize, it doesn't matter why the Lisbon sisters chose to end their lives. Only that they did, and the devastating aftermath is as nonsensical as the deaths themselves, which feel like the ultimate act of defiance in a world where their autonomy was consistently denied. ◾

THE

BEGUILED

1–2
A wide establishing shot shows
Amy (Oona Laurence) walking
alone in the woods, where
she comes across the injured
union soldier, Corporal John
McBurney. She resembles
Little Red Riding Hood with
her basket—which would make
McBurney the Big Bad Wolf.

3
Alicia, played by Elle Fanning,
and her fellow pupils take
a lesson. Alicia in particular
seems bored by schoolwork,
and McBurney's presence is
a fascinating distraction.

4
The facade of Farnsworth
Academy in Virginia.
The austere building is
reminiscent of the Lisbon
house from *The Virgin
Suicides*, but the presence
of fencing and a gate
suggests material threat
in *The Beguiled*; is it a refuge
or a prison? Does it keep
the danger in or out?

5–6
The women warily treat
the injured John McBurney,
an interloper in their space.

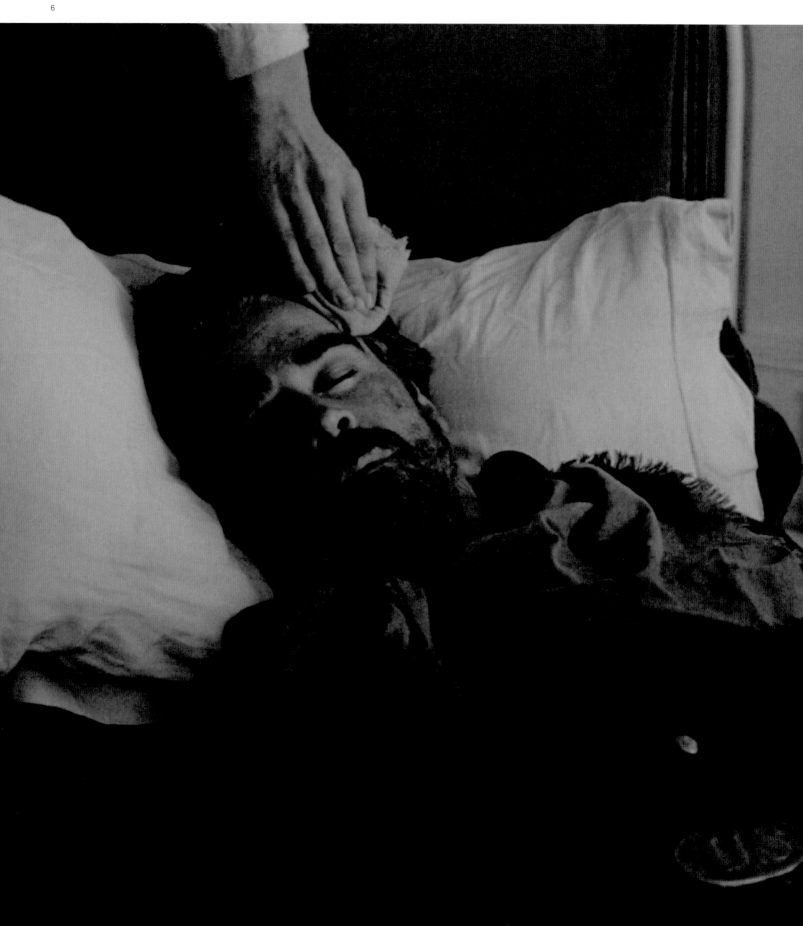

6

7-10
As well as lessons, domestic chores are part of life at the academy. The wide frames resemble the paintings of nineteenth century American landscapist Winslow Horner whose subjects frequently included women engaged in agricultural work.

SOFIA COPPOLA: FOREVER YOUNG

11
Edwina and McBurney's relationship grows. While in the original film McBurney played the women against each other to gain an advantage, his affection for Edwina in Sofia's film appears genuine.

12
Alicia sits on the edge of the woods. Sofia cites the artist John Singer Sargent as an inspiration for her vision of *The Beguiled*; in particular his painting *The Black Brook* bares a distinct resemblance to this scene, echoing an air of quiet contemplation, possibly boredom.

13
The pupils gather after dinner and perform the Civil War ballad "Lorena" for McBurney. There's an air of hesitance or bashfulness about their recital, which is swiftly interrupted by a visit from a group of Confederate soldiers.

14
The women gather for a special dinner to say goodbye to McBurney, dressed in their finery. It's the first time they have been permitted to wear fancy gowns in some time, and Alicia seems particularly keen to win McBurney's attention.

15
In anticipation of McBurney
paying her a late night visit,
Edwina wears a new, more
revealing nightgown, the sort
that might ordinarily be worn
on a wedding night.

16
Martha amputates
McBurney's broken leg.
Covered in his blood, she
resembles Lady Macbeth
after staging the murder
scene of King Duncan.

20

17–18
After McBurney catches Amy tying a blue cloth to the gates to alert Confederate soldiers to his presence in their home, he chases her down and interrogates her about Martha Farnsworth's intentions.

19–20
The threat McBurney poses to the girls is realized, as he lambasts Martha for amputating his leg.

21
The women and McBurney gather for a somber final dinner before he is to leave; but the potential risk of him returning with reinforcements and seeking revenge for his amputated leg is too great for Martha Farnsworth to endure.

22
The sun resembles fire as it peeks through the treeline. As dawn breaks the women take McBurney's body to the roadside, where it will be collected like any other dead soldier during wartime.

The Beguiled

2017
93 minutes

Budget $10.5 million
Box Office $27.8 million

23

23
Without a car or a carriage, the Coppola shot this time comes in the form of Edwina Morrow gazing out of the window, obscured by lace curtains.

24
The Sleepwalking Lady Macbeth by Henry Fuseli, depicting the resulting madness of Shakespeare's villainess after Duncan's murder. Not only does Sofia's shot of Martha Farnsworth after McBurney's amputation resemble the painting, Siegel's depiction of the headmistress's fantasy about having a sexual encounter with McBurney and Edwina evokes it as well.

IN THE IMMEDIATE aftermath of Duncan's murder in William Shakespeare's *Macbeth*, the Thane of Cawdor confesses his overwhelming feelings of guilt to his wife, who swiftly rebukes him for his cowardice. "Tis the eye of childhood / That fears a painted devil" she admonishes before disappearing offstage to ensure the servents are framed for the King's murder. American author Thomas P. Cullinan borrowed the latter part of Lady Macbeth's line in naming his first novel; *A Painted Devil* was published in 1966, telling of the fallout within a girls' boarding school in Virginia when a wounded enemy soldier comes into their care. The book would later become known as *The Beguiled* before it was adapted into a 1971 western by Don Siegel (and much later, a 2017 drama by Sofia Coppola) but the implications of Cullinan's original title are curious.

To Lady Macbeth, the "painted devil" is a perceived but imaginary threat; something that only scares children. Perhaps, in this case, the Union soldier who disrupts the rural idyll is ultimately harmless due to his injuries. A different interpretation: are the female residents of the Miss Martha Farnsworth Seminary for Young Ladies the painted devils, masquerading as beautiful, harmless creatures until their sudden inherent violence is unveiled? It does sound a little like something the injured Corporal John McBurney might shout during his late-stage confrontation with the women. Given that to "beguile" is to charm in a deceptive manner, and considering that Siegel saw his adaptation as playing on "the basic desire of women to castrate men" it seems an apt explanation that the women are the villains of the piece. But in Coppola's 2017 iteration of this Southern Gothic tale of gender trouble, the lines become a little more blurred, inviting a consideration of who's beguiling who.

Coppola was introduced to Siegel's film by her longtime friend and collaborator, production designer Anne Ross, who told her she needed to remake it. "I thought that was funny because I'd never remake someone else's film," she told the *Los Angeles Times*. Despite her initial apprehension, Coppola took Ross's advice, and was spellbound by the film's plot of seduction and secrets in the dying days of the Civil War. She turned to Cullinan's novel and began to envision how she would tell the story of a group of sheltered, genteel ladies squaring off against a wily veteran in the American South: "What if you really looked at that story about these women from their point of view, and instead of hysterical, cartoonish women, they were real, human women with stifled desires?"

The story also appealed to Coppola's desire to do something radically different from her previous film, *The Bling Ring*. "I knew that after that movie I wanted to do something beautiful—that's all I knew," she told *Entertainment Weekly* during the press tour for *The Beguiled*. "That movie was in such a tacky, ugly world, and I wanted to cleanse myself. I wanted to do something beautiful, so that was my starting point. . . . It was so depressing shooting in those kitchens in Calabasas." So she descended upon Louisiana (doubling for Virginia) to the Madewood Plantation House, which coincidentally provided the backdrop for Beyonce's visual album *Lemonade* one year earlier. Interior scenes were filmed in actress Jennifer Coolidge's grand New Orleans home, and Coppola reunited with previous collaborators Kirsten Dunst and Elle Fanning, plus Nicole Kidman (who she had previously wanted to work with on her short-lived *The Little Mermaid* adaptation) and Colin Farrell, to bring her reimagining of *The Beguiled* to life.

In Cullinan's novel ("not really worth reading" in Coppola's mind) the narrative is presented from multiple perspectives. There are the sisters Martha and Harriet Farnsworth, who run the school, and their young charges, Amelia "Amy" Dabney, Marie Devereaux, Alicia "Alice" Simms, Emily Stevenson and Edwina Morrow, plus the Farnsworth's Black slave, Matilda "Mattie" Farnsworth. This is how we come to know John McBurney, and understand his intentions and actions; through the accounts of various witnesses, each with their own unique understanding of the situation and personal bias against one another, as well as the intruder in their refuge. The most reliable is Mattie, who, owing to her race and social standing, is at once an insider and outsider. She seems to have a much better grasp on what's going on than her white counterparts, who are torn between suspicion and seduction due to the sudden presence of a man in a place where there has been none for quite some time.

It is Mattie's perspective of the harrowing climax that concludes the novel, and she is the most suspicious of McBurney's intentions. When he suggests that a Union victory will result in not only liberation but wealth and fortune for Mattie, she glibly replies, "You are the craziest man." She also appears to be the most troubled by the events which occur over the course of McBurney's stay, remarking at the novel's outset, "I didn't have any notion then how much evil we got in us, all of us." No admission of guilt ever comes from the novel's white characters, who justify their actions as a necessary evil.

Siegel's adaptation renames Mattie as Hallie (played by Mae Mercer) and she similarly acts as the film's moral compass. Impervious to McBurney's charms, she maintains a healthy (and justified) suspicion of him. When he threatens to rape her, a flashback reveals a previous attempted sexual assault on Mattie by Martha's brother Matthew Farnsworth. Disgusted but defiant, Mattie replies to McBurney, "You better like it with a dead Black woman, because that's the only way you'll get it from this one." This isn't to say that Siegel's portrayal of Blackness is perfect. Hallie is only a supporting character and given little backstory beyond mentioning her relationship with another slave named Ben, and while Edwina Morrow was portrayed as a mixed race seventeen-year-old in Cullinan's novel, Siegel reimagines her as a white teacher played by Elizabeth Hartman—a choice which would be repeated by Coppola. Similarly, Cullinan's writing is not without fault; he uses eye dialect in Mattie's chapters, creating a sense of otherness between her and the novel's white counterparts, and even though her voice is strong within the novel, there isn't an awful lot of it. Like Hallie, we learn very little about Mattie's life or identity beyond how she serves the school.

It's important to note all this because of *The Beguiled*'s setting; to erase the Black experience from stories about the Civil War is to portray a narrative which is at best myopic and at worst actively racist. Coppola is no stranger to criticism about how she addresses (or fails to address) race within her films. Critic Inkoo Kang called *Lost in Translation* "an insufferable, racist mess," and even before *The Beguiled* was released, people had picked up on her casting choices.

In Coppola's *The Beguiled*, Kirsten Dunst plays Edwina Morrow, here a composite of the naive, yearning student of the same name and Martha's sister Harriet, who teaches the pupils. Fanning is the precocious Alicia, nicknamed Alice in the novel and renamed Carol in Siegel's film, while Nicole Kidman plays a slightly softer version of Martha Farnsworth, who was something of a harridan as played by Geraldine Page in the 1971 film. There are four other pupils: Emily, Jane, Marie, and the youngest, Amy, who stumbles across McBurney while picking mushrooms in the woods, but the film very much centers upon the dynamic between the older characters.

"The slaves left," Amy tells McBurney when he asks who lives with her at the seminary. This is the only explicit reference to race—or slavery—made in Coppola's *The Beguiled*, and has been viewed by many as a lazy excuse on the writer-director's part for excluding any sort of Black perspective from her narrative. This stirred Coppola to address the criticism in an essay published on IndieWire, and she defended her decision to not include Mattie's character: "I did not want to perpetuate an objectionable stereotype where facts and history supported my choice of setting the story of these white women in complete isolation, after the slaves had escaped. Moreover, I felt that to treat slavery as a side-plot would be insulting." This may be true, but it doesn't quite let Coppola off the hook, as Edwina's biracial identity is one of the most interesting elements of Cullinan's novel; it's her feelings of "otherness" from the rest of the women that McBurney latches onto, playing on her insecurities in order to manipulate her. In Coppola's version, Edwina's yearning is more generalized. She just longs to be far away from the horrors of the South.

Responding to Coppola's decision "just to focus on the women" in *The Beguiled*, Nadra Kareem Nittle states that "it never crossed Coppola's mind that Hallie is a woman, too." Ever since *The Virgin Suicides* it has been suggested that Coppola's interests as a filmmaker only extend to the willowy, conventionally attractive blonde girls who front the majority of her films, and it's easy to understand the justified frustration and anger among viewers—particularly Black women—regarding *The Beguiled*'s very  24

limited scope. Yet Ira Madison asked what exactly is expected of white directors regarding race: "In an era where we can now task Black filmmakers with telling our own stories, like Ava DuVernay, Steve McQueen, and Barry Jenkins, why should we have white filmmakers depict Black bodies in situations as harsh as the Antebellum South?"

That doesn't mean that race is absent from the film's narrative, intentionally or not. In an essay for *Vulture*, critic and self-confessed Southern broad Angelica Jade Bastién presents a compelling reading of how the film inadvertently addresses race by presenting its white female characters as "emblems of whiteness and its toxicity." Whether it's Martha Farnsworth yearning for the glamour of her youth in Southern high society or Alicia whining about having to do chores in the absence of the slaves who did them previously, Bastién sees the *The Beguiled* as "a curious reckoning of the myths of white womanhood—how they use fragility as a shield for deviousness and insulate themselves from the horrors of a world that they, too, are responsible for."

Interestingly, another film exploring womanhood in the strict confines of historical high society emerged shortly before *The Beguiled*, and the two share a few similarities. William Oldroyd's *Lady Macbeth* stars Florence Pugh as Katherine, a young woman trapped in a loveless marriage to a wealthy older man; as in *The Beguiled*, she uses mushrooms to rid herself of a threatening male presence, and the title is an obvious reference to the machiavellian matriarch of Shakespeare's eponymous play (though the book was adapted from Nikolai Leskov's 1865 novella, *Lady Macbeth of the Mtsensk District*). *Lady Macbeth* was also praised for its piercing depiction of racial tensions and violence; Katherine's relationship with her Black maid, Anna, is particularly complex, as she embarks on an affair with the farmhand implied to have raped Anna. Later in the film, a shocking act of violence Katherine inflicts against her husband's illegitimate son (a mixed race child) and subsequent framing of Anna as the perpetrator emphasizes her monstrous nature, and—as in *The Beguiled*—how white women have inflicted physical and emotional violence on Black bodies for centuries. It makes for a fascinating companion piece to Coppola's film.

In the film's first scene, young Amy wanders alone through the dark forest at dawn, humming the Antebellum favorite "Lorena" (previously featured in *Gone With the Wind*, as well as Ken Burns's epic television documentary *The Civil War*), looking for mushrooms. It's an eerie sight reminiscent of a horror film. She stumbles across the wounded Union soldier McBurney, who asks her "Are you frightened?" Amy quickly answers 'no' before changing her mind. McBurney replies "So am I." Though she may lack the costume, Amy evokes Little Red Riding Hood, stumbling across the Big Bad Wolf on her way to Grandmother's house. Much like the wolf, McBurney infiltrates the home of these seemingly benign ladies— and much like the wolf, he meets a rather unpleasant end. It's no surprise that Coppola's films often feel like fairy tales, although *The Beguiled* has more in common with Angela Carter's feminist short story anthology from 1979, *The Bloody Chamber*, emphasising the women over their handsome interloper. Carter's reimagined fairy tales see the previously weak and innocent Gothic heroines as being quite capable of rescuing themselves; in a similar vein, the women of *The Beguiled* prove more than capable of holding their own against a perceived threat.

It makes perfect sense that Clint Eastwood was the star of Siegel's film, given that it was his idea to adapt the story in the first place. The film plays up the scandalous elements of the source material, fabricating an incestuous relationship between Martha and her brother and imagining a ménage à trois between Martha, Edwina and McBurney. The opening scene sets the tone: McBurney asks Amy how old she is, and when she tells him she's nearly thirteen, he replies "Old enough for kisses" and gives her one on the lips. The women are whipped up into a frenzy by McBurney's presence, constantly vying for his attention and affection. While Amy wants him to be her friend, the teenage Carol—a nymphette in the *Lolita* vain—makes overt advances towards him. It's jealousy between the women that fuels most of the conflict, and indeed brings about McBurney's ruin. Siegel said of *The Beguiled*, "Any young girl who looks perfectly harmless is capable of murder" but in his mind, the motivation is sexual jealousy rather than fear. In his Southern potboiler, Hell hath no fury like a woman scorned.

Mae Mercer as Hallie—the slave character omitted from Coppola's film—tending to McBurney. Her defiant attitude toward him is a contrast from the women of the house who fawn over McBurney's presence before they turn on him.

26
Clint Eastwood and Elizabeth Hartman as John McBurney and Edwina Dabney in Don Siegel's 1971 adaptation of *The Beguiled*.

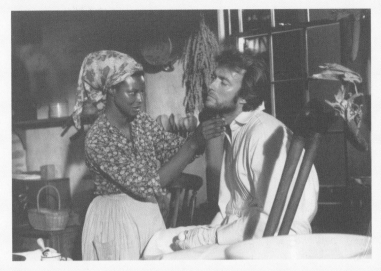

25

There's more ambiguity in Coppola's version, in which Colin Farrell plays McBurney, softer-spoken than Eastwood with a less predatory leer. His impact upon the women is more subtle; alluded to by the fact that the film's poster barely features him at all. While Eastwood's McBurney spins a yarn about how he was a nonviolent army medic (contradicted by the concurrent flashback, which shows him shooting an enemy soldier) Coppola positions him as a less obvious threat. To begin with, at least. While Farrell has a modern cultural sex symbol status comparable to Eastwood's in the 1970s (Coppola herself has referred to him as "the thinking woman's hunk"), his McBurney is more tender, less smoldering, and Coppola's interest is fixed more to how the women react to his presence than how McBurney perceives his situation. He seems to fully understand that the women of Farnsworth Seminary are in charge.

In an on-set interview, Farrell spoke about the decision to incorporate Cullinson's portrayal of McBurney as a Irish immigrant: "I think the greatest danger for McBurney was nothing to do with North or South, nothing to do with geography, politics, war—it was just that he was a man." This evokes an observation made by Margaret Atwood:

"'Why do men feel threatened by women?' I asked a male friend of mine . . . 'men are bigger, most of the time, they can run faster, strangle better, and they have on the average a lot more money and power.' 'They're afraid women will laugh at them,' he said. . . . I asked some women students in a poetry seminar I was giving, 'Why do women feel threatened by men?' 'They're afraid of being killed.'"

Subtle changes to the story make this very real fear evident. By centering the women's daily routines, Coppola highlights how disruptive McBurney's presence is to them. Early in his stay, Jane expresses an immediate suspicion of John: "He's probably a spy and will let the blue bellies in at night to raid our garden." Edwina admonishes the girls' bad manners in using this term to describe the union soldiers, highlighting how they are expecting to be genteel, polite ladies even when afraid. Yet the tension between the poor Irish soldier and the well-heeled women of Virginian high society places all the characters on their guard; Martha is resolute for much of the film in her desire to send McBurney on his way, only thawing after John appeals to her

26

ego by highlighting how strong she must be to run the school single-handedly. He warms to Edwina the quickest because they both possess a desire to leave the South far behind, and her inexperience around men makes her susceptible to his promises about running away together.

But Coppola's film does not pit these women against each other in the way Siegel's version—and to an extent Cullinan's novel—insists upon. Shortly after McBurney arrives in Siegel's film, Edwina catches Carol sneaking down to visit the soldier. When she coyly suggests "I might sponge parts of him you wouldn't" Edwina is incensed. She slaps Carol across the face and says "I knew what you were the minute you came to this school. A hussy is a hussy." Martha, Edwina and Carol all invite John to visit them under the cover of darkness. Their advances towards him are obvious and salacious—but it's Carol who ultimately tempts him, thereby signalling McBurney's fall from grace.

Coppola chooses to depict this climactic moment more subtly. McBurney tells Edwina to wait up for him, and she does, selecting a nightgown by candlelight and expectantly listening for his footsteps on the stairs. Instead, she hears a disturbance and leaves her room to find McBurney in bed with the teenage Alicia. A scuffle ensues as McBurney tries to explain himself to Edwina, and in the darkness of the house (naturally lit, obscuring our view of the commotion) he tumbles down the stairs, shattering his already injured leg. It's impossible to tell if he fell or was pushed, and Edwina seems utterly devastated in the aftermath. Siegel, ever the dramatist, has Edwina beat McBurney with a candlestick until he tumbles down the stairs, screaming "You lyin' son of a bitch! You bastard! You're a filthy lecher! I hope you're dead!" while he lies motionless on the floor.

In the aftermath, Martha assesses McBurney's injuries and decides her only option is to remove his leg before it becomes infected with gangrene. While Page's Farnsworth is calculating and practically revels in the act of amputating McBurney's leg, Kidman's character is far more frantic, while Dunst's Edwina is hysterical, in sharp contrast to Hartman's school teacher who seems unmoved by Martha's decision. The grotesque spectacle of the surgery itself is omitted; we are shown only the girls burying McBurney's severed limb in the woods, echoing the film's opening and foreshadowing the bloodletting still to come. This decision plays into Coppola's aesthetic sensibilities; even the violence in *The Virgin Suicides* is seen in snatches. Her concern lies instead with the aftermath of unspeakable acts—in *The Beguiled*, this manifests as the agonized scream we hear when McBurney awakens a few days later and realizes what's become of his damaged leg.

"You wanted to punish me for not going to your room," he spits at Martha when she defends her decision. "Now you have me at your beck and call!" The amputation of McBurney's leg—in his view—is a castration, not dissimilar to old misogynistic adages about how when a man marries he loses some facet of his masculinity. "You didn't tell me it was a house of mad women," he sobs as Edwina and Martha scurry out of the door. It's here that McBurney's attitude towards the women becomes more complex, alternating between violent threats and desperate bargaining. He hectors Alicia when she visits him (Coppola omits Siegel's choice to have Carol lie to the others, claiming McBurney forced himself upon her) and begs Jane to put in a good word for him so that "maybe things will be able to go back to the

27

27
The cast of *The Beguiled* with Sofia on set.

way they were before." His behavior becomes more desperate and unsettling, though Edwina is still attracted to him, initiating a frantic, wordless sexual encounter. Changed by the sudden violence, Edwina no longer feels the need to maintain her goodness and manners above all else; her and John give into their passion.

At the same time, Martha and the other pupils try to decide how to deal with what they perceive to be a growing threat to their safety. "We have to rid ourselves of him," Martha tells the girls. "We're not safe here while he's in the house." Ironically (and suggesting she truly sees the amputation as a necessary evil), when Emily proposes hanging McBurney, Farnsworth seems shocked, replying firmly "We cannot resort to brutality."

It's Marie who realizes they could use McBurney's love of wild mushrooms to their advantage, and young Amy is duly dispatched to pick the poisonous ones from the forest where she first found the Corporal so they can prepare a special dinner which will serve as the solution to their problem. When they eat this final meal together, they do so in relative silence; a contrast to the chatter and excitement of their previous meals with the soldier. McBurney and Edwina glance at each other fondly, having resolved to leave the school together, while the other women shared furtive looks. While Siegel's dinner scene is bombastic, Coppola's is dark and intense, with no music, only the sound of cicadas chirping outside. "I think women especially communicate through gestures and glances," Coppola has said of her intention. "Hopefully [you] can feel what they're not able to say." Their silence is necessary for another reason beyond avoiding John's suspicion: Edwina is not involved in their plan. When John collapses from poisoning, she is genuinely shocked and looks askance at the other women, who can only stare sombrely at their plates. They gently sew McBurney's body into a cloth bag, and leave him at the gates for a passing patrol to find. The final shots of the film show the women sitting on the front steps of the house, just beyond the gates which encase this prison of their own making.

But the damage is done; the sanctuary and tranquility of Farnsworth's Seminary has been breached. Bound by the knowledge of what they've done, we are aware that things can not simply return to the way they were before at the school, and the last shot of them sitting together—as in a family portrait—is haunting. There is no happily-ever-after in wartime.

If Siegel's take on The Beguiled is obsessed with obsession, Coppola's is fuelled by desperation. There is a naivety displayed by all the women in the way they interact with McBurney, whether it's Martha fancying he might stay and help around the house, Edwina expecting him to spirit her away to some better place, Alicia pursuing a romance despite the age difference between them or Amy assuming he's her best friend. The Corporal, too, displays a lack of understanding for how his presence impacts upon the women; for so long they have lived in relative safety, going about their lessons with no need to concern themselves with the outside world. McBurney's presence is not only a reminder of the gender imbalance in the world beyond their school gates, but also the reality they don't seem to want to face: one of warfare and injustice. They are as keen to rid their safe space of external politics as Coppola herself was when she removed the source material's racial element.

Usually in tales of women exacting violence on men, it's positioned as revenge for crimes committed against them. There's something less triumphant and more devastating about The Beguiled and its paradise lost, in which a group of women who have been able to lock themselves away from the rest of the world are confronted by the reality of it. If it wasn't McBurney, it would have been a different man; the South they knew was in its dying days, and they are a relic of it. Coppola has referred to the South of The Beguiled as "exotic" and appears to have a fairly romantic view of it, but her Southern Gothic vision of life in the Antebellum is a creeping nightmare in the same vein as The Virgin Suicides, where feminine innocence is shattered by vicious experience. Both films also feature the home as a prison, escape from which is ultimately futile, regardless of the gallant men who enter it to try and save you.

Although the politics and history of the Civil War extend far beyond Coppola's lens—especially the impact of the War and violence against Black men and women across the South—The Beguiled's myopia is still relevant today. The women holed up in Farnsworth only care about the War to the extent that it directly affects them, and indeed plenty of women like them still exist today. When The Beguiled was being filmed, Coppola remarked on the number of Trump placards she saw during filming in Louisiana; after the election, statistics revealed white women had turned out in droves to vote for him. Coppola's film provides a possible explanation as to why—a desire for self-preservation, even at the expense of others. Lady Macbeth would have done exactly the same. 🍄

INSPIRATIONS

↓ *Lolita*, Stanley Kubrick *&* *Picnic at Hanging Rock*, Peter Weir ↓

"HOW DID THEY ever make a movie of *Lolita*?" asks the tagline for Stanley Kubrick's 1962 adaptation of Vladimir Nabokov's seminal novel, published seven years earlier. It's a fair question; the book was infamously rejected by prominent publishers Viking, Simon & Schuster, New Directions, Farrar, Straus, and Doubleday before finding a home at Olympia Press in France. While the novel received praise from literary luminaries including Graham Greene, it also attracted a considerable amount of controversy, decried as "sheer unrestrained pornography" by John Greene, then-editor of the London *Sunday Express*. While the book continues to generate considerable praise and criticism even in the present day, Kubrick's cinematic rendering of the disturbing relationship between Professor Humbert Humbert and teenager Dolores "Lolita" Haze considerably strips back the novel's more provocative aspects.

Nonetheless, Lolita serves as a key influence on Sofia Coppola's work, in particular *The Virgin Suicides* and *The Beguiled*. The most obvious comparison might be Lux Lisbon's resemblance to Sue Lyon as the "nymphet" subject of Humbert Humbert's infatuation, but it's also worth considering how the behavior of Elle Fanning's mischievous Alicia in *The Beguiled* echoes that of Dolores Haze. Sheltered and impatient for experience of the real world, it's unsurprising that Lolita and Alicia quickly latch on to Humbert and McBurney, viewing them as intriguing masculine figures in a world that seems humdum by comparison. Humbert and McBurney seem to offer the possibility of escape, at least at first; it becomes clear that for all their perceived maturity, these are still girls rather than women, and do not hold the power in their relationships with older men.

The idea of domineering masculinity as a repressive force also echoes between *The Virgin Suicides* and *Lolita*. While the neighborhood boys of Grosse Pointe, Michigan fantasize about the Lisbon sisters, they remain cooped up inside their home, only allowed to exist as avatars of idealized womanhood. When they do escape for one night of freedom at their high school prom, Lux's newfound liberty is all but destroyed when she has sex with Trip on the football field. When she falls asleep he leaves her there alone; Lux's missed curfew plunges all four sisters back into lockdown, the consequence of being a woman with sexual agency. Similarly, towards the end of *Lolita*, Humbert arrives at the home Lolita now shares with her husband and attempts to convince her to leave with him once more, incredulous as to how Lolita could possibly be happy living a pauper's life with a humble mechanic. The impulse to control a young woman's life remains; ultimately Humbert murders Clare Quilty, partly out of disgust for his treatment of Lolita, but jealousy is undeniably a factor as well.

A similarly pertinent point of comparison is Peter Weir's 1975 adaptation of Joan Lindsay's 1967 novel *Picnic at Hanging Rock*, about a group of schoolgirls who vanish during a trip with their teacher to a geological site in Victoria, Australia. Coppola has made no secret of Weir's influence on her work: the floaty, delicate dresses of her heroines in both *The Virgin Suicides* and *The Beguiled* evoke Judith Dorsman's costume design, while the detail of ill-fated schoolgirl Miranda's butterfly belt buckle in Weir's film has a connection to the butterfly motif in Nabokov's *Lolita*; the great tragedy of this beautiful creature being its fragile and fleeting nature. Meanwhile, Rachel Roberts's austere headmistress Mrs. Appleyard is a dead ringer for Kathleen Turner's Mrs. Lisbon, or even Nicole Kidman's Martha Farnsworth, matronly authority figures attempting to curb the curiosity and yearning of young women in their care.

In the opening to *Picnic at Hanging Rock*, student Miranda quotes a poem by Edgar Allan Poe: "What we see and what we seem are but a dream, a dream within a dream." This verse, written two years after the untimely death of his wife Virginia (his first cousin whom he married when he was twenty-seven and she thirteen) and seven months before the writer's own mysterious end in 1849, suggests an ambivalence towards life, based on the notion that we can't truly distinguish between reality and imagination. The poem brings to mind an observation made in Eugenides's novel about Cecilia Lisbon ("What we have here is a dreamer; someone completely out of touch with reality") but is also reminiscent of Coppola's gauzy aesthetic in *The Virgin Suicides* and *The Beguiled*, where the quiet of dusk and dawn is as threatening as it is beguiling; a time for sneaking out to see boys, or watching the treeline for encroaching enemy soldiers.

Crucially, the dreamy ambiguity of Weir's film is reflected in Coppola's work, which never offers a concrete reason for the Lisbon sisters' deaths, or any neat conclusion to the saga of Farnsworth Seminary. Freedom for the Lisbon sisters—and the young women of Appleyard College—only seems possible through ascension, be it in death or disappearance. ☁

MARIE

ANTOINETTE

2

1
A wide shot shows Marie
Antoinette—aged fourteen—
arriving at the Palace of
Versailles, with the large
French entourage who
picked her up from the
forest of Compiègne.
The majestic palace looms
in the background, an
inescapable presence.

2–4
The Dauphine endures
the scrutiny of the French
court, who seem distinctly
unimpressed with the
Austrian princess. In
particular, Louis XV's
daughters Madame Victoire
and Madame Sophie are
perturbed by her arrival.
Still, the palace represents
an ornate, colorful future,
in contrast to Marie's cool,
quiet Austrian home.

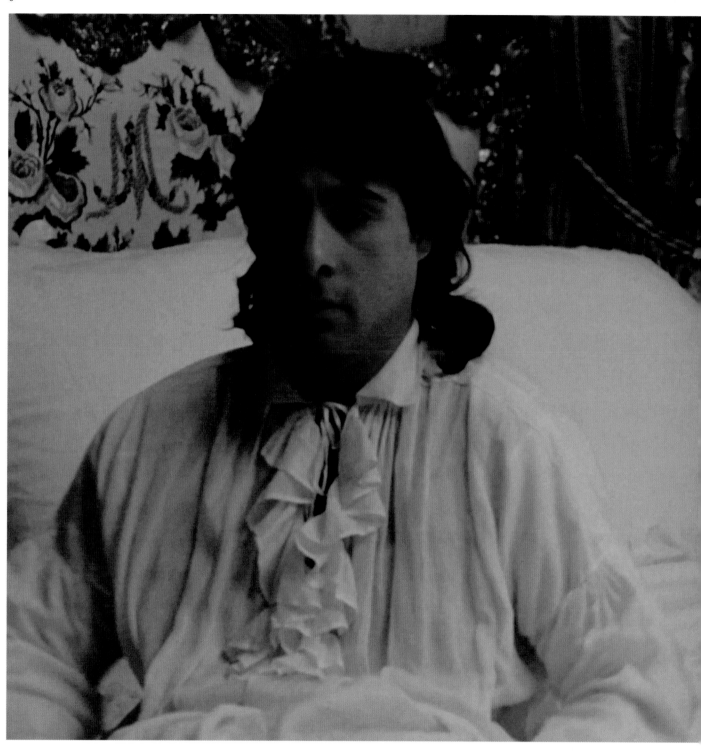

5
The future king of France
and Marie Antoinette marry
in a lavish ceremony, which
should mark a bright future
for the couple, but their union
gets off to an inauspicious
start when they are unable to
consummate their marriage.

6
Sofia Coppola's cousin
Jason Schwartzman as
the awkward King Louis
XVI, whose interests lie with
locksmithing rather than love.

SOFIA COPPOLA: FOREVER YOUNG

7–8
Dunst and her editor, Sarah Flack, decided to pay homage to Bob Fosse's *All That Jazz* in this scene which depicts the queen's morning dressing routine, using the same piece of Vivaldi music. Marie is baffled by the extravagant and complex ceremony; her decision to bring about change within the palace creates further friction.

9
The prince and princess eat all their meals with an audience, becoming a spectacle themselves.

10
Louis XV, played by Rip Torn,
and his mistress Madame
DuBarry, played by Asia
Argento, don't face any
of the relationship woes
his grandson and Marie
experience.

11
Louis and Marie settle into
married life, developing an
amicable relationship despite
rumors at court about their
failure to produce an heir.

12
After Louis's younger
brother Charles and
his wife Maria Theresa
welcome a baby son, Marie
is devastated by her lack of
a child but maintains a stoic
front at court. In private, she
knows the precariousness
of her position.

13-14
Still without a child
and frustrated by her
husband's interest in his
hobbies over his marriage,
Marie Antoinette turns to
extravagant pastimes:
eating, drinking, shopping,
and gambling.

15
Marie poses for a portrait with her children, Marie Terese and Louis Joseph, at the Petit Trianon. The chateau—formerly the residence of Madame DuBarry—allows Marie to entertain her friends informally, affording her a degree of privacy but also causing tension in the royal court.

16
After meeting at a masquerade ball, Marie embarks on an affair with the dashing Count Axel von Fersen, played by Jamie Dornan. It's the first time she has experienced genuine romance, although he soon departs to fight in the American Revolutionary War.

17
In Marie's daydream about von Fersen, Sofia recreates Jacques-Louis David's portrait, *Napoleon Crossing the Alps*. Marie Antoinette would die several years before Napoleon's ascent to power in France, but the reference is befitting of von Fersen's New Romantic styling in Coppola's film.

18
Tensions in France begin to reach a fever pitch and the French public turn against the queen, seeing her as emblematic of the crown's reckless spending. She is nicknamed "Madame Deficit" by the press.

SOFIA COPPOLA: FOREVER YOUNG

19-20
Where once Marie Antoinette was the guest of honor at the Parisian opera, she becomes persona non grata toward the end of her reign, abandoned by the aristocrats who once fought to win her favor.

21
As the court leaves the Palace of Versailles, the royal family opt to stay, until a mob descends upon the palace, forcing them to flee to the Tuileries in Paris.

22
On their final night in
Versailles, Marie and Louis
sit down for a somber dinner,
as they have done countless
times before.

23
The final shot of the film:
Marie Antoinette's ransacked
bedroom in the aftermath of
the storming of Versailles.

Marie Antoinette

2006
123 minutes

Budget $40 million
Box Office $60.9 million

24

24
The Coppola shot returns:
Marie Antoinette gazes out
of the carriage window
en route to her new life in
France. This moment is
recalled in the final scene of
the film, when Marie and her
husband leave Versailles.
Staring out of the window,
Marie informs her husband
she is "saying goodbye."

25
Lady Antonia Fraser, author
of *Marie Antoinette: The
Journey*, who corresponded
with Sofia over the course of
several years prior to *Marie
Antoinette*'s production.

26
Norma Shearer in W. S. Van
Dyke's troubled 1938 film,
Marie Antoinette. One of the
most expensive films of the
1930s with a budget over
$2 million, it recorded a loss
at the box office despite its
popularity with audiences.

"LET THEM EAT cake, she says, just like Marie Antoinette," croons Freddie Mercury in the opening verse of "Killer Queen," an ode to—as he told it—a high-class call girl. "I'm trying to say that classy people can be whores as well," he explained in a 1974 interview with *NME*. "Though I'd prefer people to put their interpretation upon it—to read into it what they like." This invitation to find one's own meaning in an artist's work holds true for Sofia Coppola's oeuvre; she has always been more interested in allowing audiences to develop their own understanding of her films than dictating where and when significance exists. But two of her films stand out as less warmly received on release than the rest: *Marie Antoinette* and *The Bling Ring*. Both based on true stories of fame, obsession and excess, they form a fascinating double feature about the Western cult of celebrity and young women vilified in the name of salacious gossip. As for Marie Antoinette . . . well, she never said "let them eat cake." As her official English-language biographer, Lady Antonia Fraser, who wrote the book Coppola's biopic was based on, explained: "It was said 100 years before her by Marie-Therese, the wife of Louis XIV. It was a callous and ignorant statement and [Marie Antoinette] was neither."

Why might Coppola be interested in the life of a European monarch who ruled several centuries ago and met a grisly end via the guillotine at the climax of the French Revolution? Given her fascination with adolescent innocence and femininity already established in *The Virgin Suicides* and *Lost in Translation*, not to mention her predisposition towards art and fashion (passions shared by Antoinette), there was certainly a precedent. But perhaps Coppola was drawn to the dethroned Queen due to another sort of kinship. As the eldest daughter of a filmmaking dynasty, Coppola was born into a position of enormous power and privilege. She grew up on film sets, counted the likes of Andy Warhol and Marlon Brando as family dinner guests, and has faced charges of nepotism repeatedly.

Indeed, contemporary criticism of *Marie Antoinette*—whether positive or negative—has tended to note the potential commonalities between Coppola and the French monarch; the headline for the *New York Times*'s profile of the director prior to release was "French Royalty as Seen by Hollywood Royalty," while Dana Stevens, in a scathing review for *Slate*, dubbed her "the Veruca Salt of American filmmakers [. . .] whose father, a nut tycoon, makes sure his daughter wins a golden ticket to the Willie Wonka factory by buying up countless Wonka bars, which his workers methodically unwrap till they find the prize."

Despite any similarities between Coppola and Antoinette, the director's love for the Rococo period developed in a thoroughly modern way. A child of the 1980s, she first encountered the aesthetics of the era as a preteen through the New Romantics; primarily Adam and the Ants (though Adam Ant himself rejected the term) and Bow Wow Wow, a band created by Malcolm McLaren to promote Vivienne Westwood's clothing line. Ironically enough, Annabella Lwin was picked to front the group at just fourteen, the same age Antoinette was when she married the French dauphin.

The movement was a reaction to the anti-fashion stance embraced by the punk movement in the previous decade, and embraced maximalism, costuming, and a reframing of romantic imagery. Their music and styling would directly influence Coppola's vision of Marie Antoinette's court some twenty-five years later. Eleanor Coppola's behind-the-scenes documentary from the set of the film features Coppola discussing how Adam Ant's New Dandy styling was a touchstone for the costuming of Axel von Fersen, played by Jamie Dornan, and the film's soundtrack combines a mixture of eighties post-punk stalwarts New Order, the Cure, and Siouxsie and the Banshees with contemporary music from Aphex Twin and the Strokes. A fusion of modern and classical iconography has become a signature of Coppola's work, and nowhere has it provoked more controversy than in her mischievous confection about the glory days and eventual demise of Versailles.

Two years before *Lost in Translation* won Coppola the Academy Award for Best Original Screenplay, she set her sights on making a film about Marie Antoinette. There had been no English-language film about her since the 1938 W. S. Van Dyke production, which starred Norma Shearer in the title role and was based on Stefan Zweig's biography, *Marie Antoinette: The Portrait of an Average Woman*. Running at 150 minutes and covering her life from betrothal to execution, the film was well received but made a loss of $750,000 due to its enormous $2.9 million budget. The film was also shot in black-and-white, as the cost of adding Technicolor was deemed to have been too expensive. A lavish modern take on the source material, then, was a canny idea.

It was Coppola's mother who suggested she read Antonia Fraser's biography, *Marie Antoinette: The Journey* (a comprehensive doorstop of a book running over 600 pages, including footnotes) as part of her research, and Coppola was suitably taken with this sympathetic approach to the oft-ridiculed monarch, who is synonymous with selfishness and frivolity. As Fraser tells it, "It had been the famous 'handover' episode [in which the young Marie is exchanged from her native Austria to the French party who bring her to Versailles] which convinced Sofia."

But the author was sceptical that Coppola would even make the film she seemed so enthusiastic about, going so far as to write a note in her diary on February 2, 2001: "But of course the film won't actually happen. Because it never does." Her doubt was not unfounded; various volumes of Fraser's historical nonfiction—including *Mary Queen of Scots* and *Faith and Treason: The Story of the Gunpowder Plot*—had acquired interest from Hollywood in the past only to amount to nothing. Nevertheless, she recalls meeting Coppola three months later in Hove, where they discussed her plans for the film. This was also the first time that Coppola mentioned to Fraser the idea of casting Kirsten Dunst (whom she had worked with on *The Virgin Suicides* two years prior) as Marie Antoinette. The pair would exchange emails and meet again several times, as detailed in Fraser's diary, with Coppola asking all manner of questions about Antoinette, and the author dutifully advising.

Almost eighteen months later in the autumn of 2002, Fraser feared the dream had come to an end: "All over! Well, it was nice while it lasted." She had been informed by Coppola's agent that the director was traveling to Asia to make a film. "The Far East! Who wants to see a movie about the Far East?" wrote Fraser. "And then she'll come back and make a movie about Marie Antoinette. And Monsieur Godot will come tomorrow. The truth is that for me the party is over once again." Yet once again her scepticism was ultimately unfounded: two and a half years later, she would be invited to the Parisian set of *Marie Antoinette*. Coppola finally bought the rights to Fraser's book on the first day of shooting.

Marie Antoinette occupies a curious space in French culture; reviled by some as the epitome of royalist ruin, she's also considered an icon, spawning large amounts of merchandise, much of which can be purchased from the little gift shops within the halls of her former palace. There's an element of protectiveness over her image, which Coppola encountered as an American seeking to tell her story. In a 2019 panel with Anna Sui at New York's Museum of the Arts and Design, she recalled an exchange with French actor Alain Delon, whom she had originally asked to play the role of Louis XIV. "He was like, 'How can you come from California and think you can make this?'" It's likely that her reputation—being both an Oscar-winning filmmaker and a member of Hollywood royalty—and the affection shown to her by French popular culture was instrumental in securing her unprecedented access to the Palace of Versailles. Producer Ross Katz points to the building's curator Pierre Arizzoli as another supporter: "He said, 'The reason I wanna support this so much is because in Sofia's movie she'll get inside the head of Marie Antoinette and that's all I care about.'"

25   26

Nevertheless, filming at a listed historical site presented a number of challenges; the production team were restricted to shooting around the Palace's tourism schedule, and couldn't use any of the existing furniture due to strict rules about its preservation. Additionally, certain rooms within the Palace cannot have their shutters open due to the threat of sun damage to fabrics and wallpaper, meaning they had to be lit artificially, and all equipment needed to be covered to prevent damage to the parquet floors. "The reality is, they're museums," said production designer K.K. Barrett in *The Making of Marie Antoinette*. "We had to show these museums as alive." A sequence in the documentary shows the crew setting up for one of the sumptuous meal scenes, cutting from the sight of Kirsten Dunst and Jason Schwartzman waiting patiently in-costume at the table to the crew diligently setting up equipment just out of frame.

True to her word, Coppola cast Kirsten Dunst as the lead, though the actor was twenty-three at the time of filming whereas Marie was just thirteen when she became engaged to the future King of France. Casting an American as France's favorite primadonna was a ballsy move, not least because Coppola then doubled down by filling out her roster with more Americans, Brits, and one Australian doing a British accent (Rose Byrne, playing Antoinette's confidant the Duchesse de Polignac). Schwartzman, Coppola's first cousin, took the role of Antoinette's shy, lock-obsessed husband Louis XVI, with Rip Torn playing his grandfather Louis XV and Steve Coogan the Ambassador Mercy, who keeps a watchful eye over Marie on behalf of her mother—a role that Antonia Fraser's husband Harold Pinter had offered to play, though his ill-health would have prevented it in any case. Rather fittingly, Marianne Faithfull, herself the daughter of an Austro-Hungarian aristocrat, played Marie's mother, the Empress Maria Theresa.

Beyond casting a member of her own family as Louis XVI (who diligently gained weight to play the famously portly monarch) Coppola's brother Roman served as second unit director. The offspring of other filmmaking talent also appear: there's Dario Argento's daughter Asia as the uncouth mistress of Louis XV, Madame du Barry; Danny "Son of John" Huston as Marie's brother Joseph II of Austria; and Bill Nighy's daughter Mary as Princesse de Lamballe, who would become one of Antoinette's closest allies. Although this was likely by coincidence rather than design, it doesn't much help the claims of nepotism which have dogged Coppola throughout her career. Still, at least when it comes to working with her brother and cousin, the director feels no need to answer to anyone: "Because [Roman] knows me so well, there's a shorthand; he can go shoot things at the same time and know how I would want them. But it's just an extension of when we were kids—Jason and Roman and I would make little movies together. And you try to approach it the same way as a professional, but you're still doing it for the same reasons and try to approach it as something fun."

Perhaps the French were right to be wary of Coppola's approach. Despite the European shooting location and creative team (including French patisserie house Ladurée who were employed to make all the intricate macarons and cakes that adorned the set) there is an anarchic American atmosphere about *Marie Antoinette*, beginning with the fact that there is virtually no French dialect (or French dialogue, for that matter) in the film. Dunst speaks with a lilting Valley Girl accent, while Coogan and Faithfull maintain the Queen's English rather than the Queen's French (or German, given Antoinette's heritage). While this was a practical consideration (removing the need for months of dialect coaching) it was also evidently a stylistic choice. This is the Hollywood version of *Marie*

27

27
Jacques-Louis David's painting of *Napoleon Crossing the Alps*, created at some point between 1801–05.

28
New Romantic heartthrob Adam Ant, a direct inspiration for Sofia's version of Count Axel von Fersen.

28

Antoinette after all—a bold, brash, candy-colored version of events, imagined as the young Queen herself might have fancied it. "It's kind of like a history of feelings rather than a history of facts," said Kirsten Dunst at a preview screening in Los Angeles. "So don't expect a masterpiece theatre, educational Marie Antoinette biopic."

The precedent for Coppola's tongue-in-cheek styling of Antoinette's court had been set decades earlier by Ken Russell's 1975 rock opera *Lisztomania*, about the rambunctious life of Hungarian composer Franz Liszt, and Miloš Forman's 1984 epic *Amadeus*, a biopic of Austrian composer Amadeus Mozart, both of which treat their historical subjects like contemporary pop stars. Russell cast the Who frontman Roger Daltrey as Liszt, and in the opening concert scene hoards of teenage girls chant "Franz Liszt!" over and over. The title itself refers to the term coined by German poet Heinrich Heine— long before the advent of Beatlemania—who observed the levels of hysteria Liszt's performances generated in the 1844 concert season, particularly among young female fans.

Coppola has cited both films as influences, saying of Amadeus, "When [. . .] they were just speaking in their regular accents, they felt like real people to me as opposed to someone living in some other era I couldn't relate to". Among the director's other influences were Stanley Kubrick's 1975 adaptation of William Makepeace Thackeray's *Barry Lyndon* and Stephen Frears's 1988 period drama *Dangerous Liaisons*, based on the 1782 novel *Les Liaisons Dangereuses* by Pierre Choderlos de Laclos, of which Antoinette herself was a fan, reportedly commissioning a special copy that was concealed inside a chaise longue. These various texts detailing historical debauchery, gossip and scandal helped Coppola to shape

her own dazzling depiction of the dying days of the French regime; in her diaries Antonia Fraser recalls Coppola asking her, "Would it matter if I leave out the politics?" Fraser responded with absolute honesty: "Marie Antoinette would have adored that."

The opening scene of *Marie Antoinette*, wryly set to Gang of Four's post-punk anthem "Natural's Not in It," shows Dunst as the young queen languidly reclining on a chaise longue, swiping the frosting off a baby pink cake while a maid puts on her matching pumps for her. In an immediate fourth-wall break—something not present in either of Coppola's previous films—Dunst spies the camera and cocks her head, smirking. The shot may only last fifteen seconds but it instantly establishes the tone of what's to come. It's an immediate challenge to the notion of the austere historical biopic, though the following scene feels more conventional, as the teenage Marie awakens in her childhood home on the morning she is to leave Austria for France. "All eyes will be on you," her mother tells her, before the young princess is dispatched with her envoy (and her adorable pug, Mops) to the handover spot in Schuttern, Germany.

It's this scene which enamored Coppola when she read Fraser's biography, and its rendering in the film is just as sympathetic. Marie cries when she's forced to leave behind her beloved dog (a symbol of Austria), and is informed by the French Comtesse de Noailles, "You can have as many French dogs as you like." Marie, wiping her eyes, nods dutifully, accepting her circumstances. Again, it's a brief scene, but one that shows Antoinette's place within Europe's ruling class: a girl of thirteen, traded like a pawn between the Austrian and French monarchies. When she leaves Schuttern in an intricate baby blue Rococo gown, the sun begins to shine through the clouds as the muted colors of her native land fade into memory, shortly to be replaced by the frivolity of the French court.

Meanwhile, Louis practices sword fighting with his friends, who comment, "Apparently, she's quite beautiful [. . .] I've heard she's really nice." In the same way that Ross Katz speaks of breathing life into the museum of Versailles, Coppola finds the humanity of her teenage subjects through closing the distance between them and modern audiences: they communicate in hearsay and inside jokes, and find themselves overwhelmed by the position of responsibility thrust upon them. While Marie speaks and dresses like a royal, Dunst offsets any pretension of regality with a vulnerability that comes through in the soft cadence of her voice and the precariousness of her movements; a quality matched by Schwartzman's own nervous energy and doleful brown eyes.

When the young dauphine arrives at the vast court she is immediately the subject of scrutiny. As she walks from her carriage to the doors of the palace, onlookers stare her down in dour silence; a scene repeated later on when she marries Louis. While her homeland is presented in earthy, muted tones, Versailles is endlessly more elaborate, with a thousand and one customs Marie must learn if she is to curry favor with her courtiers and be accepted as the wife of the soon-to-be king.

In one of the film's most enduring scenes, Marie Antoinette is introduced to the ritual of the morning dressing ceremony, in which a roomful of women assist her in preparing for the day. Against the frenetic strings of Vivaldi's "Concerto in G major," the bewildered princess endures an excessively choreographed morning routine. At its end, she declares to Comtesse de Noailles, "This is ridiculous." The Comtesse, aghast, responds, "This, Madame, is Versailles." Played for comedic effect (something not usually associated with Coppola as a filmmaker) the scene establishes Versailles as a place of pomp and pageantry, with Marie quite at odds with its fussy rituals.

In time the princess finds her feet, partaking in gossiping about the King's mistress and indulging in decadent meals. Yet Marie remains painfully aware that her place is precarious, as—despite her best efforts—she fails to consummate her marriage with clueless Louis, who is more interested in pursuing his hobbies of hunting and locksmithing. "Nothing is certain about your place there until an heir is produced," her mother reminds her in a letter. This anxiety reaches a head when Marie's sister-in-law, the Comtesse de Provence (though in reality, it was Princess Maria Theresa of Savoy) gives birth to the "first Bourbon prince of his generation." After congratulating the happy couple, she retreats to her private chambers and sobs, collapsing to the floor.

The emphasis on the twenty-year-old dauphine's insecurity and unhappiness tracks with Coppola's recurring interest in how young women are subjugated by society, from the demise of the Lisbon sisters in *The Virgin Suicides* to Charlotte's sense of ennui in *Lost in Translation*. A similar sensation of being trapped in a gilded cage runs throughout *Marie Antoinette*, who finds similar material pleasures to Charlotte on her travels around Tokyo, or the strident teenage thieves of *The Bling Ring*. Despairing over her situation at court, Marie turns to a tried and trusted coping strategy: retail therapy. Immediately after she is shown weeping with frustration and sadness, a montage sequence of Marie shopping with her friends, set to Bow Wow Wow's "I Want Candy," begins.

Antoinette would earn the unfortunate moniker Madame Deficit in France, due to her (not entirely unfounded) reputation for spending money as the rest of the country experienced profound poverty. The shopping sequence, in which Marie indulges in champagne and cakes while admiring shoes, dresses, wigs and jewels, is a feast for the eyes, playing up the popular image of the Queen as a spoiled, carefree ruler with no concept of life beyond the palace walls—an image pedalled by the slanderous libelles which were circulated at the time. It also includes a fleeting shot of baby blue Converse sneakers next to a pair of ornate period-accurate shoes, which was Roman Coppola's idea. He shot the sequence and included the anachronism to amuse his sister, who decided to keep it in, emphasizing Antoinette's youthful capriciousness as well as the idea of the film as a fantasy rather than a historical document. It's the MTV's *The Real World* version of *Marie Antoinette*, based in reality but embellished for entertainment's sake, and quite possessed of its own design—just look to Roman Coppola's spoof episode of the channel's flagship real estate show *Cribs*, shot at Versailles with Schwartzman in character as Louis XVI and included in the DVD extras.

But for all its playfulness, sorrow still creeps into *Marie Antoinette*, even after the Queen has begun spending and partying. In the aftermath of her extravagant eighteenth birthday party, in which she and her friends gambol through the palace grounds (filmed with a gauzy handheld camera evocative of Terrence Malick's *Days of Heaven*), she awakens hungover and alone. She seems despondent. The next two scenes show real life encroaching on the charmed life of the young royals: Marie is warned about her lavish spending by Ambassador du Mercy, and the King agrees to send funds to America, currently in the throes of its own revolution, despite pondering whether it's a good idea to assist "those who are rejecting their sovereign."

Marie is finally granted her wish for a child after her brother gives Louis a lesson in husbandly duty. Although she is still subject to the court's notions about what is and isn't proper behavior for a queen, motherhood does change her. After Louis gifts her the Petit Trianon château, she trades her gowns for more "simple, natural" dresses, and enjoys gentle farmwork with her young daughter. As she recites from Rousseau's *Discourse on the Origin and Basis of Inequality Among Men* her hand trails through tall grass (another likely reference to *Days of Heaven*). She appears totally at home in her comparatively modest country idyll. "This is my escape from all the protocol," she protests when du Mercy explains that her absence from the court is causing friction among the nobles.

But even as she attempts to break free from the constraints of royal life (be it through her country retreat or her affair with the dashing Count Axel von Fersen) the writing is on the wall; Louis must contend with the demands on the royal purse strings while Marie becomes the subject of increased public scrutiny and accusations. Addressing that most famous and wrongly attributed quote, Coppola depicts Antoinette dripping in jewels, wearing dark lipstick as she reclines in a bathtub before flippantly uttering the words "Let them eat cake." Antoinette herself, hearing the rumor while having a manicure, scoffs: "That's such nonsense, I would never say that."

Things go from bad to worse for Antoinette as she falls out of favor with the French public and her second daughter, Princess Sophie, perishes before her first birthday. It's too late for Marie, who prostrates herself in front of an angry mob that gathers at Versailles, prompting the King and Queen to leave their home for good. As they depart, the sun rises over Versailles. Louis asks if she's admiring her lime avenue out of the carriage window. Marie, in a small voice, utters "I'm saying goodbye." The final shot of the film shows Antoinette's ransacked bedroom while birdsong filters through the trees—a moment of calm after the flurry of loud music and even louder costuming. It could just as easily be the aftermath of one of the Queen's parties but is in fact the end of her reign.

When *Marie Antoinette* premiered at the Cannes Film Festival in 2006, it was booed—though as Coppola pointed out, "There was a standing ovation, too. I think the booing was not really that loud. It was picked upon and reported because, you know, it's a better story than a standing ovation." Cannes courts nothing like controversy, but critical opinion was nevertheless split. Writing in the *Guardian*, French political correspondent Agnès Poirier was outraged: "The film is shocking because it is empty, devoid of a point of view, because the person who has made it has no curiosity for the woman she is portraying and the time that her tragic life is set in." The *Observer*'s Philip French had a similar view, decrying the film's "tedious vacuity, uncritically rendered." It wasn't just critics; the Marie Antoinette Association feared "the film is going to set us back many years" in their quest to debunk myths about the Queen being a indulgent, cake-eating libertine. This obsession with *Marie Antoinette*'s perceived shallowness and lack of historical formality seems like a blatant refusal to meet Coppola halfway.

There were some vocal defenders of the film, notably Roger Ebert, who highlighted that *Marie Antoinette* was Coppola's third work "centering on the loneliness of being female and surrounded by a world that knows how to use you but not how to value and understand you." Of course, all of Coppola's films—from *The Virgin Suicides* through to *On the Rocks*—are concerned with some sort of longing, be it for freedom, romance, honesty or human connection. Coppola set out to make a film not about how the Queen's reckless spending and growing distance between the monarchy and general public may have contributed to the French Revolution, but how being thrust into a position of immense power, wealth, and luxury and left to one's own devices might breed apathy. If Charlotte in *Lost in Translation* is at a fork in the road, Marie drives her carriage straight down the pathway to ruin, hemmed in by circumstance. It's a sympathetic look at inherited celebrity, but not one as shallow as its critics made out. Rather, a rebel yell that captures what it is to be young, fabulously wealthy, and hurtling rapidly toward disaster. Everyone knows the Queen of France lost her head—this is a film about what else she lost, too. ♛

29

THE

RING

BLING

1–3
Designer goods in
Rachel Bilson's house,
later collected as evidence.
There is an aesthetic
similarity to the "I Want
Candy" montage from *Marie
Antoinette*, which depicts
the queen's growing
shopping obsession.

4
The washed-out mansions
of Calabasas, where the
teenagers live. Its proximity
to Los Angeles has made the
neighborhood popular with
Hollywood-adjacent types,
though since *Keeping Up
With the Kardashians*, the city
has exploded in notoriety.

5
Emma Watson as Nicki Moore
giving her speech outside the
courthouse, verbatim from
Alexis Neiers's interview with
Nancy Jo Sales.

SOFIA COPPOLA: FOREVER YOUNG

6
Part of Rhonda Byrne's
The Secret is creating
"vision boards" to "manifest"
your goals; here Laurie
Moore, played by Leslie
Mann, encourages her
daughters to make their own.

7
The Moore sisters at
home. These aspiring
celebutantes were
homeschooled according
to Byrne's teachings, but
their real ambitions were to
pursue fame; they weren't
really concerned with the
particulars of how they
achieved said fame, though.

8–9
Marc and Rebecca read
celebrity gossip on the
internet, and use this
information to determine
their targets. Their victims'
addresses are easily
found online.

10
The key to Paris Hilton's mansion, famously found under her doormat.

11
A scene shot on location in Paris Hilton's home. She was the most frequent victim of the burglaries, robbed four times over the course of a few months.

12
This enchanting sequence shot by Harris Savides, who previously worked with David Fincher, shows the teens robbing reality star Audrina Partridge. Shot to resemble CCTV footage, the characters appear like rats in a maze as they scamper through the property—or perhaps avatars in a video game, adding to the sense of detachment.

13–15
Incriminating photographs
of the teenage thieves were
uploaded (by them) to social
networking sites, showing
off their crimes. Their
compulsion to brag about
their escapades ultimately
led to their capture, as
their acquaintances and
classmates informed police
of their identities.

A recreation of the CCTV
footage released by Audrina
Partridge to try and identify
the thieves.

17–18
Mugshots of Nikki Moore
and Rebecca Ahn, played
by Katie Chang. Although
not quite replicas of their
real-life counterparts, their
expressions—defiance
for Nikki, and concern for
Rebecca—do mimic the
actual police booking photos.

The Bling Ring

2013
90 minutes

Budget $8 million
Box Office $20 million

19

THE TEENAGERS CHOSE to rob Paris Hilton first because they thought she was the sort of person who wouldn't give much thought to home security. "Like, who would leave a door unlocked? Who would leave a lot of money lying around?" Nick Prugo told Nancy Jo Sales, who profiled the so-called "Bling Ring" for *Vanity Fair* in March 2010. One night in October 2008, they found the key to Hilton's mansion under the doormat, and proceeded to steal bras, dresses, vodka, and cash from her purse—planning to take just a few things so that she wouldn't notice and they could return in future. Over the course of multiple burglaries, they pinched close to two million dollars in cash, jewelry and clothes. "We found about, like, five grams of coke in Paris's house," Prugo told police after his arrest. They proceeded to "[drive] around Mulholland, having the best time of our lives."

From the fall of 2008 until the summer of 2009, a gang of teenagers from the affluent Los Angeles suburb of Calabasas ran riot in the Hollywood Hills. They targeted celebrities while they were out of town filming or at parties—as advertised on social media—and used internet searches to find their addresses. While Paris was their initial target, they later moved on to reality star Audrina Partridge, actor Orlando Bloom and his then-girlfriend, supermodel Miranda Kerr, actor couple Brian Austin Green and Megan Fox, and Lindsay Lohan.

Once inside their homes, they relieved their famous targets of cash, clothing, jewelry, handbags, shoes, drugs, and, in one instance, a gun, to the tune of three million dollars. Seven individuals would ultimately be indicted for the robberies and for handling stolen goods: Nick Prugo, Rachel Lee, Alexis Neiers, Diana Tamayo, Courtney Ames, Johnny Ajar, and Roy Lopez Jr. Of the seven, Ajar, Neiers,

19
The Bling Ring's Coppola shot: Marc arrives in Calabasas.

20
The Simple Life starring Paris Hilton and Nicole Richie, which ran from December 2003 until August 2007.

SOFIA COPPOLA: FOREVER YOUNG

20

Lee, Lopez, and Prugo were sentenced to jail time. By the spring of 2013, they had served less than four years between them, and were released into probation programs.

Sofia Coppola read Sales's article about the case, "The Suspects Wore Louboutins," on a flight in 2010, and immediately saw the story's cinematic potential. "I always love stories about teenagers getting into trouble, and this one seemed so absurd," she explained to controversial artist Richard Prince (who would later become embroiled in a scandal around celebrity culture and social media when he used strangers' Instagram posts without their permission in a 2014 art exhibition). Having wrapped on *Somewhere*, which would go on to win the Golden Lion at the Venice Film Festival, Sofia was fascinated by the salacious nature of the teens' ten-month crime spree. "I was in the mood to do something obnoxious and faster, and something kind of in bad taste. And the story seemed to say so much about what's happening in our culture today."

That culture Coppola speaks of—the one that birthed reality television and saw the internet morph from a nerdy curio into an inescapable part of everyday life—was by turns fascinating and repugnant to her: "All the interest in reality stars and kids posting pictures on Facebook all the time. This idea of having an audience all the time. And the kids get busted because they were posting pictures of themselves with all of the stuff they stole." Having come of age in the 1970s and '80s, long before the advent of social media, this brave new world didn't resemble the one Coppola knew (she was thirty-five when Facebook launched to the public in 2006, having previously existed as a college social network). But as a filmmaker preoccupied with adolescent ennui, it's easy to see why she would be attracted to a real-life story of teens gone wild.

When it was announced in December 2011 that Coppola would be adapting Sales's article into a feature film, she had just finished shooting a campaign for Italian clothing brand Marni's collaboration with H&M. While the Swedish fast fashion giant had been working together on affordable capsule collections with big name designers since 2005, the mid-aughts saw the trend really take off; British designer Christopher Kane pronounced a range for Topshop in 2009 while Mulberry teamed up with budget retailer Target in 2010. Diffusion lines offering designer names at discount prices were nothing new by the peak of the mass market fashion house boom, but these collabs placed the glamour of high fashion alongside $9.99 T-shirts and lycra-rich jeggings, becoming prime hangout spots for teenagers in the process. Even if younger shoppers couldn't afford these cut-price designer-endorsed pieces, there was no escaping the message that it doesn't matter what you wear, but who you wear. The bigger the price tag, the bigger the social cache.

The reality television and social media boom were instrumental in amplifying this message. By 2008, when the burglaries began, shows such as *Laguna Beach* and *The Hills* had made stars out of wealthy Los Angeles teens, and online tabloid TMZ was providing rolling coverage of the lifestyles of the rich and famous. At the click of a button fans could look up a celebrity's name, favorite designer brands, social schedule, and—thanks to sites like celebrityaddressaerial.com—even their address.

It didn't start with celebrities though. When Nick Prugo and Rachel Lee (the ringleader, according to her former friends/accomplices) met in 2006, they were troubled teenagers attending Indian Hills High School in Calabasas. Prugo had been kicked out of his previous school for "excessive absences" and had been diagnosed with ADHD as well as "anxiety issues." Lee's parents were divorced—her father living in Las Vegas—and she didn't get along with her stepfather. A shared love of fashion brought the teens together, and for a while they spent most of their time smoking weed, going to house parties, and hanging out at the beach. The way Prugo told it to Sales, the break-ins didn't start until the summer after their sophomore year, when Lee suggested they rob a boy Prugo knew was out of town. "Lee found a box with $8000 in cash under a bed," Sales wrote, "The next day, they went shopping on Rodeo Drive."

The pair started stealing from unlocked luxury cars they spotted parked in their neighborhood, spending the proceeds at the same boutiques their celebrity idols frequented. Prugo also stated that he stole to fund a growing cocaine habit. But the celebrity heists started—at least according to Prugo, since Lee refused to be interviewed for Sales's article—because they envied the designer wardrobes of the women they saw on MTV. Prugo and Lee had proximity to stardom; Prugo's father worked at a film and television distribution company, and Calabasas was fast becoming synonymous with its famous reality star residents, the Kardashian family, whose reality television show *Keeping Up with the Kardashians* had premiered on E! in 2007. But living in proximity to stardom was no substitute for actual column inches. In breaking into the homes of the people they saw on television, the Bling Ring became a part of their world—no matter the eventual consequences.

It's not like the blueprint for social climbing in SoCal didn't exist. Although Paris Hilton was the It Girl at the time, her enduring legacy is as the woman who first introduced the world to Kim Kardashian. The second daughter of OJ Simpson's famed attorney Robert Kardashian had risen to prominence after initially appearing as Hilton's stylist and friend on episodes of *The Simple Life*, but became more well-known after a sex tape she recorded with singer Ray J was leaked in 2007. This was four years after Hilton's own scandal, involving the release of *1 Night in Paris* which featured the heiress having sex with then-boyfriend, professional poker player Rick Salomon. Both had emerged from these incidents more in-demand than ever, though while Paris received no money for the leak of her tape, Kim allowed the distribution of hers after settling for a reported $5 million payday, and the release formed a central part of the narrative on the family's reality television series.

By 2008, the reality television bubble showed no signs of bursting. *Laguna Beach*, with its tagline "The Real Orange County," had promised viewers insight into the world romanticized by Fox's successful teen drama *The OC* (starring Bling Ring target Rachel Bilson) and spawned numerous spin-offs. Lindsay Lohan was becoming just as known for her criminal record as her film credits. Fame and notoriety were different names for the same thing.

Like Sales's article, Coppola's film opens with the robbery at Orlando Bloom and Miranda Kerr's house. From the vantage point of a CCTV camera, the gang brazenly walk up to the security gate and hop the fence, one by one. Hoods obscuring their faces, they try various doors before one finally opens and they pile inside. Navigating the house as if it's their own, one of their number (Katie Chang as Rebecca Ahn, based on Lee) finally turns to the group with a grin and announces, "Let's go shopping." The distorted electric guitars of Sleigh Bells's "Crown on the Ground" blare like an alarm while the teens rifle through drawers and closets, picking out whatever they want. The footage is intercut with real paparazzi shots of their celebrity victims and mocked-up social media posts from the group (using authentic captions from their real-life models. Scenes of their

SOFIA COPPOLA: FOREVER YOUNG

21
The Secret by Rhonda Byrne; a popular 2006 self-help book based on the "law of attraction."

22
The music video for Madonna's "Deeper and Deeper," featuring Sofia.

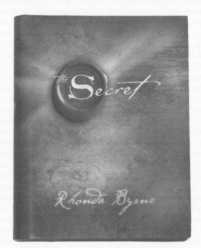

21

22

subsequent trial are included, too; Marc Hall (based on Prugo and played by Israel Broussard) leaves court, swarmed by reporters, dressed in a sharp suit and shades as though he's a celebrity himself. Slow pans over designer shoes and jewelry—reminiscent of similar shots in *The Virgin Suicides* and *Marie Antoinette*—are followed by night-vision footage of the teens calmly leaving the property the way they came in, making off with their loot. One of them (Taissa Farmiga playing Sam Moore, based on Alexis Neiers's adopted sister Tess Taylor) is carrying a painting under her arm.

As far as opening sequences go, it's one of Coppola's longest. Clocking in at almost four minutes with a self-contained narrative, it could easily be a music video or—given the array of designer goods on show—a commercial. Coppola's interest in the aesthetics of short-form video is well-documented; she had directed five music videos (and starred in a further four) by the time she came to make *The Bling Ring*. The one that has the most in common with this film is the 1992 Studio 54-inspired video for Madonna's "Deeper and Deeper," in which Coppola played a party guest. As Sydney Urbanek notes, "Forged by MTV culture, Coppola has clearly never been able to kick it." But in the case of a story about celebrity-obsessed adolescents running amok in Beverly Hills, it feels apt that the characters might want to feel like they're in a music video.

Beyond its audacious opening, *The Bling Ring* marked a departure for Coppola in other ways. The film's nonlinear structure jumps between the robberies and scenes of the gang partying to their trials and subsequent *Vanity Fair* profile, interspersed with celebrity interview footage and more social media screengrabs. It's an approach that mimics the one employed by reality television, creating a narrative out of hours of (scripted and unscripted) footage that best serves the producers' goals. Coppola's approach, as detailed by her cast and crew in the film's making of documentary, seems to have much in common with the staged-unstaged nature of a reality television production. "I feel like she wants to capture something that's very real and very authentic," said Emma Watson, who plays Nicki Moore, based on the most famous member of the Bling Ring, Alexis Neiers. "So she tends to just let us improv things and she pulls out and captures those special moments."

Another notable difference is the look of the film. "I showed it to a friend's teenage daughter and she said, 'Oh, it doesn't look pretty like your other work,'" Coppola said in 2013. It's true that *The Bling Ring* feels like an outlier amid the gauzy, lingering shots and soft aesthetics that dominate Coppola's work. Where her four previous features exhibited a tenderness even in turmoil, *The Bling Ring* is—as Coppola herself put it—"obnoxious and faster." Her long-time production designer Anne Ross was baffled by the project at first. "When Sofia told me about the idea I was completely uninterested and couldn't believe that she wanted to spend all this time living in this world [. . .] It was so repellent to me and it was repellent to her, too, so I was confused about it." But the two found a way to explore the banality of the SoCal bourgeoisie.

Drawing inspiration from a washed-out, peach-hued photograph of two neighboring Calabasas McMansions, Coppola and Ross achieved an aesthetic of blandness that extends to how the characters discuss their crimes. In one much-referenced scene, Nicki declares "I wanna rob" with the flat intonation any other young woman might declare she wants to go to the mall. The homes of the teenage thieves and their families, while superficially grandiose, all look the same (Coppola even noted the mansions they shot in had very similar layouts). It's not dissimilar to the affluent Michigan neighborhood depicted in *The Virgin Suicides*, with middle-class cookie-cutter houses, manicured lawns and teens yearning to escape lest they become their parents eventually. But the sunny, stifling sprawl of Grosse Pointe was viewed through the lens of tragedy, seeking to return to a rosier time when the Lisbon sisters were still alive (and subsequently interrogating the idea that the past was ever really that pretty to begin with). *The Bling Ring*'s suburbs are Los Angeles on benzodiazepine—lethargic and spaced out. Compared to the maximalism we see in the homes of the celebrity targets, it's an imitation of life, in the same vein as the filtered fashion designs that end up on the rack at H&M.

"I think that was a hard thing for Sofia," Ross said. "She normally makes things she finds beautiful, and I think it was a struggle for her to accept that she was shooting something that was just this beige, washed-out box." It's a stark contrast from the homes of their celebrity targets, which are invariably ostentatious—the most prominent being Paris Hilton, who was introduced to Coppola via Steven Dorff and allowed the director to shoot in her home because she was a fan of her work.

A featurette included with *The Bling Ring*'s DVD release shows Hilton giving a tour of her home. She sits on a pink and gold throne as she speaks about how the thefts affected her and confirms that her housekeeper had indeed left her front door key under the doormat the night of the first robbery. They returned a further five times; it was only then that Hilton noticed that her jewelry closet had been cleared out. She speaks in her familiar southern Californian accent as she glides around the house, pointing out the various rooms Coppola filmed in, including her "nightclub room" and her walk-in wardrobe. Standing amid rows and rows of designer clothes, she reflects: "Most robbers would just want money or jewelry, but with these kids, they wanted everything they had seen in magazines."

While it's clear that the invasion of her personal space did have an effect on Hilton (she describes attending the Cannes premiere and being upset as she watched the film for the first time), there's something slightly comical about her discussing the impact of the robberies while surrounded by a staggering hoard of luxury items, like a particularly well-dressed dragon in a cave with wall-to-floor mirrors. "This film really shows just how celebrity-obsessed some of our culture is," she says. "When I was a little girl I wanted to be a veterinarian, I wasn't obsessed with any celebrities, I could care less about that. We were definitely living in a different world."

Of course, Paris Hilton did not become a veterinarian. Hilton (and indeed Sofia Coppola) are alienated by the world of celebrity obsession: they exist within it, rather than outside of it. The great-granddaughter of hotel magnate Conrad Hilton, Paris was proclaimed an It Girl when she was roughly the same age as the teens who robbed her in 2008. Coppola grew up in a similarly rarefied world. This isn't to say that those born into such a world can't experience pain and tragedy (and when they do, we often hear all about it), more that their outlook on fame and fortune is inherently different from that of outsiders; particularly ones who came of age under the spotlight of the modern entertainment industry, exposed to a mainstream media that reveled in conspicuous consumption.

None of this makes the Bling Ring gang themselves candidates for absolution. They still came from money (albeit less than Hilton and Coppola), and seem to epitomize the concept of affluenza, a term used to describe a psychological malaise in the middle and upper classes brought about by the "dogged pursuit of more." The "beautiful, gorgeous things" the teens stole weren't all that they coveted—they yearned for star power itself. "Just as in the past, in religion, you wanted to touch the holy shroud, to wear [. . .] some garment that

23
A bird's eye view of Calabasas's upmarket suburban sprawl.

24
The cast of Harmony Korine's *Spring Breakers*, released three months before *The Bling Ring*.

23

the star was wearing, pulls you into that star's aura, makes you a kind of doppelgänger," cultural historian Leo Braudy noted in an interview about the burglaries ahead of the film's release.

The group's desire to move in the same circles as celebrities is established early in the film; the first nightclub scene contains cameo appearances from Kirsten Dunst and Paris Hilton, and an amusing throwaway remark when Nicki, staring down at her phone, complains loudly to the rest of the group, "Oh my god, Jude Law totally keeps texting me. I'll probably meet him later." With this set-up, there's a sense of escalation: If you're a teenager who's already finessed your way into brushing shoulders with celebrities in the hottest Beverly Hills nightclubs, where next do you turn for kicks? These weren't crimes of necessity, they were crimes of audacity, fueled by that same parasocial feeling that fed the TMZ boom and entitlement stemming from upper-middle-class inertia.

Nine months before *The Bling Ring* premiered, Harmony Korine's *Spring Breakers* had made its bow at the Venice Film Festival. Although set on America's opposite coastline and dealing with different social classes, there are definite similarities between the two films: both portray a group of beautiful teenage girls who, bored with their lives, turn to a life of crime to fund their hedonism and quickly find themselves in over their heads. Korine is no stranger to stories about adolescent turmoil, having directed *Gummo* and written the scripts for Larry Clark's nineties teensploitation dramas *Kids* and *Ken Park*. But *Spring Breakers* is perhaps his most melancholy film—a stylized neon headrush that can only end in tragedy. While psyching themselves up to rob a restaurant, one of the girls suggests they, "Pretend it's a video game. Act like you're in a movie or somethin'." This sense of detachment between crime and self is apparent in *The Bling Ring*, too: the actions don't seem real to the teenagers. The act of consumption doesn't have any consequences, just as reality television only ever shows the highlights.

For the scene in which the group ransack Audrina Partridge's mansion, esteemed cinematographer Harris Savides (who passed away from brain cancer before the film was completed) suggested to Coppola they try a different approach. The scene unfolds in a single, slow-zooming wide shot of the house, as the tiny figures scurry through the rooms moving with a frantic determination. While the framing evokes a security camera, the nighttime LA soundscape of sirens, crickets and howling coyotes create a sense of eeriness, stripped of the pop music Coppola often uses in her films. This voyeuristic moment is more reminiscent of Savides's work with David Fincher on *The Game* and *Zodiac* than the dreamy, ethereal cinematography widely associated with Coppola, but given that *The Bling Ring* is her take on a true-crime story, it seems entirely appropriate. The scene, which occurs roughly midway through the film, also illustrates the gang's detachment from their actions; when Partridge publishes CCTV footage of the burglars to the media and the teens aren't apprehended, they come to believe they're untouchable, and their crime spree continues.

In the end, the gang's detachment from their actions and their potential consequences is their downfall. More CCTV footage is leaked to the media; anonymous tipsters (in the film it's suggested to be the group's peers and former classmates) tell the police about the incriminating photographs the group posted on social media, posing with designer clothes and accessories. While Coppola previously spared Marie Antoinette the walk to the guillotine, here she spares none of the unseemly details. The teens turn on each other, each claiming someone else was the ringleader. It's as vicious and asinine as high school, Coppola using the transcripts from police interviews and

24

Sales's conversations with the teens to illustrate this point. "I'm a firm believer in karma," opines Emma Watson, putting on her best Valley Girl drawl. "And I think this situation was attracted into my life as a huge learning lesson for me, to grow and expand as a spiritual human being." This line of dialogue is lifted verbatim from Alexis Neiers, as she sat in her lawyer's office speaking to *Vanity Fair*.

At the time of her arrest, Neiers had just finished filming the pilot for her own reality show, *Pretty Wild*. It was produced by E! (who had also broadcast the final two seasons of Paris Hilton's *The Simple Life*) and detailed Neiers's life in Calabasas alongside that of her younger sisters and mother who homeschooled them with a curriculum she composed based on the 2006 pseudoscience documentary *The Secret* (a core tenet of which is the belief that everything one wants or needs can be satisfied by believing in an outcome, repeatedly thinking about it, and maintaining positive emotional states to "attract" the desired outcome).

Neiers's arrest did not stop the show from being filmed; over the course of ten episodes she juggles modeling, partying, and dating with her upcoming day in court. It's a difficult watch, in part because of spoilt, self-centered attitudes of the girls, but also because of the creeping feeling these young women were never really in control, despite their proclamations about how much they want to be famous. They date much older men, they pose in their lingerie for a Haitian relief charity, and late in the season it's revealed that Alexis has a drug addiction. After the show she would be arrested for possession of black tar heroin and enter a treatment programme.

None of this is covered in Coppola's film. Similarly, she omits entirely the character of Diana Tamayo, who was an undocumented Mexican immigrant at the time and threatened with deportation unless she cooperated with police. While it could be argued that Coppola quietly removed the character of Tamayo to avoid perpetuating any harmful stereotypes about undocumented immigrants, it equally could have been an opportunity to challenge those very myths. "Including her in the movie may have actually helped to chip away at this unfair standard of perfection to which we hold undocumented immigrants," argued Meagan Hatcher-Mays in Jezebel. "Yes, immigrants make mistakes! They are regular, normal people who sometimes do things that are ill-advised."

While it's clear that the film doesn't feel much affection toward its young hooligans (except, perhaps, the wide-eyed newcomer Marc, desperate to just fit in with his chic new friends), it does feel like Coppola somewhat sanitized their circumstances. Neiers in particular was vocally critical of the film, even as recently as 2020: "The problem I had was the comments that [Emma Watson] made about me and the role, despite the fact that [. . .] my drug addiction [. . .] had already come out. I was actually in treatment at the time that they were filming that movie, and [. . .] I think she said something along the lines of 'This girl is the epitome of what I'm totally against, and she's disgusting.' At that point I already came out with the fact that I had been sexually abused throughout my childhood and was like a full blown heroin addict at the time."

In the same vein as a hundred reality television shows that spawned the culture it examines, *The Bling Ring* became an entirely constructed narrative—"Based on real events" as the title card states. But with so many conflicting versions of events, how would Coppola have ever been able to tell it any other way? She met with Nick Prugo and Alexis Neiers prior to shooting, as well as Officer Brett Goodkin from the LAPD, who ended up having a cameo in the film (which ironically landed him in hot water, having failed to disclose his involvement with Coppola to his employer). Similar to her dramatisation of the life of Marie Antoinette, Coppola doesn't pretend otherwise; the teens of *The Bling Ring* might not be as sympathetic as the young queen of France, but then she did have three decades to grow up.

Although it's easily lost amid the shiny jewels and sky high heels, there's still a sense of loneliness that presides over *The Bling Ring*. Throughout the film it's as if the teens purposefully keep each other (and us) at a distance, communicating in celebrity tittle tattle and flicking through social media in silence while they sit together. Sam and Nicki's mother hands out Adderall like it's candy and spouts New Age nonsense about visualizing success rather than working for it, and even when they're having fun, there's a preoccupation with perception: staring into the webcam after a successful robbery, Nicki painstakingly applies lip gloss while Marc checks his hair. The robberies are the only time they seem to come alive, finding a sense of connection with each other through their shared criminality but also with their idols through the most extreme iteration of a parasocial relationship.

To date, *The Bling Ring* has divided audiences more than any other Sofia Coppola film. While Watson's performance was praised—particularly in the context of its departure from her previous work in the Harry Potter series—many have perceived the film as shallow, while John Powers in *Vogue* cried, "Morality be damned, I kept wishing *The Bling Ring* was juicier" and Catherine Shoard described it in the *Guardian* as "a Tinseltown stitch-up that exonerates all involved by understanding the plight of the crimes in terms of simple celeb worship." But Coppola has never painted in black-and-white; she always opts for those dreamy pastels, even if she settled for washed-out peach and Louboutin red this time. There's no real moral stance to her take on a sordid tale of the pursuit of more, but then again, Coppola seems to understand more than most that the truth can only ever be subjective in a city as capricious as Los Angeles. ◆

25

25
A variation of Ed Ruscha's
Hollywood painting. Francis
Ford Coppola owns one,
which was used in the film
when the gang robs Orlando
Bloom. The visual metaphor
of literally stealing Hollywood
can't be undersold.

A

VERY

CHRISTMAS

MURRAY

A Very Murray Christmas

2015
56 minutes

2

ON SEPTEMBER 11, 1977, David Bowie turned up at Elstree Studios in London to record an appearance on Bing Crosby's forthcoming Christmas special, *Bing Crosby's Merrie Olde Christmas*. Bowie was on the promotional trail for his *Heroes* album, while Crosby was a veteran of the variety show format, having recorded forty-one Christmas specials previously. It was the forty-second that would become the most famous, when their odd pairing resulted in one of the most charming moments in television history. In a somewhat awkwardly staged skit, Bowie pays Crosby a visit at the quaint London home he's staying in, and the pair talk briefly about the festive season and music before performing a very special rendition of the carol "Little Drummer Boy." Crosby passed away just under six weeks later, before the special aired on television, but the duet became a Yuletide favorite around the world, and a prime example of what makes the Christmas variety show such an enduring format.

Almost forty years later, Sofia Coppola would pair her old friend Bill Murray with a variety of unlikely costars in a similar fashion for her Netflix holiday special, *A Very Murray Christmas*. The project came along at a strange time in Coppola's career. In March of 2014, *Deadline* reported that she was to helm a live-action adaptation of *The Little Mermaid*; by October the Christmas special project with Murray had been announced, too. Ultimately only the latter would come to fruition (although her version of Hans Cristian Andersen's classic tale was imagined in an online parody sketch for Funny Or Die). In the years since Coppola has mentioned her disappointment about the abandoned project, saying to *Variety* during *The Beguiled* promotional tour, "I would have liked to have done that. We couldn't agree on some elements. When it's smaller, you can have exactly what you have in mind. For me, it wasn't a good fit."

1
Bill Murray and musician Paul Shaffer on the set of *A Very Murray Christmas*. The pair previously worked together on *Saturday Night Live* and *Scrooged*.

2
Bill Murray frets over the fate of his Christmas special in his hotel room.

3
Bing Crosby and David Bowie in *Bing Crosby's Merrie Olde Christmas*.

SOFIA COPPOLA: FOREVER YOUNG

3

Perhaps the notion of Coppola writing and directing a Christmas television special with Bill Murray seemed equally strange on paper. Dreamt up by Coppola after she remarked to Mitch Glazer that she would love to see their old friend Bill do a week-long residency at the Carlyle Cafe, "singing, crooning, doing old standards and Chet Baker love songs." Glazer and Murray were already working on a treatment for a television special, and with Sofia's input, the seasonal setting took shape: "I got excited by the tradition of the Christmas variety show. We all loved that they had no logic, when Bing Crosby and David Bowie are singing by the piano. We tried to embrace that and just get together all the people that we liked and wanted to work with."

Sure enough, in a tight fifty-six minutes, Coppola, Glazer and Murray assemble a sparkling cast, pulling in favors from Chris Rock and George Clooney alongside Rashida Jones, Maya Rudolph, Amy Poehler, Michael Cera, Jenny Lewis, Miley Cyrus, Julie White, and New York Dolls legend David Johansen (who also played the Ghost of Christmas Past in Bill Murray's first Christmas-themed outing, *Scrooged*, cowritten by Mitch Glazer). Coppola's cousin Jason Schwartzman and her husband Thomas Mars's band Phoenix also star, while her brother Roman helped with the logistics of shooting the performances. The entire show was shot on location at the Carlyle Hotel in four and a half days; a far cry from the twenty-seven spent shooting *Lost in Translation* at the Tokyo Grand Hyatt, or the three weeks in Los Angeles's Chateau Marmont filming *Somewhere*—Coppola's previous hotel-based stories.

The loneliness of the weary traveler explored in her past work resurfaces in *A Very Murray Christmas*, as Murray—playing a caricature version of himself—anxiously waits in his suite at the Carlyle, ahead of his live Christmas special. A snowstorm in New York has caused most of his guests to cancel their appearances, and he's feeling blue about the prospect of staging a flop; an idea Coppola attributes to Murray. Although the film predates Coppola's screwball comedy *On the Rocks*, it undoubtedly shares some of the same DNA, beyond the casting of Murray and Rashida Jones and the Carlyle Hotel as a setting; *A Very Murray Christmas* is one of her more whimsical works, playing on the celebrity and charisma of its central star while also serving as a tribute to the genre.

The film's second number is perhaps the best example of this, in which Murray bumps into Chris Rock and coerces him into performing "Do You Hear What I Hear?" in matching festive turtlenecks. "Where's George Clooney? Matt Damon or John Goodman? Your boys!" Rock incredulously asks him. According to Coppola, it was watching an Andy Williams special that inspired the skit—though it feels equally comparable to Bing and Bowie's iconic (and only slightly awkward) performance. "They're always surreal," Coppola said of the Christmas television specials of yesteryear. "We watched the Carpenters, and Dean Martin—Dean Martin looks sunburned, like he just drove through Burbank in a convertible, but it's on this snowy Christmas set."

That specific brand of strangeness is what Coppola sought to emulate and update, which may have come as a surprise to viewers more familiar with her ethereal aesthetics and melancholic storylines. The duet between Murray and Rock is only the first of these surreal moments, with Rock appearing visibly uncomfortable as they croon their way through the carol, until the power goes out and he seizes the chance to run off into the night, leaving Murray alone once more. "I just wanted to see them both in matching turtlenecks," Coppola joked. A fan of Rock (a clip from his 2004 special *Chris Rock: Never Scared* is shown at the beginning of *On the Rocks*), she knew Murray was a friend, so asked if they could call in a favor.

It's little surprise that so many stars were eager to find time to join the production, given the talent at the helm. "I just feel like when you say, 'Oh, will you come be in Bill's show?' or when Bill asked them, everyone said, 'Yes, when?'" Coppola explained. But one guest proved most elusive—rapper Rick Ross. Glazer brought him on board after the pair worked together on the television series *Magic City* to duet with Murray on a cover of Albert King's funky hit "Santa Claus Wants Some Lovin,'" but on the day of recording, Ross was nowhere to be found. Murray's old friend George Clooney stepped in to replace him for the strange dream sequence portion of the film, in which the star and musician Miley Cyrus cavorts around a festive set with a bevvy of dancers in matching silver outfits. It might be an unintentional reference, but the scene is particularly reminiscent of

a scene in Richard Curtis's festive romantic comedy *Love Actually* in which Bill Nighy's aged rocker Billy Mack records a seasonal version of the Troggs's "Love is All Around" (retitled "Christmas is All Around"). Styled as a festive version of Robert Palmer in his "Addicted to Love" get-up, Nighy swaggers and croons his way through the song; in the stage segment of Coppola's film, Murray prowls about the stage in a similar manner. It's the most extravagant part of an otherwise quite low key affair, and particularly taps into the imagery and staging usually associated with the televised Christmas variety show. The format has remained virtually unchanged since the days of Bing Crosby and Bob Hope; nowadays stars like Dolly Parton, Mariah Carey, and John Legend are the main attraction, but the focus is on pageantry rather than plot, with lavish musical numbers and beautiful costumes, the order of the day and a message of togetherness invariably at the core.

"I wanted it to be fun, but not kitschy," Coppola said of her special, but perhaps that's an impossible dream in American popular culture. Consider the dominant western image of Santa Claus, as a jolly bearded elder in a red suit. Created by German-American cartoonist Thomas Nast in the late nineteenth century, this image was standardized when Haddon Sundblom adapted it for the Coca-Cola Company's marketing in 1931. Nearly a century later, there is still a strong association between Old Saint Nick and Coca-Cola; a beverage which has precious little to do with the holidays, but through the strange magic of affective advertising, achieved brand recognition all the same. Christmas, as typified by the spectacle of indulgence and presence of a jolly, charismatic figure decked in red and white as master of ceremonies, does seem to possess an inherent kitschness from which no auteur is immune.

In fact, there's something a little kitsch about Murray himself; his deadpan delivery and well-documented eccentricity off-screen have earned him considerable popularity among audiences, and developed into a sort of cult status, as evidenced in the 2018 documentary *The Bill Murray Stories: Life Lessons Learned from a Mythical Man*. Even in 2021, there's a strong market for merchandise bearing his likeness—coloring books, candles, mugs, and T-shirts are among the most popular examples—and countless anecdotes tell of a man who makes impromptu house party appearances and midnight trips to Prague. There are small nods to this in *A Very*

4

4
Bill Nighy as aging rocker Billy Mack in *Love Actually*.

5
Sofia Coppola and Zoe Cassavetes in their short-lived Comedy Central show, *Hi Octane*.

6
Dean Martin's 1980 Christmas special. L-R: Dean Martin, Beverly Sills, Mel Tillis, Andy Gibb, Erik Estrada.

Murray Christmas, but Coppola herself admits it's hard to know where "the fantasy version of Bill" starts and ends. This makes him a fitting stand-in for Santa Claus then— a charming, ultimately benevolent figure steeped in history and mythology.

5

Responses to *A Very Murray Christmas* skewed positive, if not a little underwhelmed, given the breadth of talent (both acting and musical) included. The flimsy premise of Murray noodling around the Carlyle was criticized for being too simplistic, while other viewers took umbrage with the perceived lack of comedy, although this complaint suggests an unfamiliarity with Coppola's work; her films don't deal in witty one-liners but rather wry situational observations. Nevertheless it is a strange sort of curio in her filmography, far more whimsical than her previous work; even that which resembles thematically.

Coppola's interest in celebrity is inescapable, dating back to her short lived Comedy Central show *Hi Octane*, which she created with her friend Zoe "Daughter of John" Cassavetes. Although it possesses a much more grungy and DIY aesthetic than the world of *A Very Murray Christmas*, it also stars a host of Coppola's close friends and family playing lightly fictionalized versions of themselves. Her cousin Nicolas Cage stars in a skit all about how much he wants to be on the show, while Martin Scorsese discusses his favorite Beastie Boy. Even Sofia and Zoe get in the act, bickering over their roles in a fashion show, and having a blast driving monster trucks. There's something delightfully unpolished and nonsensical about the whole production, which borrows from the anarchic skate culture videos Coppola was familiar with (her partner at the time, Spike Jonze, was a veteran of the scene) and suggests that these lauded stars are as silly and strange as the rest of us. Or perhaps the very concept of celebrity itself is the strange thing; from *Lost in Translation* to *Somewhere*, her fictional (or in the case of *Marie Antoinette*, fictionalized) stars seem continually bemused by the frenzy their very presence creates.

"I don't really know how they let us develop it," Coppola said of *Hi Octane*, in a 2020 interview with *Vogue*. Her critics might suggest it's by virtue of her name, and it's not an unfair assumption, considering how much of the show rests on the connections between Sofia and her milieu. But even if Coppola is emblematic of a privilege unfathomable to the majority, her work provides glimpses into that world, reckoning with a genuine desire for human connection not predicated on holding court in Hollywood. When asked if she should change anything about *Hi Octane* with the gift of hindsight, Coppola declined: "I think if anything has sincerity and heart, this is it." The same is true of *A Very Murray Christmas*, which may lack the depth of her other work, but retains a festive charm, and provides a little insight into the creative partnership between Sofia Coppola and Bill Murray. If Christmas is all about togetherness and spending time with the ones you love, what statement is more fitting for a director as intimate as Coppola than a film made with her nearest and dearest. ▥

6

INSPIRATIONS

↓ *Amadeus*, Milos Forman & *To Die For*, Gus Van Sant ↓

SOFIA COPPOLA: FOREVER YOUNG

IN 1762, DURING their three-year grand tour of Europe, Leopold and Anna Maria Mozart received an audience with the Viennese royals where their prodigious children Nannerl and Wolfgang Amadeus performed for Empress Maria Theresa. During this visit, according to Mozart biographer Eric Blom, young Wolfgang was introduced to Maria Theresa's seven-year-old daughter, Maria Antonia. She assisted Mozart when he slipped on the palace's polished floor; in return, he proposed marriage. Needless to say, Maria Antonia did not take up young Mozart on his offer; in 1770 she would marry the Dauphin of France, and take the name Marie Antoinette.

This meet-cute between two of Austria's most famous cultural figures didn't quite make it into Sofia Coppola's portrait of the ill-fated French queen, nor Milos Forman's semibiographical *Amadeus* from 1984. However, the latter's influence on Coppola's film is well-recorded. Adapted from Peter Shaffer's 1979 play of the same name and described by the playwright as "fantasia on the theme of Mozart and Salieri," Forman's film stars F. Murray Abraham as Antonio Salieri and Tom Hulce as Wolfgang Amadeus Mozart, the upstart composer who causes a commotion when he announces himself in Salzburg as a transcendental talent.

From *Amadeus*, *Marie Antoinette* inherits a raucous sensibility, based on emotional truth rather than historical fact. Coppola's decision to write a screenplay using modern language and cast the majority of roles with non-French actors was directly inspired by Forman, while *Marie Antoinette*'s aesthetic owes a debt to costume designers Theodor Pistek and Christian Thuri, as well as makeup/wig impresario Paul LeBlanc. A baby-pink bouffant Mozart wears while conducting may have no basis in historical fact, but it remains one of the most enduring images of Forman's film; in the midst of her Petit Trianon phase, Marie Antoinette sports a similarly colored wig

with a matching gown. Likewise: "They're all so beautiful! Why don't I have three heads?" Mozart remarks while deliberating over which wig to buy; a scene that comes to mind during *Marie Antoinette*'s "I Want Candy" montage when the young queen overcomes her sorrows by indulging in some retail therapy.

Both *Amadeus* and *Marie Antoinette* have been criticized for their lack of historical accuracy with regards to costuming (Mozart rarely wore wigs, and when he did they certainly weren't pink, according to his more stringent devotees), but Forman and Coppola share a desire to capture the vivacious, rebellious nature of youth, not to mention a sense of the past as present, away from the buttoned-up formality of similar period productions.

If *Marie Antoinette* is Coppola playing with notions of historical celebrity and excess, *The Bling Ring* is a thoroughly modern take on the price of fame, based on a true story. But real-life criminality has inspired cinematic cautionary tales for decades; as early as 1906, Charles Tait was recounting the life of Australian outlaw Ned Kelly in *The Story of the Kelly Gang*. But it's Gus Van Sant's 1995 dramedy *To Die For* that had a key impact on *The Bling Ring*, inspiring not only the film's format but also Emma Watson's central performance.

Based on Joyce Maynard's novel of the same name, *To Die For* has its roots in the strange case of Pamela Smart, a woman from New Hampshire who conspired with her fifteen-year-old sexual partner, William Flynn, to murder her twenty-four-year-old husband Greggory in 1990. Smart was convicted of conspiracy to commit murder, witness tampering, and accomplice to first-degree murder, and is still serving a life sentence in prison. In Van Sant's film, Nicole Kidman plays ambitious TV-obsessive Suzanne Stone, who

marries Larry Maretto (Matt Dillon) to keep herself financially stable while pursuing her dreams of becoming a broadcast journalist. While filming a news project with teenagers at a local high school, she meets student Jimmy Emmett (Joaquin Phoenix) and the two begin an affair. When Larry asks Suzanne to consider giving up her career so they can start a family, she convinces Jimmy and his friends Russell and Lydia to murder Larry, claiming he abuses her.

Much like *The Bling Ring*, *To Die For* employs the mockumentary format, using direct-to-camera monologues that mimic interview footage. (It's also worth questioning whether Coppola was inspired by Michael Patrick Jann's 1999 beauty pageant mockumentary *Drop Dead Gorgeous*, starring Kirsten Dunst.) Kidman's opening speech where she describes her ambitions to be a superstar reporter is particularly chilling—a masterclass in portraying a specific sort of white female narcissism unrivalled until, perhaps, Watson's turn as Nicki Moore in *The Bling Ring*. Watson confirmed that Kidman's performance inspired her turn as the apathetic, celebrity-obsessed teen burglar who treats her day in court like an appearance on a talk show.

It's interesting that Coppola's examinations of celebrity should point to such cautionary, salacious sources of inspiration. Having grown up in the spotlight, Coppola knows all too well the tempestuous relationship between the rich and famous and the little people. Yet it's not that her sympathies lie more with the likes of poor little rich girl Marie Antoinette than the scheming would-be socialites of *The Bling Ring*. Instead, these films serve as an exploration of volatile girlhood and what women are brought up to covet and value. ◣

FATHERS &

SOME-

WHERE

1
A wide shot shows Johnny
Marco (Stephen Dorff)
driving his Ferrari through
the Californian desert, with
the vastness of the landscape
particularly evident.

2–3
Kristina and Karissa Shannon
as pole-dancing twins Johnny
hires to perform in his hotel
room; there are no cuts or
lingering body close-ups in
this sequence, which gives it
a strangely comedic tone, as
if Coppola is emphasising the
sleazier side of Marco's life.

SOFIA COPPOLA: FOREVER YOUNG

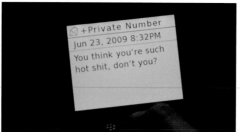

4–7
Throughout the film
Johnny receives strange
text messages from an
unknown number. The plot
is never resolved, but he
doesn't seem particularly
rattled by them; it helps set
the scene for what life in
Hollywood is like.

8
Cleo, played by Elle Fanning, arrives for a day with her father. Unlike most women who encounter Johnny, she's pleased to see him.

9
Johnny takes Cleo to ice
skating practice, where she
performs a routine set to
Gwen Stefani's break-up
ballad "Cool." Compared
to the previous dance
sequence, this one is sweet,
and Johnny seems to show
genuine interest in his
daughter's hobby.

10
Johnny showering at the
Chateau Marmont—holding
his arm out to keep his cast
dry, it feels more than a little
ridiculous, contrasting from
his glamorous public persona.

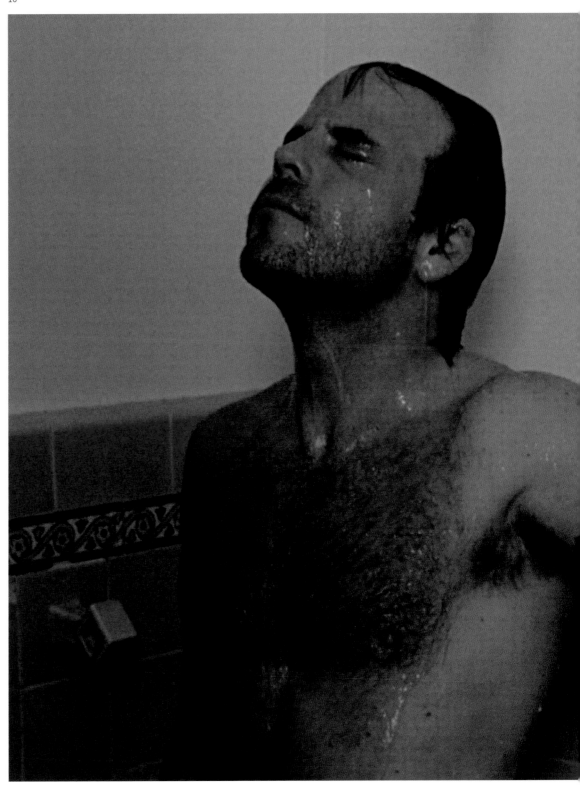

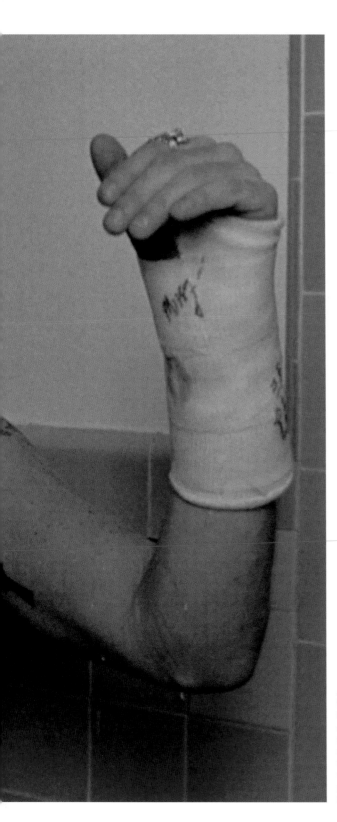

11
Johnny attends a fitting
for a prosthetic mask that
involves having plaster
applied to his face for
a period of time. In a
claustrophobic-feeling long
take, he waits alone, with
the ambient noise of the
production office implying
he might have been forgotten.

SOFIA COPPOLA: FOREVER YOUNG

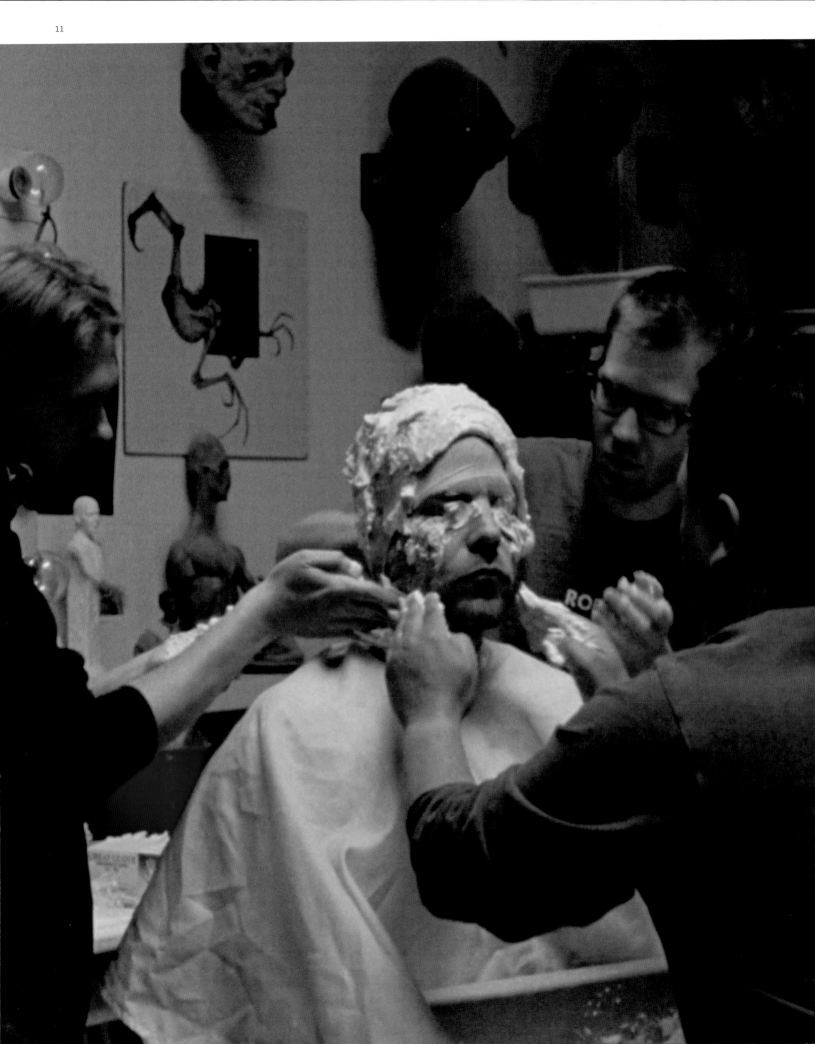

12
Johnny and Cleo play
Guitar Hero in his hotel
room; Johnny seems more
invested in the game than
his daughter is.

13
Johnny and Cleo attend the
Telegatto award ceremony
in Milan—inspired by Sofia's
own experience attending the
same ceremony with
her father.

14
While in Milan, Johnny sneaks
out to see an old girlfriend,
unable to quite avoid
temptation even though
he's with his daughter.

FATHERS & DAUGHTERS

15
Cleo is unimpressed by her father's philandering. Her silence implies it's probably not the first time she's been through this routine.

16
Cleo cooks for her father for the second time. Her care is obvious; she makes hollandaise from scratch and delicately cuts chives with scissors, displaying a maturity beyond Johnny's.

17
In a montage set to the Strokes' "I'll Try Anything Once" Johnny and Cleo spend time together at the hotel. The pool shot is reminiscent of a scene in Mike Figgis's drama *Leaving Las Vegas*— a less reaffirming story of a woman saddled with an unstable Hollywood figure.

18
After a magical few days together, Johnny drops Cleo off for summer camp. He apologizes for his absence in her life; it's unclear whether or not she hears him.

19
Alone again, Johnny opts to spend time at the Chateau rather than partying—but the sun doesn't shine quite as brightly without his daughter around.

20–21
Inspired by Cleo's presence in his life, Johnny cooks his own dinner for the first time in the film. He makes too much pasta, and eats alone at the table in his suite, which contrasts with the loving, meticulous way Cleo prepared eggs benedict for him. But at least Johnny is starting to try.

Somewhere

2010
97 minutes

Budget $7 million
Box Office $14.7 million

22

22
The Coppola shot: Johnny
gazes out at California.

23
Helmut Newton, famed
photographer and a key
influence on Sofia Coppola.

24
The Chateau Marmont hotel
in Los Angeles, California.

WHEN SOFIA COPPOLA was a child, she accompanied her father on a number of his work trips, which afforded her a variety of lavish experiences that would entertain any youngster—even the daughter of Hollywood royalty. She recalls sampling all the gelato flavors on a Milanese hotel's room service menu and a spontaneous helicopter ride; details which would be recreated in her fourth feature, about Johnny Marco, a hot property young actor whose listless life of debauchery changes dramatically with the unexpected arrival of his preteen daughter, Cleo. Despite using details from her own childhood in *Somewhere*, Coppola rejects the notion it's about her family, describing the film as "personal but not so autobiographical." Still, it was a tonal departure from the opulence of her previous feature, *Marie Antoinette*, and her second original screenplay after *Lost in Translation*—a sun-drenched sojourn at Los Angeles's legendary Chateau Marmont hotel, inspired by films by Chantel Ackerman and Federico Fellini.

After making *Marie Antoinette*, Coppola was living in Paris with her husband Thomas Mars and their two young daughters, but found herself homesick for California. She began to reflect on Los Angeles—not the city of *The Long Goodbye* or *Rebel Without a Cause*, but the modern version, beneath the frivolous party town she saw depicted on television and had frequented in her youth. "The flip-side of *Entourage*," she summarized, referring to Doug Ellin's dramedy television series about a young actor trying to make it in Hollywood. "It looks like these guys are having this fun party lifestyle, but what would that really be like? What it's like the next morning?"

To understand *Somewhere* it's necessary to first understand the Chateau Marmont, where star-on-the-rise Johnny Marco (played by Stephen Dorff) has taken up residence. Located at 8221 Sunset Boulevard and modeled after the Château d'Amboise in France's Loire Valley, the building was completed in 1929 and has a storied history in Tinseltown. After its conversion from an apartment building into a hotel in the 1930s, it attracted a decent amount of business in the subsequent decades, "populated by people either on their way up or on their way down" according to *Newsday*'s Jerry Parker, reporting in 1979. True enough, John Belushi died of a drug overdose at the Chateau in 1982, and renowned photographer Helmut Newton passed away after suffering a heart attack while leaving the hotel in 2004. As it happens, Sofia Coppola was actually at the Chateau that day—she recalls meeting Newton—one of her heroes—in the elevator: "I was excited to meet him because he was a hero of mine, and I was glad to thank him for a photo he had sent me. . . . Then, I left the hotel and when I came back, his car was crashed into the wall at the entrance with flowers around it."

23

Following its 1990 acquisition by American businessman André Balazs, the hotel was modernized, and its popularity only increased. Anyone who's anyone has a story about staying or partying at the Chateau, many of which are richly detailed in Shawn Levy's *The Castle on Sunset* which documents the Chateau's seven decade history. Its popularity with the rich and famous stems from its meticulously intact traditional decor and sensibilities, plus the sense of exclusivity afforded by its small size (there are only sixty-three rooms, plus one bar and one restaurant). Away from the hustle and bustle of the Sunset Strip but maintaining a close proximity to it, famous guests obtain a degree of privacy without the pomp and circumstance of more opulent surroundings.

24

Sofia has a history with the Chateau, having visited since childhood. According to Levy, at one point her father "toyed with the idea of buying the place and turning it into a kind of artist colony" and during her college years at the California Institute of the Arts, the Chateau was a frequent hangout spot. The paparazzi extensively covered her twenty-second birthday party, which was held at the hotel, attended by friends including Ethan Hawke, the Beastie Boys, Red Hot Chili Peppers, *Vogue* editor Marina Rust, and fashion heiress Tatiana von Furstenberg. While she never lived at the Chateau, Coppola understood its status within Los Angeles society: "It's sort of a rite of passage for an actor to live at the Chateau Marmont. It means you've made it, but you're still down-to-earth."

Stephen Dorff had experienced this exact scenario, having stayed at the hotel for two months when he was nineteen, after filming Iain Softley's Beatles biopic *Backbeat*. "I got back from England, and I didn't want to go home. I had all this money, so I decided to just stay at the Chateau until [my agent was] like, 'Uh, Stephen, you have to go get another job.'" Fifteen years later, Dorff was working steadily in the industry, but mostly in smaller roles opposite bigger stars—but Sofia thought of him while writing the script for *Somewhere*, having met him years earlier. It was serendipity that she should picture him while writing a story about a drifting Hollywood actor, given that Dorff was struggling to cope following the death of his mother: "I was not in a good place at all. [. . .] I was very lost." After Sofia reached out to him with the script, he flew out to Paris to meet her and discuss the project. He found out he had got the part on the one year anniversary of his mother's passing.

After the maximalism of *Marie Antoinette* (with its enormous cast, bespoke shoe designers and specialist pastry chefs) Coppola sought a more minimalist aesthetic, which is in part reflected by the film's budget—a relatively slight $7 million, compared to the

$40 million that her previous film had cost. She also returned to working independently, after Sony had financed and distributed her previous film.

Beyond the finances, *Somewhere* is perhaps the most impressionistic of Coppola's films to date; its plot and script are sparse, the majority of its music is diegetic, and the familiar intricacy usually present in her production and costume design are replaced by something that feels more in line with its almost monosyllabic protagonist, who's grown tired of the party scene but doesn't quite know how to escape it—no doubt exacerbated by the fact he resides in a hotel synonymous with the rich and famous. It's something Dorff says is accurate to his own experience: "I think being an actor is a very lonely job, and that's probably the reason why you read about a lot of people that go off the deep end. In a hotel room, when the party stops, when the camera stops, when the junket stops, it's like, what now?"

Although the Chateau had been featured in films before, it was never to the extent of which it appears in Sofia's film. In the spring of 2009 the entire fifth floor of the hotel was rented out for three weeks for the shoot; an unprecedented move, given how selective the Chateau is about filming in the grounds. "The Chateau doesn't allow a lot of filming," commented G. Mac Brown in the film's production notes. "If and when they do, they can charge a very high location fee and it probably has to be done in the middle of the night. None of this was the case with *Somewhere*."

Sofia, who had already shot films in the Tokyo Grand Hyatt hotel and the Palace of Versailles, approached André Balazs, who understood her long standing relationship with the building—and more importantly, its staff. General manager Philip Pavel attested to as much: "What spoke to me was Sofia's appreciation for Romulo Laki. He's been at the Chateau for well over thirty years and is known as "the singing waiter." He loves to serenade the guests with his guitar. Sofia had a memory of him singing "Teddy Bear" to her in the lobby, and incorporated that into her script. I'm excited for people to see that in the film, because they might not know about the Chateau's sweet side. I believe it's what makes the place so special; there is a homey feeling, and a feeling of safety."

Various members of the hotel staff, including Pavel and Romulo Laki, appear within the film as themselves, lending an authenticity to *Somewhere* that makes the film feel lived-in; the building is a breathing ecosystem which exists with or without Johnny Marco, but welcomes him back every time he drifts away. When he and daughter Cleo return exhausted from a trip to Milan, they rest for a moment in the lobby—and Romulo serenades them with Elvis Presley's "Teddy Bear," just as he had Sofia Coppola many years before. It's the dichotomy at the heart of the Chateau Marmont that Sofia manages to capture within the film: its reputation as a hotspot for Los Angeles cool kids, but its enduring warmth and familiarity which creates a sense of being a home for the waifs and strays of Hollywood who aren't quite ready to find a place to call their own.

Sofia's interest in hotels as homes is enduring, having begun in 1989 when she cowrote the script for *Life Without Zoe*, her father's segment of the anthology film *New York Stories*. The short film—about a precocious twelve-year-old girl who lives in the Sherry-Netherland hotel while her parents are away working—was generally considered the weakest of the three (the other two provided by Martin Scorsese and Woody Allen) but would foreshadow Sofia's later work in *Lost in Translation* and *Somewhere*; two films about drifting individuals in a state of melancholia, who reevaluate their lives in the wake of an unexpected meeting with a charming young woman. In *Somewhere*, it's the arrival of Johnny's eleven-year-old daughter, Cleo, who comes

25

to stay at the hotel with her father after her mother declares she needs some time alone.

The father-daughter relationship is a recurrent theme for Coppola, from the gentle figure of Mr. Lisbon in *The Virgin Suicides* to debonaire Felix Keane in *On the Rocks* (which feels like a spiritual successor to *Somewhere*). There is always a distance between the two—a sense of failure to connect, be it through Mr. Lisbon's inaction in *The Virgin Suicides*, or Felix's old-fashioned ideas about sexual politics in *On the Rocks*. In *Somewhere*, the fractures in the relationship between Johnny and Cleo are revealed slowly, without any of the blazing arguments or temper tantrums audiences have come to expect from depictions of familial relationships on screen.

Cleo appears exactly fifteen minutes into *Somewhere*, writing her name on her sleeping father's arm cast, which he's sporting on his arm after drunkenly falling down the stairs at the Chateau. She draws a love heart and signs her name with a sharpie. When her father stirs, she smiles brightly, and says, "Hi dad." They lie on the same sheets he'd shared with a stripper the night before, and when his ex, Layla, enquires about his arm, he claims he received the injury while doing stunt work.

Another connection between *Life Without Zoe* and *Somewhere*: while walking in New York with her mother, Zoe pauses to watch a blonde woman in a blue costume, ice skating at Rockefeller Plaza. "She's what I call the ideal woman," Zoe tells her mother. The image is recreated almost perfectly in *Somewhere*, when Johnny takes Cleo to an ice skating lesson. She performs a routine to Gwen Stefani's "Cool"—a synth-pop ballad about a post-breakup friendship developing between two lovers. The song plays in full while Cleo completes her routine (performed entirely by Elle Fanning, who learned to skate for the role) and while Johnny is initially distracted by his phone,

he becomes absorbed watching her—just as Zoe was watching the stranger at Rockefeller Plaza. "When did you learn to ice skate?" he asks her in the car, on the drive back to her mother's house. Cleo looks over at him and replies, with a certain amount of incredulity: "I've been going for three years." Johnny seems surprised, indicating how little he really knows about his daughter.

While the moment serves as a signifier of the distance between Johnny and Cleo, and his realization that his daughter is growing up and he's already missed a lot of her life, it's also interesting to consider the moment in contrast with the two dance scenes which precede it. The film's second scene shows Johnny recuperating from his accident in bed, while a set of blonde twins named Bambi and Cindy (real life Playboy Playmates Kristina and Karissa Shannon) perform a pole dancing routine to Foo Fighters's "My Hero" (a rock ballad about the ordinary people you look up to, according to frontman Dave Grohl). By the time the twins finish their first dance, Johnny has fallen asleep. Six minutes later they are shown performing a similar routine—inexplicably in tennis outfits—to R & B song "1 Thing" by Amerie. Johnny is a little more receptive this time; he applauds gently and says "That was amazing" before promptly forgetting which twin is which.

Like Cleo's skating scene, the routines play out in full, but the motionless camera and sharp cuts to Johnny's listless expression in the bedroom scenes create a contrasting sense of awkwardness. Cinematographer Harris Savides was inspired by Chantal Akerman's *Jeanne Dielman, 23 quai du Commerce, 1080 Bruxelles* to create a sense of the monotony within Johnny's life, and certainly pole dancing—usually portrayed as lascivious, per films such as *Showgirls* and *Closer*, or even Sofia's sultry black-and-white video for the White Stripes' cover of "I Just Don't Know What to Do With Myself," starring Kate Moss—plays out as a remarkably unerotic act in the context

26

of Johnny's bedroom. It's a distraction to him; a transactional attempt at closeness that leaves him feeling empty. In contrast, the natural light and gliding camera in the scene at the ice rink give a sense of freedom and innocence, which is recurrent throughout Cleo's appearances in the film.

Johnny's interactions with women throughout the film aside from his daughter are strained. It's hinted that he has a difficult relationship with his mother, who is publishing a book about him. Reunited with a costar at a press junket, it becomes clear he's hurt her following an intimate relationship, and when he meets his neighbor at the Chateau, it's as though he's powerless to resist her flirtatious advances. He passes out in bed before he can have sex with a woman he meets at a party, and when in Milan with Cleo, he upsets his daughter by sneaking off to a tryst with an old flame, who joins them for breakfast. Cleo glares daggers at him across the table, but as is Sofia's trademark, the moment goes undiscussed. There's a sense that Johnny attempts to combat his loneliness through sexual relationships, but these don't bring him any fulfillment. Everything—success, parties, intimacy—is only temporary.

Coppola is a master at conveying a sense of vulnerability on-screen; her first three films provided crucial insight into the agony and ecstasy of being a young woman in a world that is often cruel to them. Although Sofia had presented a male protagonist (and indeed a celebrity one) in *Lost in Translation*, Johnny Marco feels every bit as raw and bruised as the Lisbon sisters or even the isolated Queen of France. His hotel room is a sanctuary in one breath and a prison in the other; extended takes of him shaving and washing his face against the cool blue tiles evoke that sense of stagnation Savides and Coppola sought to emulate from Jeanne Dielman.

For most of the film there's a sense of Marco holding back, allowing experiences to wash over him, stumbling from junkets to parties, drinking and dropping pills with a nonchalance that evokes any number of elegant bad boys in the films which Coppola frequently cites as inspiration. One notable example is Mickey Rourke's Motorcycle Boy from *Rumble Fish*, which Francis Ford Coppola directed in 1983; a quiet, intense reformed rebel who feels alienated after he returns home from California to Tulsa, Oklahoma. It's not quite a motorcycle, but in *Somewhere*'s opening, Johnny loops around a desert road in his black Ferrari, the engine whirring loudly. It's easy to believe the film was part of the inspiration for Coppola, particularly given she cites it as her favorite of her father's work, and she used the same lenses her father used to shoot her movie.

The difference Cleo's arrival makes to Johnny's life is apparent from that first scene where she signs his cast, but comes more into focus when she comes to stay with him. Cleo frequently can be seen cooking for them, and while Johnny plays video games with his friend Sammy (played by Chris Pontius, who Sofia first met through her ex-husband Spike Jonze back in the glory days of *Jackass*), Cleo does her homework. She's the more responsible party at eleven years old, while her father is in a state of arrested development, but there's also a sense that kids in Los Angeles just grow up faster. When Johnny wonders if the black SUV behind them in traffic is following them, Cleo calmly remarks "There's kind of a lot of those in LA," but notes down the license plate number, just in case.

In the behind-the-scenes documentary for *Somewhere*, Dorff holds up a DVD of Peter Bogdanovich's *Paper Moon*, which she asked him to watch to gain a sense of the relationship between Johnny and Cleo, but a less obvious connection comes in the form of Mike Figgis's *Leaving Las Vegas*, about an alcoholic screenwriter who decides to slowly drink himself to death in Sin City and crosses paths with a empathetic sex worker along the way. It's a similar film about a woman taking care of a despondent man against the backdrop of a city where glamour and seediness sit side by side. Both also feature a pool scene in which the protagonists share a moment of connection underwater, but perhaps *Somewhere* is the flip-side to *Leaving Las Vegas*; if Ben Sanderson had decided to live after all.

The true turning point for Johnny and Cleo comes in Milan, after they travel to Italy so Johnny can accept a Telegatto award. At the ceremony Cleo's peach-colored dress stands out amid a sea of dark, sequined gowns, highlighting her purity in a world overrun with falsehoods and fakery. On their return to the Chateau, Johnny finds a naked woman waiting in his bed—for the first time, he chooses his daughter over the possibility of sex, and they go down to eat and play cards in the lounge. Following this, there's a montage scene set to the Strokes' "I'll Try Anything Once" (Sofia had previously used their song "Whatever Happened" in *Marie Antoinette*) in which Johnny and Cleo spend time together at the Chateau, playing ping pong and relaxing by the pool. It's the happiest they've both looked all film—the sort of moment one imagines a young woman looking back on fondly in her memory, like Sofia recalling sampling Milanese gelato or the singing waiter who had charmed her in her own youth.

When they leave Los Angeles to drive to Cleo's summer camp, the young girl finally breaks down, crying in the car. "I don't know when Mom's coming back," she sobs. "And you're always gone." Johnny, realizing the impact of his continued absence on her life, decides to stop in Las Vegas with Cleo, where they play craps in a casino (despite Cleo being told to stand away from the table) and take a spontaneous helicopter ride. He pauses before Cleo leaves for camp, shouting against the roar of the helicopter engine: "I'm sorry I haven't been around." It's not clear whether or not Cleo hears him, but she waves goodbye, and Johnny returns to the hotel.

His apartment seems colder and emptier without Cleo in it—another shot of Johnny shaving in the bathroom suggests the possibility of a return to his excruciating routine. He calls Cleo's mother, and tearfully expresses his insecurities. "I'm fucking nothing," he tells her. When she declines to come over, he hangs up the phone, and cries alone in his room. But a return to his previous life isn't inevitable; inspired by Cleo, he cooks dinner for himself, possibly for the first time during his tenure at the hotel (a previous shot of stacked room service dishes suggests as much) and makes a comical amount of spaghetti. The scene stands in sharp contrast from how delicately his daughter had cooked eggs benedict, cutting up chives to top the homemade hollandaise. Cooking is often an act of love (and interestingly, not one we see often in Coppola's films, even if food and the politics of mealtimes are) and if Cleo did so to show her affection for her father, Johnny's emulation suggests a desire to now care for himself.

Johnny leaves the Chateau the next day. "Shall we put your things in storage until you return?" the concierge asks. Johnny declines and takes off on the freeway in his black ferrari—the only constant in the film for him, besides his daughter—and seems to drive forever, until he's out of the city, back in the desert that opened the film. The purr of the engine returns, but this time it's undercut

by the sound of Phoenix's score—the synthy, extended instrumental opening to "Love Like a Sunset Part II." When he pulls off the road and gets out of the car this time, he walks away—smiling. The guitars kick in as the screen cuts to black, but there's something hopeful about this ending, even in its ambiguity. Perhaps Johnny is turning his back on Hollywood, if only for a little while (the concierge's offer suggests a cyclical nature to life in Tinseltown) or just has a clearer sense of where he's going: forward, rather than back.

Somewhere premiered in competition at the 67th Venice Film Festival, where it received a warmer reception than *Marie Antoinette* had at Cannes four years earlier. So much so, Sofia became the first American woman—and only the fourth overall—to win the festival's top honor, the Golden Lion. Her victory was somewhat overshadowed by nepotism claims, as the jury president that year was Quentin Tarantino, whom she had briefly dated in 2003. Tarantino denied the suggestion of course, claiming that *Somewhere* was chosen by a unanimous vote, but Coppola's success is so frequently credited to the men in her life it seems almost inevitable that her achievement would be detracted from in this way.

The sparsity of *Somewhere* can be mistaken for coolness; Johnny Marco seems largely indifferent to everything around him. The girls are interchangeable (we don't even learn some of their names) and while he's a fixture at parties, he doesn't seem present. Criticisms around the film suggested Johnny is an unsympathetic protagonist due to his success, but it's rare to find such a naturalistic portrait of the creeping depression familiar to many men. Statistically men are three times more likely to die by suicide than women, and the stigma that still exists for many around expressing feelings of loneliness and anhedonia is likely a contributing factor.

It's an old adage that money can't buy happiness (though it certainly makes the search for it more comfortable) and Sofia's work wrestles with ennui within the rarefied world she understands best. She's always been quite upfront about her inspiration and intentions, and seems to understand the absurdity of modern Hollywood better than perhaps any other contemporary filmmaker; both *Somewhere* and *The Bling Ring* point out the absurdities of the city and the lifestyle, even if they're affectionate. Her observational tendencies create portraits, rather than paragraphs; here the subtle tension between a father and daughter with a strained relationship and the acute sensation of drifting at an age where you're supposed to have life figured out.

Where is that place the title refers to—is it the Chateau Marmont, where Johnny lives in faux anonymity, or the destination he seeks at the end of the film? Coppola cites Ed Ruscha as her inspiration—"I [. . .] was trying to think of something in that spirit, and the idea is that the main character needs to go somewhere else, but doesn't know exactly where. It's the vague idea of somewhere other than where he is right now." It's a similar yearning experienced by the Lisbon sisters, Charlotte and Bob, and even Marie Antoinette; that desire for escape from a gilded cage, even one that presents the illusion of freedom. We never find out where Johnny's going, or where he'll end up. But wherever it is, Cleo is there, too. ★

27
Mickey Rourke in *Rumble Fish*, directed by Francis Ford Coppola in 1983.

28
Nicolas Cage and Elisabeth Shue in *Leaving Las Vegas*, Mike Figgis's film about an alcoholic screenwriter who opts to drink himself to death in Sin City.

ON

ROCKS

THE

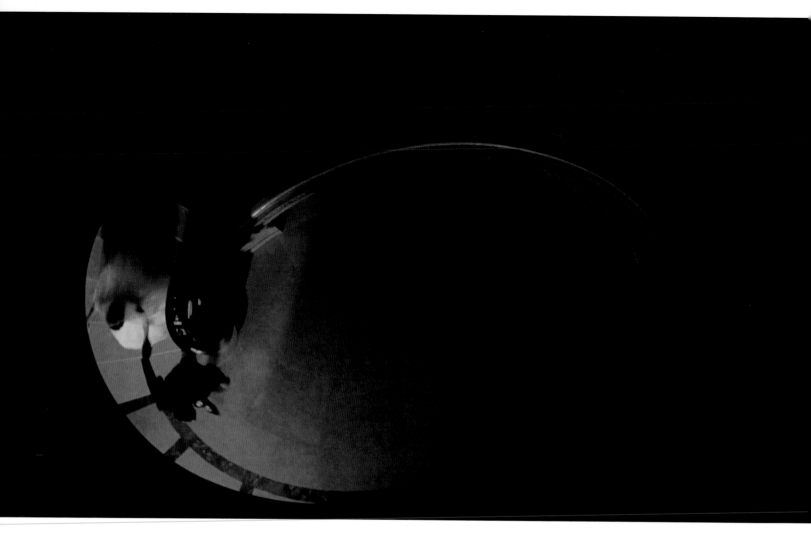

1
Laura, played by Rashida
Jones, and Dean, played by
Marlon Wayans, marry in
a lavish ceremony.

2
An exhausted Laura tries to
juggle motherhood and her
writing career.

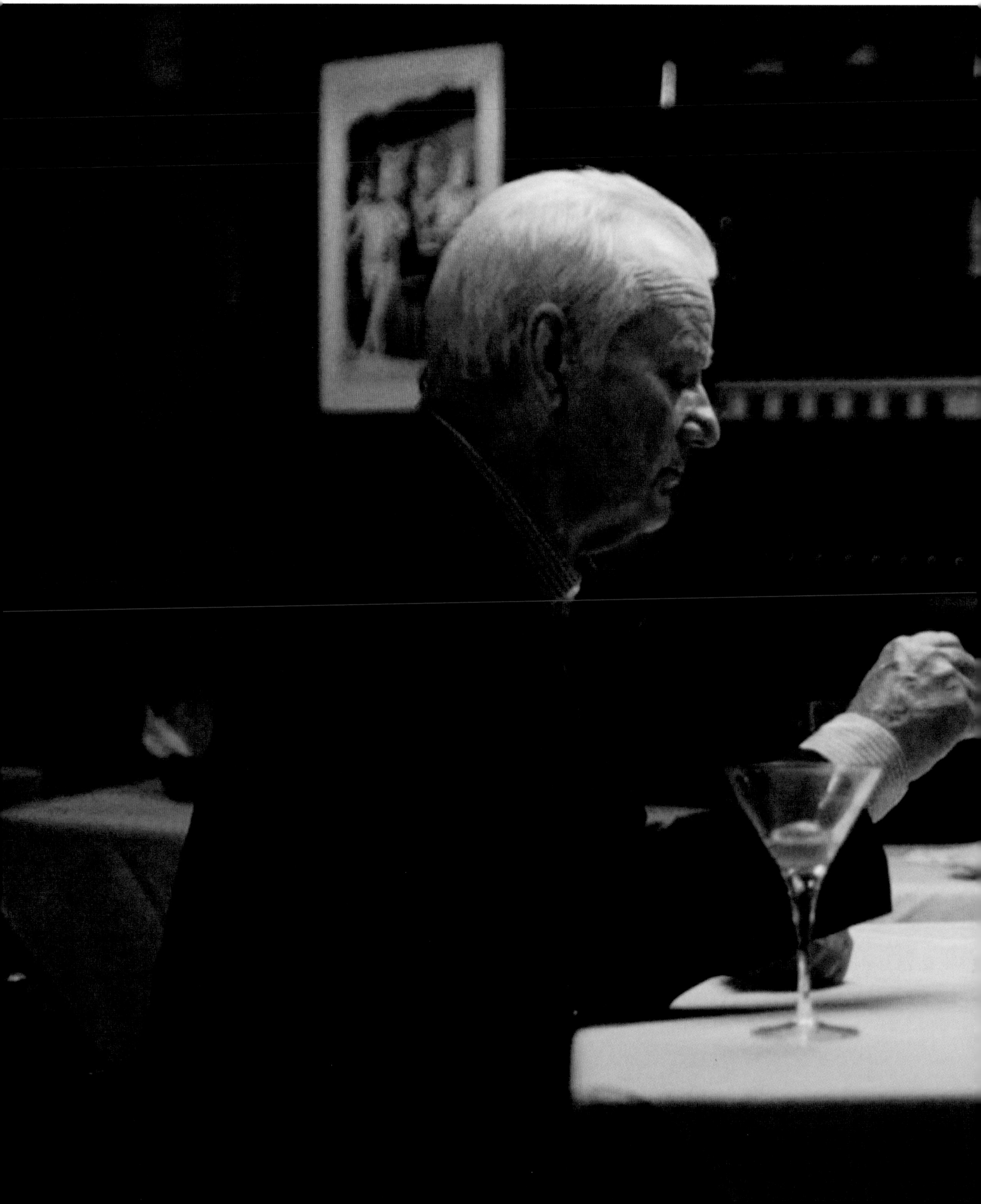

3
Laura and Felix, played
by Bill Murray, share her
birthday ice cream. While
Dean is too busy with work
to really celebrate Laura's
birthday with her, Felix insists
on giving his daughter a day
to remember.

4
Laura and Felix stake out
Soho House, where Dean
is attending a work event.

5-7
New York by night. Philippe
Le Sourd's cinematography is
reminiscent of how Tokyo was
shot by Lance Acord in *Lost
in Translation*, but presents a
more tranquil version of New
York City than we're used to
seeing on screen.

8
Laura contemplates her
father's suggestion that
Dean is having an affair.

9
Laura's drink of choice:
a martini.

10
Laura and Dean enjoy some
rare time as a family with their
daughters prior to him leaving
for a conference in Mexico.

11
Felix relaxes in Mexico, after he and Laura decide to follow Dean and see how hard he's really working.

12
After fighting with her father, Laura awakens on a beach in a scene that echoes Lux Lisbon on the football field in *The Virgin Suicides*.

13-14

Laura and Dean reconcile; it's
revealed that his mysterious
trip to Cartier was to buy her
an engraved birthday watch.
Their failure to communicate
feels a little reconciled by this
scene, but Dean's suggestion
Laura "make time for herself"
feels hollow.

On the Rocks

2020
97 minutes

Box Office $1 million

15
Felix arrives in New York;
this shot is reminiscent of Bill
Murray in the back of a cab in
Lost in Translation.

16
Murray on *Saturday Night Live*.

THE SUPPOSEDLY MYRIAD differences between men and women have provided material for entertainment for millennia. For as long as humans have been telling stories, comedy and tragedy have centered around these intricacies, from the epics of Ancient Greece through to Jane Austen's romance novels. The twentieth century and the advent of film brought with it a new medium to explore gender trouble, and by the 1930s, a new genre had emerged within it: the screwball comedy. The Great Depression had brought about a desire within American audiences for films that provided social critique while simultaneously presenting a little escapism, and out of this came a slew of titles that saw men and women sharpen their wits against each other in a variety of outlandish situations. Plenty of these titles have become enduring classics, including *It Happened One Night*, *His Girl Friday*, and *The Philadelphia Story*, described by Andrew Sarris as "sex comedies without the sex." Sharp dialogue, strong women, and plenty of slapstick: that was the screwball way.

It makes sense that the earliest definition of the genre may seem antiquated now, as our collective understanding of gender as a societal construct and views on sexual politics have developed to a point where simply pointing out potential differences between the "female" and "male" brain is at best old-fashioned and at worst exclusionary. The debate continues among film critics about whether or not the genre truly ended with the onset of the Second World War, or simply became known to modern audiences as the black comedy, with the Coen Brothers in particular cited as an example of modern filmmakers inclined towards screwball elements in their work (*The Hudsucker Proxy*, *Intolerable Cruelty*, and *Hail, Caesar!* are among the most commonly cited examples.)

16

If Joel and Ethan Coen are the directors most committed to keeping the screwball spirit alive, perhaps Bill Murray is a contender for the acting crown. His deadpan delivery has been a trademark since he rose to fame on *Saturday Night Live* during his three year stint in the late seventies, but it's his turn as Phil Connors, the curmudgeonly weatherman caught in a time loop in Harold Ramis's 1993 fantasy *Groundhog Day*, that best evidences this. The fantastical premise might be a little more elaborate than those familiar in the 1930s films, but audiences have studied its rich thematic possibilities for decades, with analysis ranging from a modern interpretation of the Myth of Sisyphus to an allegory for Jesus Christ. Combined with the chemistry between Murray and his female foil (Andie McDowell playing his assistant and love interest, Rita Hanson) and the whip-smart dialogue written by Ramis and Danny Rubin, it's a screwball comedy in all but name.

Despite the film's roaring success both critically and commercially, Murray was dissatisfied with it, and a rift had grown between himself and close friend Ramis during production. While the pair would later reconcile before Ramis's death in 2014 and Murray gave his approval to the *Groundhog Day* musical which opened on Broadway in 2017, Murray's career perhaps didn't follow the expected trajectory, as he sought supporting roles over the leading ones which might have been anticipated following such a star turn. Five years later he would give an equally well-received performance as the disillusioned businessman Herman Blume in Wes Anderson's 1998 bildungsroman *Rushmore*, and become a mainstay of Anderson's eclectic troop of repeat performers, appearing in every one of his films to date.

When Sofia Coppola cast Murray in her sophomore feature, *Lost in Translation*, he had given his word he'd take the part, but with no contract signed she was sceptical he would actually turn up for the Tokyo shoot. She turned to her old pal Wes for advice; "If he says he's going to do it, he'll show up" he assured her. The rest, as they say, is history—the film would go on to become perhaps Coppola's best-known work, and sparked a friendship between the two which resulted in two more collaborations: a Netflix variety special entitled *A Very Murray Christmas*, and her ode to the bygone era of the screwball comedy, *On the Rocks*.

The way Coppola tells it, *On the Rocks* was inspired by an anecdote from a friend, who had noticed her husband was traveling with a female coworker a lot. "She really went and spied on her husband with her dad. They were hiding in bushes," she recalled to *Vogue*. "Hearing that, I thought I would love to see a father-and-daughter detective movie." Fueled by her love of the *Thin Man* films popularized in the thirties and forties, Coppola registered the film's title seven years ago, and began to write the script two years after that, before she had shot *The Beguiled*. In time it became a more complex proposition, dealing not only with goofy romantic foibles through the lens of father-daughter relationships, but the shift in self-perception that comes with marriage and motherhood; concerns she had come to grapple with since having children. "I used to stay up all night writing," Coppola said. "Now I had to wake up early, and then you find yourself in this whole new world of schools and people you wouldn't know otherwise. It's like a foreign land."

Staying true to Coppola's experience in writing what she knows, *On the Rocks* centers on Laura Keane (played by Rashida Jones), a writer approaching forty, juggling her career with motherhood, matrimony, and the return of her charismatic father, who breezes into New York once he hears that his daughter has doubts about her marriage. Given the long-standing partnership between Coppola and Murray, it makes sense she would cast him as a stand-in for her own dad, though while conducting press for the film, Sofia was quick to play down any substantial resemblance between Felix Keane and Francis Ford Coppola. She did, however, acknowledge how details from her own life made it into the script, as they had in *Somewhere*: "I have this really vivid memory from my twenties going out with my dad having martinis," she told *EW*. "I was caught up on some guy. [My dad] was like, 'Let me tell you what's really going on and what he's thinking.' It's so fascinating for a man to have a grown daughter that's dealing with relationships and to have these different perspectives."

Of course Murray's comedic chops have been proven over a career spanning some four decades, but *On the Rocks* was only the second leading film role for Rashida Jones (her first had been in the 2012 romantic comedy *Celeste and Jesse Forever*, which she also cowrote).

Coppola and Jones first met at a workshop years previously, when Jones played the role of Charlotte in a read-through for Coppola's *Lost in Translation* script. They would later work together in 2015 on *A Very Murray Christmas*, in which Murray played himself and Jones played a distraught bride hoping to reconcile with her fiance, which is where the director first got a sense for the chemistry between the pair. Of course, Jones—the daughter of music legend Quincy Jones

18

17

William Powell and Myrna Loy in the 1939 screwball mystery film, *Another Thin Man*.

18

Katharine Ross and Dustin Hoffman in *The Graduate*.

19

Signs from the 2020 Black Lives Matter protests.

17

202   SOFIA COPPOLA: FOREVER YOUNG

and actress Peggy Lipton—knows a thing or two about living in the shadow of a larger-than-life character. "I had completed a six-year project directing a documentary about his life," she told the *Los Angeles Times*. "So all of that kind of intensity and of feeling, and also really being able to put that on screen in a way where I was like, 'OK, you know what? I think I've done a good job as a daughter, whatever happens, that's forever immortalized, that I made a movie about him,'" Jones said. "And now I can try to be my own person in a way that doesn't feel like it's completely tied up in him and his success and his love for me."

On the Rocks follows in a tradition for Coppola, having navigated the choppy waters of father-daughter relationships in the widely derided *Life Without Zoe* as a teenager working with her own father, then in her 2010 drama *Somewhere*. If the latter is an impressionistic portrait of a father learning how to parent his daughter amid personal crisis, *On the Rocks* feels like a companion piece; it's easy to believe Cleo and Johnny Marco could have conversations similar to Laura and Felix in their hypothetical future, where the generational divide becomes a contentious issue in light of personal turmoil. From the film's opening this becomes apparent, as Felix warns a young Laura in voice-over, "And remember, don't give your heart to any boys. You're mine. Until you're married. And then you're still mine." She laughs, doubt evident in her response of "Um, okay Dad."

This might be a joke that echoes patriarchal sentiments handed down for generations, but Coppola chooses to directly follow the exchange with footage of Laura and her husband Dean (Marlon Wayans) on their wedding day set to Chet Baker's "I Fall in Love Too Easily," which has a melancholic edge in opposition to the cliche of a wedding being the happiest day of your life. A shot of Laura and Dean after the ceremony resembles the ending of Mike Nichols's *The Graduate*, in which Dustin Hoffman and Elaine Robinson flee her wedding ceremony on a bus. Initially ecstatic, their smiles fade as they realize what they've done. "What happens after the glamour?" asked Stephen Marche, revisiting the scene for *Esquire* in 2014. "What happens beyond the storybook ending? What happens when everything has worked out and you find out that you're just a couple of people sitting on a bus, wondering who the hell you and the person beside you are?" There's a similar sort of expression shared between Laura and Dean, even as they escape their nuptials to go skinny-dipping in a moonlit pool. In prefacing the title card with this apprehensive beginning to their marriage, Coppola sets the tone for a more rigorous interrogation of relationships than her past films have allowed.

This is partly possible through the film's script, which is a departure from Coppola's trademark sparsity; *On the Rocks* is her second-longest work at 117 pages, behind *Lost in Translation* at 138, and some way ahead of her shortest (*Somewhere*, which comprised just 44 pages). In fact, it was Buck Henry, cowriter of *The Graduate*'s screenplay, who encouraged Sofia to experiment with her writing. "I've always been drawn to finding a way to express emotion through visuals and atmosphere. I was talking to Buck Henry about this idea early on, and he said, 'Why don't you write some dialogue?', she explained to *Vogue*. "I thought I'd try writing something dialogue-driven that was almost like a play for me. *On the Rocks* started with just Felix and Laura sitting in different restaurants and bars having conversations."

These meetings between father and daughter take place in various iconic New York establishments, including the Sentinel Association, Bemelman's Bar (which featured on the film's poster, and was also a setting in *A Very Murray Christmas*), and 21 Club; Felix is

19

an art dealer, and has a particular affection for the New York of yesteryear, one populated by classy joints with live music and plenty of dark corners for clandestine conversations—"A time before athleisure," as Coppola describes it. Felix expresses an incredulity at the modern city, declaring of trendy hotspot Soho House, "I still don't understand why anyone would want to go there, with all the great clubs in New York? Not only the Sentinel—have you ever been to the Architectural League? Now that's a place to go . . . and the Knickerbocker, they have great readings . . . " with a despairing shake of his head. Felix moves through these establishments with the ease of old money, flirting with waitresses and greeting staff by name. Laura—more removed from this world—is simultaneously amused and incredulous at his brazen attitude. When the pair are pulled over by a police officer while tailing Dean in Felix's extremely conspicuous vintage Alfa Romeo sports car, Felix manages to talk his way out of trouble by revealing he knows the man's father. The police officer lets them go with a warning, and Laura, dumbfounded, comments to Felix, "It must be very nice to be you." Her father, without missing a beat, replies "I wouldn't have it any other way."

After the film's release, Coppola reflected on the scene to Indiewire, and expressed an air of regret over her approach in light of the Black Lives Matter protests of 2020, which highlighted white privilege particularly related to law enforcement. "I probably wouldn't have written it in today's climate because it brings up so much violence that we're talking about right now," she told Indiewire. "It's very specific for that kind of guy who's a real representation of privilege, in the way that he breezes through life and doesn't see it for other people." Yet the scene's inclusion does drive home the point that Felix lives on a different plane of reality from his daughter, a biracial woman with a Black husband and two young biracial daughters; it isn't mentioned, but the implicit differences in their experiences navigating New York City are there in every well-timed eye roll or sigh from Laura.

It's also the first time Coppola's work has focused on a Black family, which is significant given the criticism she has faced previously for choosing to cast predominantly white actors (and in the case of *The Beguiled* and *The Bling Ring*, even remove canonically non-white characters from the narrative). When asked if her casting for *On the Rocks* was a response to these criticisms, Coppola demurred: "I was just thinking about how to make a beautiful American family that represents families I see living in New York and in the world around me."

The Keanes certainly are a modern family—they have a Bernie 2016 sticker on their door, and Dean is a high flyer for a publicity start-up—but it has to be said that Coppola is still preoccupied with the rarefied world she knows best. Laura is a comfortably middle class woman, who can afford to dedicate large portions of her time to spying on her husband or drinking cocktails midweek with her father; it's every bit as fantastical and escapist as Coppola's previous work, but that doesn't mean the anxieties and miscommunications don't translate on a wider scale. In fact, Felix's hare-brained schemes appeal to Laura in the same way *On the Rocks* appeals to audiences, retaining that outlandish element which made screwball comedies a sensation throughout the 1930s and '40s.

In a twist on the screwball formula, it's Jones who plays the straight man, while Murray pinwheels across New York City showcasing the charisma which made him a Hollywood legend. But his return to Laura's life comes at a time where she's experiencing writer's block, familial burnout and insecurity in her marriage; Felix's propositions of cocktails and stakeouts turn her life into something more fantastical, rather than facing the potential reality that "Dean's just busy and I'm in a rut."

But the appeal is twofold; it also offers Laura a chance to reconnect with her father, whose absence in her life has had lasting effects. It's revealed that he cheated on her mother Diane with a younger gallery assistant when Laura was a child, which led to the breakdown of their marriage. This caused heartache for Laura and her younger sister Amanda, who remarks "I don't know how you can deal with him" when he comes up in conversation. Later, when Felix laments that men who have affairs are seen as sordid, and that he did so because he felt he wasn't loved enough by his wife and family, Laura is incredulous. "It's exhausting to try to love you enough," she tells him. There seems to be a look of acknowledgement in Felix's expression, but even when Laura asks him if it was worth it, he refuses to accept responsibility for his actions, cryptically replying "It was heartbreaking for everyone." This rejection of accountability fits into Felix's old-fashioned view of relationships that he espouses throughout the film, citing bonobo chimpanzees and the historical significance of the bangle as an indication of man's "ownership" of women throughout the film. Laura is initially tolerant of his diatribes, but becomes increasingly frustrated. When Felix claims he's becoming unable to hear women's voices, she's particularly perturbed, eventually responding "And no one goes deaf to just the frequency of women's voices! You have daughters and granddaughters, so you better start being able to hear them! You already drove Mom away, do you want to drive us all away?!"

Although pitched as a comedy—and certainly more akin to one than any of Coppola's past work—there is a melancholy edge to *On the Rocks* which comes through in the moments Laura and Felix clash with one another. Realizing your parents aren't necessarily good people (and in turn realizing your children are old enough to see through your charade) is a crucial part of growing up. Although most of Coppola's coming-of-age stories concern adolescents or young adults, *On the Rocks* makes the case for one with an older protagonist, suggesting we're all works-in-progress, and that it's okay to not have life completely figured out, even when you're raising a family of your own. In a heated argument, Felix reprimands Laura by saying "What happened to you? You used to be fun"; the inference being that Laura had to grow up while Felix continued his arrested development indefinitely. That's often the way it goes for women who do marry and have children, and ties in with Coppola's admission that she experienced something like an "identity crisis" after having kids. Even Dean remarks, with no trace of irony, "You have to make time for yourself," while Laura raises their daughters alongside writing a book.

By her own admission Coppola attempted to show more through her dialogue this time, but trademarks of her aesthetic remain; when Felix and Laura follow Dean to Mexico in an attempt to catch him in the act, the idyllic resort is bathed in cool blue light that reflects her growing sense of unease. A shot of Laura awakening on a deserted clifftop also brings to mind Lux Lisbon alone on her high school football field, having been left alone by Trip Fontaine; these experiences leave our heroines changed in the harsh light of morning.

Ultimately Laura returns to New York, and finally discusses her anxieties with her husband, who is surprised but sympathetic, recognizing her burnout and his own workaholic tendencies which have led to an imbalance in their relationship. It's perhaps a fairly trite resolution to the past ninety minutes of intrigue, but it does suggest that reality is often much more mundane than the stories we conjure to explain our situations, and that the rat race's demands on parents are increasingly hard to manage. While *On the Rocks* really doesn't interrogate the idea of how long office hours and demands on working parents can lead to relationship breakdown, it actually shows something even rarer in the movies: a rocky marriage which manages to find its stride again.

This is made possible through Laura reconciling her desire to connect with her father with her own identity as a wife and mother. She declines Felix's offer to take a spontaneous cruise, and reconnects with her husband over martinis, where he presents her with an engraved Cartier watch. This replaces one her father had given her earlier in the film; a symbol of Laura embracing her own family, as well as her future, over the past.

Of course the past isn't totally forgotten; we glimpse it in details such as the vintage band T-shirts Laura wears around the house, and her collection of tote bags from beloved New York institutions such as the Strand and Greenlight Books. These gestures are less glamorous than the Louboutins of *The Bling Ring* or Johnny Marco's Ferrari in *Somewhere*, but tell us plenty about Laura's character, and in turn, the way Sofia Coppola views New York compared to her take on Los Angeles. Where the Californian city is washed-out shades of peach and cerulean, New York is the greys and blues of concrete and skyscrapers, punctuated by the glimpses of color in the restaurants and bars visited—such as the murals that adorn the walls of Bemelmans, or the Monet painting Felix and Laura sneak off to look at in the Sherry-Netherland Hotel. "Philippe [Le Sourd] and I found our way as we went shooting the cityscapes and finding the contrasts between Felix and Laura's worlds," Coppola explained to *Vogue*. "Showing her walking down the street with the construction sounds then Felix shielded off in his town car gazing up into all those old uptown spots." This contrast makes *On the Rocks* a fascinating study in the changing landscape of New York, and suggests that it's hard to really appreciate the romantic elements of the city when you're weighed down by the responsibilities that come with balancing a career and family life. But unlike Felix, Laura has chosen to embrace these difficulties—she seems happiest when she's spending time with her daughters—and by the film's close, her marriage seems to have course-corrected.

On the Rocks premiered at the 2020 New York Film Festival, which was presented in a slightly different format due to the COVID-19 pandemic. Rather than opening with a glitzy red carpet at Lincoln Center, the premiere took place at the Queens Drive-in, with Coppola, Murray, and Jones in attendance (though, it's perhaps fitting that the film would premiere at a drive-in, given that a substantial number of scenes show Felix and Laura driving around the city as they reconnect). The film was then distributed by Apple TV+—a first for Coppola—bypassing cinemas in most territories due to shutdowns prompted by the pandemic. "We didn't know we were making a period movie," Coppola joked at the time, yet there is a sort of other-worldliness to her filmography even beyond her obvious period films, *The Virgin Suicides*, *Marie Antoinette*, and *The Beguiled*. It speaks to her fascination with bygone eras and the history of movie making; in particular the films she chooses to draw character and visual references from, such as Peter Bogdanovich's filmography for *Somewhere* and W. S. Van Dyke's *Thin Man* series for *On the Rocks*. Combined with the timeless themes Coppola is most interested in exploring (innocence, secrets, celebrity, familial discord, and the constant work of growing up) this creates a distinct sensibility about her work that transcends the period of its production and is likely the reason her films have endured, gaining traction with new audiences over time.

Of course the valid criticism remains that Coppola's worldview is often narrow, offering us glimpses into a world populated by the haves rather than the have-nots, and *On the Rocks* in particular is unlikely to change anyone's perceptions of Sofia as a benefactor of Hollywood nepotism who doesn't have much interest in really interrogating the structures and world that made her. In her *On the Rocks* review for American socialist magazine *Jacobin*, Eileen Jones—who also disliked Coppola's version of *The Beguiled*—summed this up as "Sofia Coppola Wants You to Feel Bad for the Very Rich and the Very Sad," a suggestion which has reappeared in various guises throughout her career. It's understandable that a publication like *Jacobin* might take umbrage with the world Coppola chooses to represent on-screen, but there's no clear solution to this quandary. Should she turn her sights to underrepresented characters and face accusations of voyeurism and insincerity, or continue to be as honest as she can regarding emotions and relationships even if it means moving in the world of privilege she knows best?

I grew up, and still reside, a thousand miles away—literally and figuratively—from the experiences Coppola depicts. The beauty of her films is in the physical (aesthetically pleasing outfits, aspirational locations, casts of impossibly attractive celebrities) but also their potential as flights of fancy grounded in more universal core themes. My own father was distinctly less charming but every bit as absent as Felix Keane, and I tried for a very long time to love him enough that he might love me back. I see in *On the Rocks* the relationship I wish I'd been able to have with my dad, but also the idea that it is crucial to move past our parents' expectations and perceptions of us in order to figure out who we are. This may not be revolutionary, but it is comforting, particularly in a time of global upheaval that's caused so many to reevaluate their identity, to disappear into a world of cocktails, charisma and conversation, and decide who we want to be. ◗

INSPIRATIONS

↓ *Paper Moon*, Peter Bogdanovich &
The Thin Man, W. S. Van Dyke ↓

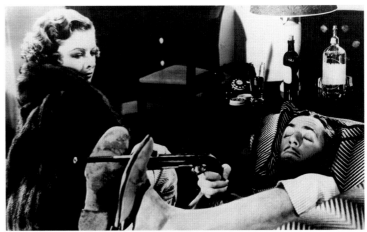

SOFIA COPPOLA: FOREVER YOUNG

GIVEN THE TIGHT-KNIT nature of the Coppola family, it's unsurprising that familial relationships should play such an important role in the cinema of Sofia Coppola. While *The Virgin Suicides* acts as a starting point in its exploration of sisterhood and the stifling impact of parental restriction, her later work focuses more closely on father-daughter relationships, with *Somewhere* and *On the Rocks* particularly inspired by her own relationship with her father—though, as Sofia has been careful to point out, there are elements of Francis Ford Coppola in Johnny Marco and Felix Keane, rather than either being a faithful biopic representation.

In preparation for *Somewhere*, Sofia Coppola gave Stephen Dorff a selection of films to watch that conveyed the spirit of Johnny Marco. Among them was Peter Bogdanovich's 1973 comedy *Paper Moon* (based on Joe David Brown's 1971 novel *Addie Pray*) about a con artist who is unexpectedly saddled with a strong-willed nine-year-old orphan after agreeing to deliver her to her aunt's house in Missouri. Starring Ryan O'Neal as the smooth-talking Moses Pray and his daughter Tatum O'Neal as Addie Loggins, it's a charming film with the O'Neals making for an irresistible double act. Similarly, while Johnny Marco might not be a con man, he is certainly stuck in a case of arrested development, and it's the unexpected arrival of Cleo in his life that provides the wake-up call he needs to change his ways. Both Addie and Cleo challenge the father figures in their lives to care about someone other than themselves for the first time.

"I loved them in that movie. It's like a buddy movie with a father and daughter," Sofia said of Ryan and Tatum O'Neal. "They have a sweet relationship in that it isn't sappy." This is certainly true; at first young Addie resents Moze, but quickly becomes fascinated with his scam artistry, and becomes a quick study in cons. Her precocious performance won ten-year-old Tatum an Academy Award for Best Supporting Actress, making her the youngest winner of all time (a feat still not surpassed at the time of writing). Elle Fanning's performance might not be as well-known as O'Neal's, but her quiet mastery of the art of looking incredulous comes into its own when her father sleeps with a woman during their trip to Milan, and she joins them for breakfast. The awkward moment feels reminiscent of Addie's run-ins with Miss Trixie, whom she is eventually able to exorcise from Moze's life by staging a con of her own.

There are similarities between *Paper Moon* and *On the Rocks*, too. Bill Murray's Felix Keane reads like an older (but no less rakish) Moze Pray, while Rashida Jones's Laura is a defiant (and only slightly less mischievous) version of Addie Loggins. There might not be any cons in *On the Rocks*, but there's certainly a fair amount of scheming as the pair attempt to discern whether or not Laura's husband is having an affair. Given Bogdanovich's own love of screwball comedies (directly before *Paper Moon* he made *What's Up Doc?*, an ode to the genre also starring Ryan O'Neal) it's no surprise that Sofia would find an affinity with his work, and while *Paper Moon* is often considered a road movie more than a screwball caper, it definitely blurs the lines between genres.

Coppola has cited other screwball comedies as her inspiration for *On the Rocks*, namely Leo McCarey's *The Awful Truth* and W. S. Van Dyke's 1934 film *The Thin Man*, starring William Powell as detective Nick Charles. Adapted from a Dashiell Hammett novel, the wise-cracking dick and his wealthy new wife Nora (Myrna Loy) begin investigating the mysterious disappearance of Clyde Wynant at the behest of his daughter Dorothy. Crucial to every screwball comedy is the dynamic partnership between two leads—be it Powell and Loy or Bill Murray and Rashida Jones. However, a clear point of deviation between the two films is their depiction of marriage; for the well-suited Nick and Nora, marriage is an effortless partnership, whereas much of *On the Rocks* hinges on the tensions within Laura's marriage to Dean. Nevertheless, the habitual imbibing of Nick Charles certainly reflects Felix Keane's attitude toward his daughter's predicament; they spend plenty of screen time holding court at New York drinking establishments, discussing Laura's fears about her husband's long hours and business trips.

The traditional function of the screwball comedy throughout the 1930s and '40s was to provide some light escapism for audiences grappling with changing attitudes toward women, challenging traditional masculinity in a similar vein to the popular film noir genre. Coppola's films often provide a similar sort of escapism through their upmarket settings and well-heeled characters, but maintain a similar sharpness; *On the Rocks* explores the pressures of trying to maintain a romance in the ever-demanding modern world, as well as the generational divide between parents and children when it comes to expectations about love. Despite the disparate plotlines, there's a singular truth present in all four films: life is a hell of a lot easier to endure with someone who understands you by your side to share the weight, or even just hand you a glass of scotch when the going gets tough. ♣

LOST

TRANSLATIO

IN

N

1
Bob Harris, played by Bill Murray, arrives in central Tokyo, where buildings are illuminated by the technicolor glow of billboards and neon signs.

2
Bob takes the elevator in the Tokyo Grand Hyatt. At 6' 2", he stands out, but the Japanese guests are indifferent to the celebrity's presence, indicating a sort of anonymity available in being so far away from home.

3
Charlotte is restless in the hotel room she shares with her husband. Jetlagged by the journey from Los Angeles, she finds it difficult to sleep; which is how she comes to encounter Bob in the hotel bar.

4
In an attempt to keep herself busy, Charlotte takes an interest in Japanese decor and crafts; but are these fleeting interests in the same vein as her attempts at photography and writing?

5
Bob joins Charlotte and her friends for a night out, which culminates in karaoke.

6
The wordless moment between Bob and Charlotte in the hallway of the karaoke bar they visit is one of the film's most tender moments.

7

A wide shot depicts Bob playing golf in the breathtaking shadow of Mount Fuji. Bill Murray is a keen golfer in real life (and of course starred in the 1980 comedy *Caddyshack*) but this tranquil moment seems to reflect how Bob is starting to enjoy his trip despite initial apprehension.

8

With Charlotte's husband away, she continues to bond with Bob. They watch *La Dolce Vita* together and he provides reassurance that despite how hard life (and marriage) is, she's on the right track.

9

After a tense lunch, Bob and Charlotte make up during a hotel fire drill.

10

Charlotte takes a day trip to Kyoto, enjoying the peaceful contrast from the overwhelming Tokyo. Like Bob's trip to the golf course, it shows a newfound willingness to engage with the outside world.

11

Bob and Charlotte say their goodbyes in the streets of Tokyo, while the world spins madly on around them.

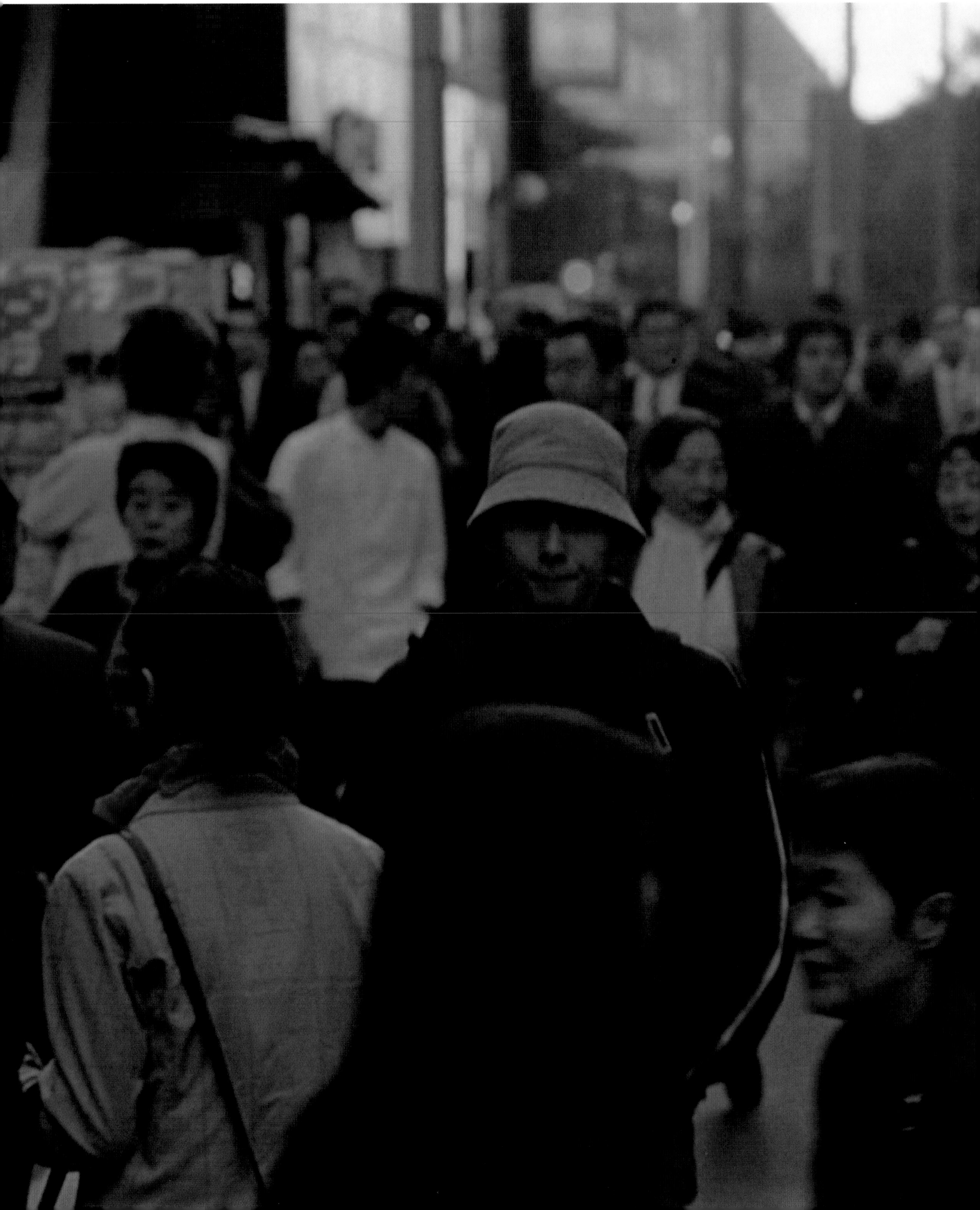

Lost in Translation

2003
102 minutes

Budget $4 million
Box Office $118 million

12

IN THE SUMMER of 1979, on the set of *Kagemusha* in Hokkaido, Japan, Akira Kurosawa and Francis Ford Coppola appeared in a series of commercials for Suntory Whisky. They sip glasses as they look over storyboards; Kurosawa directs an epic battle sequence while Coppola observes from the sidelines. "There's no stronger friendship than between these two men," the Japanese voiceover states. Coppola was certainly a major influence in bringing *Kagemusha* to the big screen, stepping in as executive producer alongside his friend George Lucas, who helped Kurosawa secure the budget from 20th Century Fox. Coppola had only recently won the Palme d'Or for *Apocalypse Now*; the following year, *Kagemusha* would share this accolade with Bob Fosse's *All That Jazz* (which would eventually inspire *Marie Antoinette*). The memory of her father's trip and his brief foray into whisky commercials stayed with Sofia; Japan would have a lasting impact on her life.

"I spent a lot of time in Tokyo in my twenties," Sofia recalled to *Little White Lies* in 2018. "I really wanted to make a film around my experience of just being there. That was the starting point." Her fashion line Milk Fed was popular in Japan and she would frequently visit, staying at the Grand Hyatt Tokyo in the upmarket Roppongi Hills neighborhood whenever she was in town. This was prior to her making *The Virgin Suicides*, when she was still experiencing feelings of directionlessness: "I'd had my share of hotel room malaise," she told *Sight & Sound* in 2003. Fifteen years later, she recalled the inspiration behind her debut feature with poignant clarity: "I got married not long before and kind of felt isolated. I was in this stage where I wasn't sure if I'd made the right choices or what I was doing in the post-college beginning of my adult life."

12
The Coppola shot: Bob Harris gazes out at Tokyo as his taxi takes him to his hotel.

13
Akira Kurosawa and Francis Ford Coppola's Suntory commercial.

After her grueling experience with *The Godfather Part III*, Sofia shied away from film, reluctant to reenter a world which had shown contempt for her. "I became a dilettante," she admitted. "I wanted to do something creative, but I didn't know what it would be." Her mother had encouraged her to study photography at the California Institute of the Arts, but it didn't stick; her foray into television with *Hi Octane* was equally brief. But the success Sofia found with *The Virgin Suicides* was encouraging. She began to work on a short story about her experiences in Japan, eventually developing it into a screenplay that explored the young adult anxieties with which she was intimately acquainted while centering a perspective quite different to her own.

The role of Bob Harris, a middle-aged movie star who arrives in Tokyo to shoot—what else—a commercial for Suntory Whisky, was written with Bill Murray in mind, though the advertisements themselves were inspired by similar ones she had spotted in the city featuring Harrison Ford. Sofia had never met Murray, and was well aware how difficult he was to contact, but she was adamant the role had to go to him. "People said, 'You need to have a backup plan,' and I said, 'I'm not going to make the movie if Bill doesn't do it,'" she told the *New York Times* in 2003. "Bill has a 1-800 number, and I left messages. This went on for five months. Stalking Bill became my life's work." But to be a Coppola is to be connected, and Sofia was friendly with screenwriter Mitch Glazer, who had worked with Murray on 1988's *Scrooged* and remained one of his closest friends. She asked him if he could grease the wheels with Bill, or at least pass along her ten-page treatment. "When she was pursuing Bill, I talked to her more than I talked to my wife. She talked to me a thousand times. In that sweet way, but persistent," Glazer said. "In more than twenty years of friendship, I never said anything was perfect for Bill, and this time, I did. But Bill is difficult. He wouldn't give anyone an answer."

Sofia enlisted another pal to her cause: Wes Anderson. She had suggested her cousin Jason Schwartzman to the director for the lead role in *Rushmore* a few years earlier, which he ended up starring in alongside Murray. Anderson was only too happy to repay the favor. The three of them had dinner in New York the evening after Sofia had been introduced to Murray by Mitch Glazer. "It was one of those patented Bill evenings," Anderson recalled. "He was driving. He went through a red light, reversed the car and then ducked into this Japanese place that only he could see. By the time the sake came, I knew he would do the movie."

Even so, with no formal contract signed, Sofia worried that Bill would be a no-show when it came time to shoot in Tokyo. "If he says he's going to do it, he'll show up," Anderson assured her. She didn't have the same concerns about Murray's costar, Scarlett Johansson, who plays newlywed college graduate Charlotte (she turned eighteen just after filming). Coppola had approached the actress after remembering her performance as a tearaway preteen in Lisa Kruger's 1996 dramedy *Manny & Lo*, and Johansson said yes to *Lost in Translation* as soon as they discussed the part. "She had that husky voice even then and seemed mature beyond her years," Coppola remembered. "There was some quality about her that stood out and I connected with. She's able to convey a lot without saying anything. I had a feeling about her."

It's Johansson who provided the film's enduring image, lying on a hotel bed in a sweater and pink, semisheer underwear. It was inspired by the painter John Kacere (particularly his 1973 piece *Jutta*) and reflects Coppola's interest in the cusp between girlhood and womanhood. Charlotte's baby blue sweater is a soft contrast to her suggestive undergarment, but the peach color is deliberate;

where Kacere often painted his models wearing lacy stockings and negligees in sultry black or virginal white, designed specifically to appeal to men without much consideration given to the wearer's comfort, Charlotte's underwear suggests an element of practicality and playfulness over seduction.

The extended length of the shot invites us to focus on Johansson's body, but there's something serene about her posture. With her back to the camera, she seems to exist in her own world; our voyeurism is accompanied by the arched eyebrow of Coppola, who acutely understands the pressures of being a young woman observed by strangers. "I was afraid to wear the underwear," Johansson told the *New York Times*. "Sofia said: 'I'm going to try on the underwear and show you what it looks like. Then, if you don't want to do it, you don't have to.' Well, I've been directed by Robert Redford, who is very handsome, but I can't imagine him suggesting that. Only a female director could get me to wear the underwear. And we shot it."

This image lasts less than a minute, with the intro to Kevin Shields's "City Girl" briefly fading in and out before the film cuts to the soundscape of an airport and the melancholy shoegaze of "Girls" by Death In Vegas. From the backseat of a taxi, Bob Harris stares out at the neon wonderland of downtown Tokyo (passing a billboard of himself in the process). This brief establishing scene succinctly captures what it's like to arrive in the Japanese capital for the first time as an outsider. By night the inner city is illuminated by technicolor signs and towering billboards; crowds bustle with salarymen heading home, teenagers heading out, and tourists snapping photographs. Tokyo feels at once familiar and foreign, a sprawling metropolis all but designed to give weary travellers a sensory overload. It is mesmerising as much as it is overwhelming; a place where the past, present and future converge. Traditional Shinto shrines nestle between imposing glass skyscrapers; patrons cram into tiny bars in Shinjuku's Golden Gai district, formerly a hub for sex workers prior to its 1958 criminalization; tourists drink in dancing robots and women posing in traditional kimonos. It's perhaps the easiest place in the world to be surrounded by people and still feel completely alone.

The shoot would prove to be a difficult one, particularly compared to the experience Sofia had filming *The Virgin Suicides* in Toronto. The language barrier and threat of an impending typhoon meant the twenty-seven-day shoot was hectic; Sofia described it as "a stealth production" as she worried that publicity might further jeopardize their tight schedule. Most of the Grand Hyatt scenes had to be filmed after 1 a.m. so as to not disturb the hotel guests, and the chaotic nature of Tokyo forced the crew to get creative, using subways, the middle of the street, and even the second floor of a Starbucks to get the shot.

When they ran late shooting Charlotte and Bob's dinner in a shabu-shabu restaurant, the owner felt disrespected by their tardiness and kicked the cast and crew out onto the street, prompting the location manager to resign. But Coppola's adaptability was her saving grace, and she found herself inspired by the location as well as challenged by it. Producer Ross Katz told *Filmmaker* magazine how a sudden downpour made it possible to shoot Charlotte walking through Tokyo's iconic Shibuya Crossing in the rain: "We shot Scarlett walking through Shibuya with 13

hundreds of translucent umbrellas, steam coming off the rooftops and the noodle shops. Afterward we had to deal with losing a location, but it was worth it."

Although most of the *Lost in Translation* crew were Japanese, Sofia reunited with several key collaborators: director of photography Lance Acord (who had worked on her short *Lick the Star*, as well as Spike Jonze's *Being John Malkovich* and *Adaptation*); costume designer Nancy Steiner; and music supervisor Brian Reitzell. This is the Coppola way—building relationships with like-minded artists who can come together to create something beautiful. "They collect interesting people," Wes Anderson has said of the filmmaking family. "They have a leader in Francis who cooks up things to do together. They work on each other's projects, and they like to add members to the family." In this spirit, Roman Coppola joined his sister in Tokyo as additional director for the Japan unit, shooting many of the neon nightscapes that bring the film to life.

If *The Virgin Suicides* is about a group of boys watching a group of girls from a distance, imprinting their own meaning on their lives from afar, *Lost in Translation* is an exercise in introspection that no less understands the power of looking. Beyond Charlotte gazing out of her hotel window at the city's breathtaking skyline, or Bob sitting in front of a camera to record his Suntory commercials, the couple first lock eyes in a crowded elevator, later spotting each other again in the hotel bar. Before they have spoken a word to each other they establish a sort of dialogue; they smile at each other and Charlotte sends a bowl of snacks over to Bob's table, which he eats in one gulp, a clownish display before he exits the bar. They finally have their first conversation thirty minutes into the film, meeting as insomniac displaced Americans who bond over a nightcap and a cigarette.

Much of the film focuses on Charlotte and Bob's blossoming companionship as they drift through the city together, reflecting on life, love and everything in between. "You're probably just having a mid-life crisis," Charlotte tells Bob when they meet. "Did you think about buying a Porsche yet?" Murray deadpans: "You know, I was thinking about buying a Porsche." The film hinges on the easy chemistry between Johansson and Murray, but it avoids romantic comedy clichés by never allowing their relationship to develop into something more. The solace they find in each other's company transcends a physical relationship—while Charlotte provides an alluring counterpoint to Bob's rocky marriage of twenty-five years, to Charlotte, Bob is attentive, charming and wise next to her distant husband. "It was about those relationships that you have that are more than friends but less than a love affair," Coppola reflected to the *Independent* at the time of the film's release.

When Charlotte invites Bob out to meet her friends, we see her unfurl. Her quiet demeanor gives way to a newfound confidence. One of the gang, Charlie Brown, is Sofia's real-life friend, and watching him perform the Sex Pistols's "God Save the Queen" at a karaoke bar

was another inspiration behind the film. Their wild night spans a foot chase through an arcade and a cosy house party (soundtracked to Phoenix's "Too Young") before ending in a karaoke booth. Music is a common language here, as the Japanese and American guests bond over familiar tunes and all thoughts of tempestuous marriages and stalling careers melt away.

The enduring image of Scarlett Johansson in a bubblegum pink wig singing the Pretenders's "Brass in Pocket" comes from this moment, showing a different side to the formerly icy young woman. But the final song of the night, Roxy Music's "More Than This," which Murray and Coppola settled on together, was chosen specifically for the poignancy of its lyrics. "Who can say where we're going?" wrote Bryan Ferry—a sentiment Charlotte and Bob evidently relate to as they share a cigarette and a long, exhausted look in the zebra-print hallway. When Charlotte rests her head gently on Bob's shoulder in a silent moment of intimacy that summarizes the film, it provides both characters a brief respite from the overwhelming demands of the real world.

Bob and Charlotte's relationship drifts over the course of the film, becoming somewhat paternal as he carries her to her hotel room after their night on the town, and shepherds her to a hospital for a broken toe. When Charlotte asks Bob if life gets any easier, he instinctively says "no" before relenting: "Yes. It gets easier. The more you know who you are and what you want, the less things upset you." Sofia tried to write minimalist dialogue that reflected real conversations, rather than the contrived, unnatural exchanges we're more used to seeing on-screen. "I don't want my movies to feel like movies," she told the *Directors Guild Association* magazine. "I want them to feel like life. People don't really express themselves articulately in real life." The film's title refers to this disconnect as much as the literal language barrier Bob and Charlotte experience in Tokyo.

When Bob drunkenly sleeps with the hotel's jazz singer (a decision he appears to instantly regret), however, Charlotte is disappointed, maybe even a little jealous. "You can talk about things you have in common, like growing up in the fifties," she needles. "Wasn't there anyone else there to lavish you with attention?" he bites back. It's as if Charlotte has finally seen a crack in Bob's charming persona—but with the knowledge that Bob is leaving in the morning, they reconcile, sharing a charged moment in the hotel bar. They accept the strange, fleeting nature of their relationship, and that it must end with Bob's departure.

Their initial farewell the following morning in the lobby is awkward and stilted, as Bob is accompanied by his Japanese attache. But shortly after getting into his car he spots Charlotte in a crowd of people and runs after her. They share a tearful embrace, and Bob whispers something inaudible to her before they kiss each other goodbye. Over the years speculation has been rife as to what precisely Bob whispers, but no conclusive answer has ever been given. The final draft of Coppola's screenplay simply states "Bob tries to tell Charlotte

14

15

he loves her but he can't muster the words." Digitally enhanced audio suggests the film's final line is "I have to be leaving, but I won't let that come between us," although neither Coppola nor Murray have ever confirmed this. "I always like Bill's answer: that it's between lovers," Sofia said. Given the director's preference for creating moments that transcend dialogue, the particulars hardly matter.

Lost in Translation was sold to Focus Features after production wrapped, premiering at the Telluride Film Festival in August 2003. It made an impressive $118 million from a $4 million budget and was nominated for four Academy Awards, including Best Picture, Best Director, and Best Actor, losing out in the former categories to *The Lord of the Rings: The Return of the King* and Sean Penn's performance in *Mystic River* in the latter. Sofia did take home the award Best Original Screenplay, however, as well as a clutch of prizes from other notable institutions and festivals.

One of the enduring debates around *Lost in Translation* is how much the narrative hews to Coppola's own experiences. Charlotte—whose sartorial style is similar to the director's—is in Japan accompanying her husband John, a celebrity photographer (played by Giovanni Ribisi) who bears more than a passing resemblance to Sofia's then-husband Spike Jonze. In Lynn Hirschberg's revealing profile of Sofia, published August 31, 2003, the journalist notes that Jonze and Coppola grew distant as their respective careers began to flourish. Sofia has confirmed this: "It's been rough being apart so much, but we have to figure out our relationship after September 12, when the movie comes out." The couple would announce their divorce three months later through Coppola's publicist.

Perhaps the most persistent rumor surrounding the film is that Kelly, a client of John's (played by Anna Faris), was based on Cameron Diaz, who had worked with Jonze on *Being John Malkovich* in 1999. The blonde actress is presented as a foil to Charlotte; animated, talkative, and faux-intellectual. She proudly tells Charlotte and John she is staying at the hotel under the name "Evelyn Waugh"—out of earshot, Charlotte smirks "Evelyn Waugh was a man." After listening in on Kelly giving a vacuous press conference to promote her new action film, Charlotte attends a flower arranging class. A juxtaposition between the two is presented: Kelly claims to like Japan "best out of all the Asian countries" because she feels close to Buddhism and reincarnation, whereas Charlotte is interested in exploring elements of Japanese culture for herself, observing and learning.

Sofia has always vehemently denied that Kelly was directly inspired by Diaz ("I could probably name eight people that she was based on, just that bubbly, extroverted blonde that you see on talk shows," she told the *Daily Beast* in 2013). Regardless, it feels like the cruelest observation in the film, a withering eye roll aimed at the sort of traits Hollywood demanded of its female stars—friendly, approachable, skinny, sweet—particularly during the nineties and aughts. Interestingly though (and perhaps as a result of casting the effortlessly charming Faris), Kelly doesn't come across as vapid in the same way the Los Angeles teens of *The Bling Ring* would do a decade later; she comes across as ditzy but perfectly good-natured in her short cameo. The way she is perceived hints at Charlotte's—and perhaps Sofia's—insecurity, stemming from introversion and displacement. Charlotte is unsure of her place in the world, and finds it easier to project her unhappiness onto those who seem more sure of themselves.

Further questions arose in the wake of *Lost in Translation* regarding Sofia's approach to Japanese culture. Two scenes in particular were the subject of much criticism: one in which Bob is directed on the set of his whisky commercial by a Japanese team

16

16
Joaquin Phoenix in Spike Jonze's *Her*.

16

Joaquin Phoenix in Spike Jonze's *Her*.

16

who have difficulty communicating with him; and a strange moment where a sex worker is unexpectedly sent to Bob's hotel room and encourages him to "lip" her stocking, reinforcing the stereotype that Japanese people struggle with certain English pronunciations. Writing for the *Guardian*, musician Kiku Day heavily criticized Sofia for "shoe-horning every possible caricature of modern Japan into her movie," and scathingly declared "there is no scene where the Japanese are afforded a shred of dignity." Day goes on to suggest that, "The good Japan, according to this director, is Buddhist monks chanting, ancient temples, flower arrangement; meanwhile she portrays the contemporary Japanese as ridiculous people who have lost contact with their own culture."

Sofia responded to the criticism with surprise. "I can see why people might think that, but I know I'm not racist," she told the *Independent*. "I think if everything's based on truth, you can make fun, have a little laugh, but also be respectful of a culture. I just love Tokyo, and I'm not mean-spirited. Even on our daily call sheets, they would mix up the 'Rs' and the 'Is'—all that was from experience, it's not made up. I guess someone has misunderstood my intentions." Her defensive explanation is understandable (and typical of white people when criticized for even unintentionally racist behavior) but the concerns of Japanese and Asian critics should not be discounted purely on the basis of good intentions.

Some Japanese critics did support the film, however, and Yasuhisa Harada disagreed with racism claims in his review for *Yomiuri Shimbun*: "In the United States, some people were concerned that the film might appear as anti-Japanese. Despite that fact, the film neither tries to dissolute [sic.] Tokyo, nor investigates it; the peculiarity and wonder of the city is accurately reflected." The film's very conceit suggests ignorance on the part of its main characters; affluent white Americans who experience a profound culture shock. Having based the story on her own visits to Japan, it makes sense that Sofia might intentionally or unintentionally display a level of ignorance herself, as well as the initial uncertainty that comes with arriving in a foreign city.

Yet there is also reverence in the way Sofia chooses to portray Japan, capturing the bright lights and noise of Tokyo but also the relative tranquillity of Kyoto, where Charlotte takes a solo day trip. There's a sense of awe in the lingering shots of Tokyo, too; the director has cited Ridley Scott's *Blade Runner* as a direct influence, emphasising the warm neon glow that means darkness never really sets in. Sofia could never profess to know Japan like a local, nor does she pretend to—*Lost in Translation* is a film about strangers moving through unfamiliar spaces as much as how they move each other.

By the end of his trip, Bob confesses to Charlotte that he doesn't want to leave Tokyo, to which she suggests, "Let's never come here again because it will never be as much fun." Bob and Charlotte will always owe the city a debt of gratitude for bringing them together, and had they not experienced the misery of jetlag and displacement they never would have met in the first place.

After his performance in the film, Murray's career experienced something of a renaissance. Similarly well-received roles followed in Wes Anderson's *The Life Aquatic with Steve Zissou*—the ending of which was inspired by a photograph of Sofia with her father at the Cannes Film Festival following his Palme d'Or triumph—and Jim Jarmusch's *Broken Flowers*. The film's soundtrack proved equally popular. Reflecting on *Lost in Translation*'s ethereal mixtape in 2010, music critic Frank Mojica wrote: "One has to wonder how much of a role the film and its soundtrack had in the rebirth of shoegaze in the mid-aughts. After all, My Bloody Valentine eventually reformed, as did The Jesus and Mary Chain, with the latter performing with none other than Scarlett Johansson at their Coachella reunion."

But most interesting are the parallels between *Lost in Translation* and Spike Jonze's 2013 sci-fi romance *Her*, in which Joaquin Phoenix stars as Theodore Twombly, a lonely writer who falls in love with his AI virtual assistant, Samantha, voiced by Scarlett Johansson. Video essayist Jorge Luengo Ruiz beautifully illustrated the similarities between these films in *Lost in Translation / Her: An Unloved Story*, noting their visual symmetry and the fact they both feature lonely protagonists adrift against gleaming cityscapes. And when Theodore's ex-girlfriend Catherine (Rooney Mara), who is strikingly similar to Sofia in style and demeanor, discovers his relationship with Samantha, she accuses him of being unable to deal with real human emotions. Just as *Lost in Translation* isn't particularly critical of Jonze, *Her* doesn't read as a personal attack on Sofia. Toward the end of the film, Theodore writes a letter to Catherine, apologizing for his past behavior and thanking her for their relationship. While Jonze and Coppola have never spoken publicly about the possible connection between their work, it doesn't seem far-fetched that *Her* is at least partially based on their relationship and Sofia's film.

After all, love and loneliness are universal human themes, transcending gender, age and language. They occupy space throughout all of Sofia's work, from the desperate isolation of the tight-knit Lisbon sisters to the social media malaise and plutomania of *The Bling Ring* teens. Although Sofia describes herself as a shy, introverted person, and her films are often quiet and meditative, the emotions at their core are intense and earth-shattering. Tokyo is a city of more than thirteen million inhabitants, and *Lost in Translation* is a story about two temporary ones who find themselves caught halfway between isolation and adoration. ❡

INSPIRATIONS

↓ *In the Mood for Love,* Wong Kar-wai ↓

SOFIA COPPOLA: FOREVER YOUNG

WHEN SOFIA COPPOLA won an Academy Award for Best Original Screenplay in 2004, she gave a characteristically succinct acceptance speech but crucially thanked several directors who had inspired *Lost in Translation*: Michelangelo Antonioni, Wong Kar-wai, Bob Fosse, and Jean-Luc Godard. While the influence of *L'Avventura* and *A Married Woman* is notable, and Sofia's love of *All That Jazz* is well-documented, Wong's 2000 romantic drama *In the Mood for Love* makes for the most interesting point of comparison.

Against the backdrop of British-ruled Hong Kong circa 1962, Chinese expatriates Chow Mo-wan (Tony Leung) and Su Li-shen (Maggie Cheung) meet when they rent adjacent rooms in an apartment building. Their interactions are initially brief, but when they realize their spouses are having an affair the two grow closer and a mutual attraction develops. While their relationship ultimately goes unconsummated, *In the Mood for Love* takes place over the course of four years, charting Chow and Su's encounters and missed connections with haunting tenderness.

Throughout the first act Chow and Su only meet briefly, usually as they pass each other on the stairs in their apartment building or eat dinner at a nearby noodle bar. Their shared isolation is established as they go about their daily routines; Chow is a journalist, while Su works at a shipping company, and their partners are often absent, citing long working hours and business trips. "It's sad to see her so lonely," Su's well-meaning but overbearing landlady Mrs. Suen notes. When the strangers finally do share more than a passing glance, Chow invites Su out for dinner. The warmth of their first real meeting is an amusing contrast from the terse lunch Bob and Charlotte share in *Lost in Translation* (the frosty atmosphere being a result of Bob's affair with the hotel

bar's singer), but it's also the moment they realize their partners are having an affair, which adds a sense of melancholy in spite of the romantic music that plays as they wander the streets of Hong Kong together.

While Chow and Su commiserate over their partners' love affair, they are also drawn together out of mutual loneliness; something they have in common with Bob and Charlotte. Kar-wai's lingering camera captures them in moments of single contemplation: Su waiting for her order at the local noodle bar; Chow leaning in an alleyway after receiving a message that his wife won't be joining him for supper. Sofia, too, loves to focus in on these moments (consider Charlotte, alone in her hotel room, or Bob drinking silently at the hotel bar) that feel familiar to all of us, depicting the strange sensation of being completely alone in a crowded city.

"I didn't think you'd fall in love with me," a melancholy Su says to Chow when they reflect on the impossibility of their situation. "Me neither," he replies. Believing Su won't leave her husband, Chow takes a job in Singapore; by the time Su decides to go with him, he's already left. Although she visits the country a year later, Su finds herself unable to meet with Chow: she calls his office, but doesn't speak when he picks up; she visits his apartment but leaves only a lipstick-stained cigarette butt. Her spectral present is felt by Chow, but ultimately he doesn't act upon it; the pair are doomed to never meet again. But in the final scene, Chow travels to the Cambodian temple of Angkor Wat. He whispers a secret into a hollow part of the wall and plugs the hole with mud, never to be shared; not dissimilar to the unheard words of Bob to Charlotte in the final scene of *Lost in Translation*. Murray's cryptic explanation of "It's between lovers" feels equally apropos for what Chow utters into the holy space.

Wong Kar-wai's and Sofia Coppola's films are masterful examples of how so much can be said without a single word. Maggie Cheung's performance is as much in her stoic posture or the sadness in her eyes as it is in Kar-wai's beautiful script. Beyond this, the framing of lost love as beautiful as well as melancholic cements the pair as a bittersweet double feature. Just because something was short-lived doesn't mean it wasn't significant; doesn't mean it isn't worth remembering.

In traditional Chinese, *In the Mood for Love*'s title is 花樣年華, which translates to "the flowery years," a Chinese metaphor for the fleeting beauty of youth and originated in the title of a 1946 song by Zhou Xuan. While this could apply easily to Charlotte, fretting so much over her future while failing to grasp the magnitude of her present, it makes for an even more apt summation of Sofia's filmmaking spirit, which so deftly explores the agony and ecstasy of being young and hopelessly alive. ☁

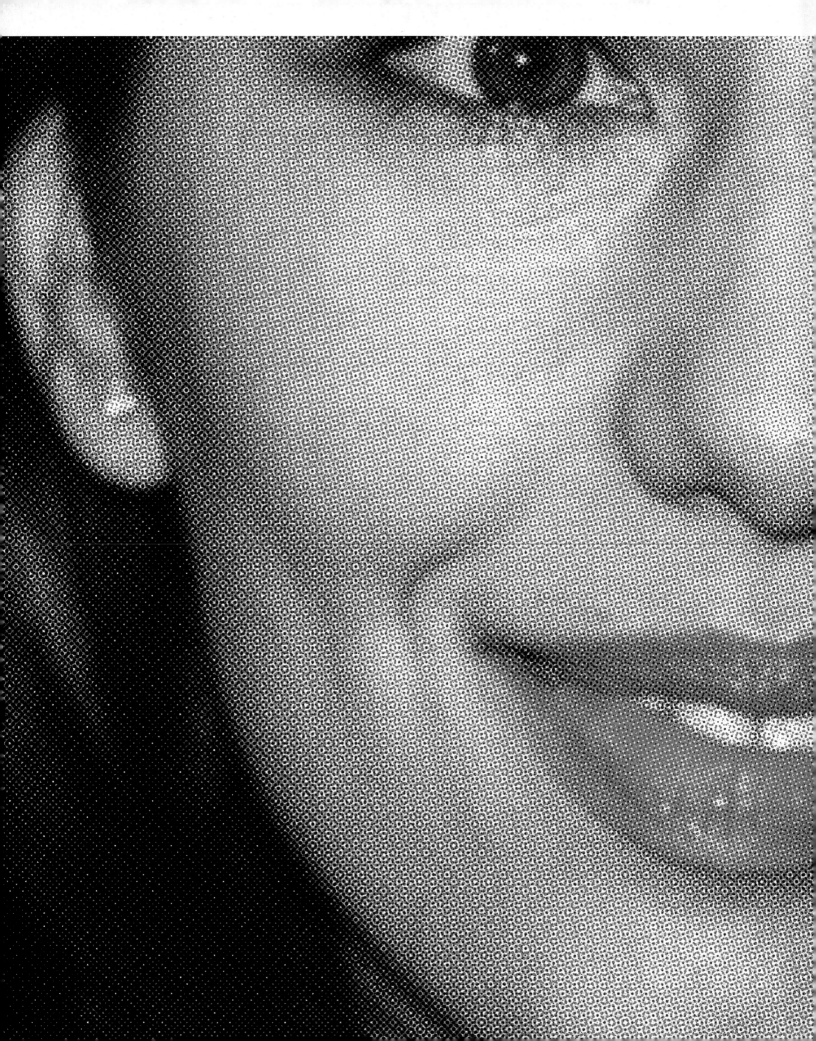

INTERVIEWS

KIRSTEN DUNST

JEAN-BENOÎT DUNCKEL

SARAH FLACK

PHILIPPE LE SOURD

NANCY STEINER

BRIAN REITZELL

Kirsten Dunst

Kirsten Dunst has been acting professionally since she was six years old, and has built an incredible career, working with filmmakers including Michel Gondry, Lars von Trier, and Jane Campion. Her breakout role came when she was sixteen as Lux Lisbon in *The Virgin Suicides*, and she has since worked with Sofia Coppola on *Marie Antoinette* and *The Beguiled*, as well as having a cameo in *The Bling Ring*.

Sofia and Kirsten Dunst on set of *The Beguiled*.

When did you and Sofia meet?

We met in Toronto. I think it was at the Four Seasons; I was shooting another movie there and I think she must've been location scouting for the film [*The Virgin Suicides*], because we shot the movie there [in Toronto]. I had read the script and I was kinda nervous because I'd never done a part where I was like, the sexy one, you know what I mean? Just the things that I had to do in the movie, I was a little scared of. Making out on a football field, or . . . just every time I read "Lux makes out with somebody" I was just like, "Oh my god, I have to make out with so many boys," and it really freaked me out.

You were so young as well.

Yeah, sixteen. And I was an innocent sixteen, so I was just nervous about kissing all these random dudes that I didn't know in front of people. There was a scene in the car where I had to jump on Josh Hartnett and start kissing him, and that couldn't be farther from my sixteen-year-old personality.

There must have been something about the script that drew you in as well.

Meeting Sofia completely put me at ease. She was just really kind and soft-spoken and I just felt that she would take care of me. I also remember the day that I had to make out with a bunch of guys, she said, "Oh, you don't have to make out with any of them, just bury your head in their jacket shoulder and we'll just make it look like you're making out with them." She was easier on me with things like that. Also, she played the music that was going to be in the scene where

I jump on Josh Hartnett in the car, so that kind of helped me because it took my mind off the sounds of getting on top of someone. I remember Josh . . . I was mortified. He was like "I think you bit me." His wig fell off in one of the takes and the sixteen-year-old me was dying inside.

None of that comes across in the film—you look so elegant.

I know, cool right? Yeah, that was a big deal, and it was such a long shot, too. They shut the lights off, they were like "Okay, go!" and it was like a whole process because it was really long. It was a long shot. There was this risk to me having to do this, too. I had to run out of the house, open the car door, and it's an old car door so it would get stuck if I didn't go for it perfectly. It was very nerve-racking.

The set was predominantly women, I imagine, which in the nineties must have been refreshing even to someone who'd been working in the industry for quite a while by that point.

I had worked with Gillian Armstrong on *Little Women* with an all-female cast and I had also worked just before this with Michelle Williams on the movie *Dick*. It wasn't like I hadn't worked with women, or with a female director before, so that wasn't really new. But what was new was the intimacy. It was a small movie, and I hadn't been part of a rehearsal like that, where we all hung out in the house. There's an atmosphere on Sofia's sets that really reflects the film that you watch.

I think that sense of intimacy is probably one of the large reasons why I love her work so much. It's also a reason that her films have been underappreciated.

I think that people are just . . . first of all, when your last name's Coppola they're gonna be harder on you. But I think it's so much harder to make a good movie when you can ask a favor of a great DP. It's so much more pressure to make a good movie, because if you don't, then . . . the fact that she made a great film, her first film was great, it doesn't matter. Either you're a filmmaker, or you're not. People were just harder on her, that's all. *The Virgin Suicides* was such a magical movie. Also, that was a time when women weren't being as celebrated as they are now in film as directors. I think that had that movie been made by a man, it would have been received in a very different way. It's very hard for men to call women geniuses. I really think that part of it is that someone like her, who has this feminine energy and who also is her own auteur, that's a sign of a unique voice and a special director. Women in general just have a different kind of poetry that doesn't translate as well in movies that are directed by men.

It's been very interesting to me reading the reception of some of her films, especially toward the beginning of her career with *The Virgin Suicides* and *Marie Antoinette*. The conversation around these films has shifted completely over time—especially *Marie Antoinette*, which has had this whole resurgence.

What's funny is it's still being discussed like, "Do you like this movie? What's your take on it?" It's awesome that at the time it was polarizing. As an artist you want to do work that's not down the line anyway. At the time the reception hurt my feelings, but now . . . when I first saw the movie I was like, "This is so awesome *[gasps]*, this is so beautiful, I've never seen anything like it!" I was alone in the theater when I saw it for the first time. I was swept away, really. To find out that other people didn't feel that way, it makes you feel a little "am I crazy?" But then I realized that it's just ahead of its time, which is great! Sofia's never gonna make a down-the-line history lesson; I don't know what everyone was expecting. It's funny that now that movie is such an inspiration for what people have done with period films since, or TV shows. *The Great*, or even *The Favourite*. I don't think Yorgos [Lanthimos] would have made that movie had there been no *Marie Antoinette*.

Marie Antoinette is also an accessible film for teenage girls, which is what it should be, you know? Marie Antoinette was a teenager.

I remember when I was young watching the movie *3 Women* for the first time, or seeing *Picnic at Hanging Rock*. These are the films for the next . . . I mean, obviously they should watch those films, too, but this is the next version of movies like *Daisies*. All these unique female movies are what Sofia gave this generation.

It's interesting that her films unlock a lot of older films for people like me. The first time I saw *The Virgin Suicides* I was about fifteen and didn't really know anything about movies. I came from a small town, and my family didn't watch movies. That's how I found out about *Picnic at Hanging Rock*. *The Virgin Suicides* has really found a home with the next generation. I was looking at Marc Jacobs' latest collection, the one with your face across it. How does it feel that the film and that character have such resonance with audiences?

You never think when you're making something that it's going to mean something to people, so when it does and it's continually watched and beloved . . . when I look back at my own career and the decisions I've made, I'm just very proud to be a part of it, that's all. It just makes me very proud of my little self. You get to see me as a sixteen-year-old, too; you get to see me at every stage of my life and not many people get to see that with their mother. It's amazing, just the documentation of my life.

The Beguiled was a really different role from the sort of things you'd done up to that point. Edwina is very quiet and reserved and quite difficult to unlock for a lot of the film. What was your reaction when you and Sofia started talking about it? Was it liberating to play as something that people didn't really perceive you as before?

I'd really play any role if Sofia was directing. For me, I know I'm in good hands so I'll play any role and find a way to make it interesting for myself. I watched [Don Siegel's *The Beguiled*] before and was into it. It made sense that Sofia would want to redo it. There was a campiness to it that I really liked. I remember Sofia saying when she was directing this music video, "I just want something on the screen that I wanna see." She was doing a White Stripes video, I think . . .

The Kate Moss one?

Yeah, with pole dancing. I remember her just being like, "I really wanted to see that, so that's what I did," which I love.

Is that how you approach your roles; these are characters you want to see?

No, I'm very director-driven, so it's not like my dream was to play Marie Antoinette. I don't really have dream roles; I have dream directors. I have a slight aversion to playing biographical people, I don't know why. It's just not my go-to.

You said you'd do anything if Sofia was directing. I'm curious to know more about how she works as a director and the environment she creates on her sets.

Well, I feel like music is a big deal for Sofia. I remember on *Marie Antoinette*, she gave me a CD of music. I feel like music is a big part of her writing process, because there's always a great soundtrack to what we're shooting before we even shoot. Sofia is very good at explaining exactly the mood she wants. She's very specific, and not many directors know how to communicate the emotion they want. It's a hard thing to do. Even I have trouble doing that myself, communicating what I'm trying to do. I'm more just like, let's feel it and do it. I don't wanna over-talk it, and Sofia's good at not overtalking things, she'll just give you a little bit of a scenario that makes perfect sense and you get it immediately. She doesn't overly direct either; in terms of acting she lets you feel it out, do another take, and then comment, rather than giving all these notes out of the gate. She lets you, kind of, marinate in it with her.

I have to ask about the shoot that you did for *W* last year. It was beautiful. You announced your second pregnancy at that shoot so it feels like something you would only really do with someone you trust, knowing it's going to be done the way you want.

And I was wearing Laura and Kate, who are two of my best friends. Also, it's nice to have a pretty pregnancy photo! I was like, *W* magazine, done by Sofia, with a beautiful dress made by my friends. . . . It's also sweet that I was wearing their clothes both times, in both of my pregnancy photos. I'm not someone who would go take pictures of myself pregnant, so to have it directed by Sofia is the best possible scenario.

Pregnancy photos directed by Sofia Coppola is a big flex.

Yeah, exactly. I didn't even think of it like that, but I was like, "This is gonna be beautiful," and it's a fun way to say, "Yeah, yeah whatever, I'm pregnant." I was just excited to have pretty pregnancy photos *[laughs]*. I looked like crap most of the time, I was mostly in sweatpants, but there was that one day when Sofia made me look beautiful.

Sofia has such a special relationship to fashion. I want you to confirm or deny a story that I heard, that she lent you a dress for your high school prom.

Yes, she did! A wine-colored John Galliano dress—like a burgundy—that she wore to the Golden Globes. My dress was very nice.

How do you think the experience of working with Sofia so young impacted your career in terms of what you took away from the experience? You said you're very director-driven, so was there a point where you were like, this is the sort of atmosphere I want to find on sets and with directors?

The Virgin Suicides was my first time working on a more independent film, and the experience of that I definitely took with me. Even the fact that my introduction as a young adult, an actress who wasn't a child anymore. . . . To have that through her eyes rather than a male director's eyes gave me the confidence when I was on set with male directors to not need that attention from them, because I felt, "Well, Sofia thinks I'm pretty, so I don't care if you think I'm pretty." I felt like the coolest girl thinks I'm cool, so I'm good. I just never needed that validation from my male directors, which I think a lot of people do, you know?

I was talking to Maggie Gyllenhaal a few weeks ago and she said something I thought was very interesting about the way women have to make concessions to fit around what male directors and producers want, which is why she made her own film. I wondered if you had a similar thing where you feel like you have to make yourself less because there's a male ego in the room.

I think that there's a nurturing that men expect and women don't because we're innately nurturing—we're easy to be like, "Oh, we'll just let them have it," like it doesn't really affect us anyway, but it does really. They're okay with demanding this thing and our nature is more accepting of certain things because . . . I don't know . . . I just know that I didn't seek validation in my beauty or talent through the men I worked with because of my experience with Sofia.

To work with someone like Sofia at sixteen, such an impressionable age where you feel "ugh" about yourself . . . I remember going into *Spider-Man* and one of our female producers actually wanted me to go to a dentist to fix my teeth and I was like, "Oh no, girl, this ain't happening." Like, no way! That's one of the things that Sofia would like, "Your teeth are so cute, I love your teeth!" I probably would've changed them had I not had that experience with Sofia.

Do you feel having that friendship with Sofia has made it easier to work together, because you understand each other and you're not afraid to challenge each other?

Yeah, we really have an understanding and similar taste and similar sense of humor. Now it's just working with a friend. She was like a big sister and I was her little sister, and I feel like it's more of a friendship now.

I read an interview with you in *W* about *On Becoming a God in Central Florida*. You mentioned that you felt your career hadn't been properly recognized, certainly at that point. Do you feel that there is still some hesitation to celebrate female filmmakers and actors who really embrace femininity and aren't afraid to be girly?

I know what you're saying. I think when you work with a female director they want to see another side of a woman that a male director doesn't necessarily always understand. With someone like Lars von Trier, he always wants a woman to play him. Maybe he feels like there's a different level of despair that a woman understands, in terms of what we go through, biologically. I don't really know. I just feel like I made a lot of movies that were . . . maybe I had a bit more fun with Sofia, you know? Now, way more women are being celebrated, female directors are being celebrated. Everything's shifting and it's great to see and I'm happy to have been part of doing this before people were scrambling to finally work with a female director. I've been doing it all my life.

Likewise, I've been watching your movies since I was a kid, and I watched *Dick* for the first time a few weeks ago and loved it. I do think it's interesting that these very fun films about young women are so often lost to history. I don't know if it's to do with there not being a lot of female film critics back then . . .

Listen, I'm just happy to be part of the resurgence. Someone told me, "*Marie Antoinette* is one of the most Instagram movies of all time," you know? It's like, "Great!" I'm so happy it finally found its audience *[laughs]*. By the way, have you watched Jason Schwartzman doing *Cribs* at Versailles?

Yes, I have! One of my favorite things. Also, that picture of the two of you on set in full costume with the MacBook . . .

I know. I wish Apple would pay us to use that for one of their campaigns, because it would be so cool!

Going back to *Marie Antoinette*, it looks to me like it must have been an insane experience, especially in your twenties. Filming in one of the most iconic buildings in the world, surrounded by this huge, incredible cast. Was that experience as crazy as it looked?

Yes, and at the time I was very overwhelmed. It was as [Marie Antoinette] would have felt. It was also a lot of hair and makeup every morning, a lot of changing decades within a day. It was like, "Oh, now I'm old . . . and now I'm young again!" We started with the "small head", as they called it, and my hair just piled up. So yeah, we worked at Versailles every Monday, and then K. K. Barrett, our production designer, recreated Marie Antoinette's bedroom at a château somewhere else in France. It was the most beautiful, decadent thing, even the food . . . I mean, macarons became popular because of the movie. Like, suddenly everyone has macarons! It's true! There was only Ladurée in France and now it's everywhere.

That millennial pink aesthetic, you can trace it back to Sofia's work on that film.

I know! Do you know, Io [Bottoms], who played one of my ladies in waiting, she was a family friend of Sofia. We became really good friends and I remember after the wrap party, which was at the Orangerie in the property of Versailles, we ended up in one of the fountains, at night. Just, you know, took our shoes off and got in, which is so crazy that we even got to do that, you know? If a security guard had seen us we would have been very very quickly taken off the property. But that was just a magical evening.

The Beguiled is so tonally different from *Marie Antoinette*. I'd like to know about the environment on set there, because again it's a very tight-knit group of women and from what I have seen of you guys hanging out on set, it looks like it was a lot of fun despite the harshness of the subject matter.

Did you see Elle [Fanning] and I with our red Solo cups? We made like a Girls Gone Wild video, but showing our ankles with our red Solo cups running though the field. I actually really bonded with Elle on that film. She became my little sister. I love her and her sister Dakota so much. Elle really became my little partner-in-crime.

You've also both got such a history with Sofia; there's a kinship there.

I just remember her telling me that her dream was to be one of the girls in a Sofia Coppola film.

What is the number one thing you've learned about yourself from working with Sofia over the years?

She's always been so true to herself, and working with her at such a young age, my impression of her was very strong but very feminine. I felt like she helped me be me and not worry about being something other than what I actually am. She was definitely a role model for me as a woman, in my teenage years. And still she's someone who I ask questions. I would still ask Sofia for advice on something.

I love when actors and directors have those relationships off-camera. It seems especially special with Sofia because her films are so personal and intimate, and it's lovely that she fosters these friendships with actors as well as working relationships.

Not many people work with the same actors. It's a very old-school thing. Listen, if you're gonna be someone's muse, it's nice to be Sofia's. We'll definitely work together again one day. ☁

Jean-Benoît Dunckel

Jean-Benoît Dunckel is a French musician and one half of the electronic duo Air. Together with Nicolas Godin, he provided the score for *The Virgin Suicides*, as well as "Alone in Kyoto" on the *Lost in Translation* soundtrack.

When did you first meet Sofia?

I don't remember exactly when but it was before the shooting of [*The Virgin Suicides*], so it might have been in 1999, probably in Los Angeles. I think she showed us some footage of the movie and we went into a room and we were introduced by Roman Coppola, who was working with Mike Mills at the Directors Bureau. Mike Mills was the artwork designer of *Moon Safari*, and Sofia had that record and told us she liked it very much and listened to it all the time. So she wanted to have the band do the soundtrack. We'd never done a film before so it was a new experience for us.

You were still at the beginning of Air weren't you?

Yeah, it was brand new, like one year old. I mean, we had major success in England and then we were trained to do promo in Los Angeles and New York, so we had done a few shoots in America already.

What was it about that footage that Sofia showed you that appealed to you and Nicolas?

I don't know if it was before or after but we already had the scenario in our heads. I'd read maybe half of [the script] and also we had the book of Jeffrey Eugenides, which for me was sort of like Bret Easton Ellis—a decadent book about young people in America. *The Virgin Suicides* is much more hardcore than the movie actually because it's filled with drugs, sex, nervous breakdowns, and these girls are locked down by their parents. It's pretty dark, and *Moon Safari* was really bright. In England some of the critics were saying that we were an easy-listening band, making nice, loungey music for adults. We wanted to prove that we were real musicians and that we could make music with a different mood, and so this was a perfect opportunity for us to play some dark chords and to really do something more with personality and more aggression.

It's the opposite of *Moon Safari* in a lot of ways, especially listening to it outside of the film—it's so ominous and so creepy at times.

Yes, it sounds creepy!
[Laughs]

You and Nicolas have said that you were keen for the music to not just feel like a soundtrack. How did you approach that?

We knew we wanted to release an album around *The Virgin Suicides*. We approached it like a proper record. At the time we were touring and we also had a new album to do [*10 000 Hz Legend*] so we didn't want to lose too much time by editing the music always to the pictures. Sofia would send us some video tapes so it was possible to synchronize the music to the pictures. We would try to do a track that somehow fit with the ambience of the video, but it was not completely edited and the mix wasn't finished. She picked two or three tracks as the main songs to use in the film, "Playground Love" and "Highschool Lover," which is an instrumental ballad version of "Playground Love."

It's interesting that you were being guided by Sofia, I think maybe that's why the score works so well on its own because it's not made just to fit in with what's on screen. The album sounds so different to what we're seeing on screen in terms of the setting and the whole seventies aesthetic. What kinds of references were you drawing from?

We had in mind sort of religious sounds, because for me the movie was about the girls' fascination with death. They were attempting to enter into a safe world which to them was death. So I was imagining sounds for churches, something really dark but bright at the same time. I think at that time we were influenced by Beck a lot, because he was our friend and we very much liked what he was doing. I think that we had in our mind the Serge Gainsbourg album *Histoire de Melody Nelson*, because there is an organ in that music, too. There's some Pink Floyd in there as well. And I was also thinking about this Roman Polanski movie about vampires [*The Fearless Vampire Killers*]. We found an American music shop called Black Market Music and we bought a lot of keyboards, a harpsichord and like a Hammond organ—the kinds of instruments you find in churches. We wanted to play with effects pedals, like guitar pedals, and we had a bit more money then so we bought some mics. And we wanted to use a real drum kit so we bought a Sonor drum kit and brought in our friend Brian Reitzell who is a drummer and the music supervisor of the movie.

It sounds like it was a good opportunity to experiment with your own sound, to try and do something completely new.

Yes exactly. Something new, something dark, something shocking, but something transcendent.

"Playground Love" has really endured as a song. I imagine there are a lot of people who hear it for the first time and then go and find the film because they love the song so much. You worked with Thomas Mars on the lyrics, and I was interested in why you decided to do a version of the song with lyrics. Is that something that Sofia suggested?

Yeah, because she wanted to have a song at the end of the movie. So we said to ourselves, "Oh shit, we have to do a proper song!" We knew the band Phoenix, who were also kind of at the beginning of their career, and so we sent the music to Thomas to do some lyrics and he came to the studio one afternoon. We recorded the drum track first in about one hour, with Nicolas on the bass, and then Thomas sang the song. It was one afternoon of recording. [Laughs]

It's funny when you speak to a musician about a piece of music that's considered very influential or iconic and they're like, "Yeah, we did it in just an afternoon."

Well, actually, music and art don't obey the rules most of the time. But I mean, if you improvise something like poetry, all your own words, all your knowledge of the English language, all the books and poetry that you've read in your life, are all synthesized into that moment. And music is like that. When you play on stage you have all this knowledge of music right in front of you, it's the result of all this internal chemistry coming up. But it takes a lot of work before you get to that moment.

What impact did this particular score have on your life? Is it still something you look back on and are proud of?

When we did it people were shocked because we were coming off the back of a massive success with *Moon Safari*, and especially in England the radio was not very understanding of this new sound. Because it's slow, you know, it's strange and the movie was not even out yet. But I knew that this music was really deep and that it would travel with the movie, and I think it's maybe now a more iconic and more respected work [than *Moon Safari*]. Even in France it changed completely, because when we did *Moon Safari* we were already on TV and all the radio stations—we were this French band having huge success abroad. In France people wanted to have a band be well-known abroad, with new music, with a new sound. It was us and Daft Punk. But when we did *The Virgin Suicides*, because of the name of Sofia Coppola and because the music was really deep, I think that we gained a lot of respect in the press and in the world of music.

It's funny to think that it was kind of a wake up call for people who had maybe dismissed Air as being an easy-listening band. You come out with this very dark soundtrack that encapsulates that feeling of depression and anxiety and isolation.

It's really melancholic, and when you are melancholic yourself you should put on a melancholic record. Suddenly your brain recognizes that somebody else has had the same experience as you—you feel like you're not alone in the world anymore. At the time we were having a lot of success but privately, I was a bit like a prisoner because I had new children and we were working like crazy. It was not that fun because we were traveling all the time, we had a lot of pressure on our shoulders; it was not about partying all the time, we were going home and taking care of the children. So I was maybe

Poster for Roman Polanski's 1967 comedy horror *The Fearless Vampire Killers*.

You got your start working with Steven Soderbergh—if my facts are straight, working as a production assistant on *Kafka*. Where did you develop an interest in editing?

I had always loved movies, and my parents exposed me to lots of films when I was growing up, but it never occurred to me to work in film. In college I started taking film classes for fun, both theory and production, but my plan at the time was to work for the State Department or a think tank in the area of my studies, US–Soviet relations and the neighboring Soviet Bloc countries. I graduated in 1989 with a double degree in film and political science, and a few months later the Berlin Wall came down. I had always loved editing our student projects, and when I realized that my original career choice might be less in demand after the fall of the Berlin Wall, I started looking for a job in editing. I was willing to take any film job though, and after cold-calling all the film companies in New York in the fall of 1989, I found a secretarial job in international distribution at Orion Pictures.

A few months later I noticed a short paragraph in the *Hollywood Reporter* announcing that Steven Soderbergh would be directing his second feature, *Kafka*, in Prague. I made more cold calls and managed to reach the producer, Stuart Cornfeld, who told me that if I got myself to Prague I could work on the film as a local hire. Thanks to my studies and interest in the former Soviet Bloc countries, I had some friends who were going to Prague to teach English. One year after graduating, and less than a year after the fall of the Berlin Wall, I traveled around Europe and finally arrived in Prague.

Stuart Cornfeld was true to his word and hired me as a production assistant. Steven was going to edit *Kafka* himself after the shooting, so one day I mentioned to him that I hoped to become a film editor. I asked if I could take notes for him in dailies, which was the only thing related to editing that I could offer to help with in Prague. He didn't need that, but it turned out to be good that he knew about my early interest in editing as he remembered it five years later.

After four months in Prague I started working as an apprentice and then assistant film editor in LA. I stayed intermittently in touch with Steven through the members of his sound team, Mark Mangini, Paul Ledford, and Larry Blake. They had been my "big brothers" on location in Prague and also were very kind to me in my early years in LA. In 1995 Steven heard through Mark that I was learning the "new" (at the time) Avid editing system, and he hired me to be his assistant editor on his very low-budget experimental film *Schizopolis*. Steven ended up being too busy to edit it himself, and started giving me scenes to edit in addition to my assistant duties. He was happy with my work and promoted me to editor, and amazingly that was my first feature credit! All because I'd had an interest in Eastern Europe in the years before the Berlin Wall came down, so in a way I have Mikhail Gorbachev to thank for my career!

How did you come to work with Sofia on *Lost in Translation*?

I lived in LA for nine years, and decided late in 1999 to move back to New York. My wonderful agent Lara Sackett, who signed me after I edited my second film for Steven, *The Limey*, introduced me to some of the producers working in New York. In 2002 one of those producers, Ross Katz, was looking for a New York–based editor for Sofia because she, too, was planning to move from LA to New York. He remembered me from our first meeting, plus two other New York producers, Jason Kliot and Gary Winick, had recommended me to Ross as a potential editor for Sofia. Ross interviewed me, then flew me to LA to meet Sofia just before she left for Tokyo to shoot *Lost in Translation*. To my great happiness, she hired me!

Reading interviews with Sofia's other collaborators, they often say she's a very visual filmmaker, and thinks more in images than necessarily in what's on the page. Is that something that you've noticed through working with her over the years?

Sofia is indeed very visual, but that is in addition to her tremendous depth of understanding of, and ability to create, story, dialogue, character, emotion, and atmosphere, much of which is not visual—she conjures entire worlds with those elements. Her visual talent is just one part of the way she creates the embodiment of the written page on film. I'm never on set so I don't know how she works with her other collaborators, but I imagine that in my job as editor, our collaboration picks up where the visual creation ends, in that we have dozens or hundreds of hours of footage from which to put the movie together. And that process is only partially visual—there are so many other elements such as pacing, clarity, rhythm, sound, and music, not to mention choosing which line reading and which character and camera angle to include at any given moment in the film. Sofia has an uncanny ability to communicate an incredibly clear vision in the fewest possible words. I've noticed this in her scripts, in emails she sends me from the set, and during our editing room conversations—it never ceases to impress and amaze me. It helps that we have similar taste and a similar sense of humor. We both are very intuitive, and often pick up on the same subtle moments in the performances that best convey the story, character, and emotion of a scene.

Does your early work with Soderbergh come into play at all when working with Sofia? They seem like very different filmmakers on the surface, but both have worked across so many genres, and seem to have a very clear directorial vision in everything they do.

My work with Steven definitely has come into play when I work with Sofia, both in general ways and specifically. He taught me so much, not only about editing but also the importance of good camera coverage of the action on set, and innovative camera angles, and how to use them. This involves choosing, while putting together the film, the best performance, the most effective camera angle, when to cut, and who or what to show at any given moment, in order to "tell the story" of the scene. There are infinite examples of this, including playing a key moment by showing a reaction shot instead of a more straightforward shot of the person speaking. I also learned, for example, when to play something in a wide shot that is not the most obvious choice yet is the most effective. There is a wide shot early in *The Limey* where the characters played by Terence Stamp and Luis Guzman exchange cigarettes, ex-prisoner to ex-prisoner. I remember Steven making a point of saving the wide shot for that moment at the end of the scene, even though we had wide coverage of all the dialogue, in order to heighten the subtle and symbolic moment of the cigarettes. Steven taught me how to know where to "be" (i.e. what shot to choose) in any given moment of the scene—how to communicate the story through the best and most correct choice among so many.

The great lesson of *The Limey* was that footage can be completely repurposed and used in ways that may not have been how it was intended at the time it was shot. I have used that concept over and over, even for small moments in a movie that are not about reconceiving the entire structure, as we did in *The Limey*. I did a bit of that in *The Beguiled*, when the shooting schedule was tightened and a few scenes were cut. When I was putting together the rough cut I wasn't sure if a key plot point would

director's cut phase, we had to find the balance between fracturing time in a way that conveyed the feeling of memory, loss, and regret, but not let the audience get lost in this experimental structure. Steven had a list of films we watched for reference and inspiration, especially Alain Resnais's films *Hiroshima Mon Amour* and *Last Year at Marienbad*. We had weekly work-in-progress screenings of *The Limey* to gauge the audience's reaction to each version of the film. It was a bit of trial and error, too, like a pendulum

Each day during the shoot, I receive and assemble the footage of the scenes Sofia filmed the previous day, or two days earlier if she is filming abroad—this timing is standard for most productions so that editors can work throughout the shoot and complete a rough cut shortly after the filming is over. That one or two-day lag allows me to incorporate the information from the script supervisor as I work my way through the dailies. Over the years I have found that I almost always gravitate towards many of the same moments in the dailies that Sofia liked, too, and noted for inclusion—they kind of leap out at me.

When I watch the dailies (which are usually two to four hours of film per day for a few minutes of screen time), I note or hold aside anything that I think would work well in the cut. This can be characters on-camera line readings, or just the audio of a piece of dialogue which I can play over another character's reaction shot, or possibly in another scene if it's needed to clarify something. Sometimes I select something just because it's so great that we need to find a place for it, as with some of Bill Murray's improvisations!

Sometimes actors do something special and unique in one of the takes, or the line reading comes out exactly as I imagined hearing it when I read the script—these are the most common things that I mark or put aside. These are almost always the same types of moments that Sofia notices, too, and she sends those notes to me herself or through the script supervisor.

When I work with other directors I always check the script supervisor's and director's notes before I go through the dailies so I can get a sense of the director's taste. But when I look at Sofia's dailies I like to wait to read those notes until after I've assembled the scene. Then I cross-check the notes with my cuts to make sure I didn't miss anything, and if I did I go back and add it. But for the most part, what we both are drawn to is almost always the same— we pick up on the same moments or subtleties in the footage. And we have a very similar sense of humor and always find the same things funny, which was especially pronounced when we worked on *The Beguiled*. We had so much fun laughing at the refined nineteenth-century ladies and girls competing for the attention of Colin Farrell's character.

Once I have my selects, I start to build the scene around the footage I like best, or the selected portions of the footage that best "tell the story" of the scripted scene. Sofia writes so well, and with such economy, that

Joe Gideon in *All That Jazz* (Bob Fosse, 1979).

often a single line of dialogue will convey the emotional subtext of that moment. I try to pick footage where not only the actors' deliveries, but also their expressions or body language or interactions with other actors, best embody what I imagine Sofia wants.

Sometimes I'll hold aside multiple versions of the same line reading or moment in the scene, but from different takes, so I have to narrow it down to the best among many great options when choosing which one to include in the rough cut. In those cases I often will take some dialogue, sometimes even a word or two from a take that won't make it into the cut, and "cheat" it into the actors' on-camera line readings which will be in the cut by swapping out some words. Or sometimes I'll create an off-camera line reading. That way we can have the best of all worlds and use as many of the selected moments as possible. Most dialogue is filmed from more than one camera angle (but usually each of those angles is filmed with a single camera at a time, rather than two cameras running simultaneously overlapping the same action). And the dialogue covered by each of those camera angles is filmed several times— so the possibilities are endless.

On the other hand, my freedom to use certain selects can be constrained by whatever camera angle any given selected moment was filmed in, and whether or not the laws of cinematic illusion will enable me to cut to a different select in a different camera angle, at whichever specific point I would like to. In other words, it's not always possible to use certain selects while maintaining cinematic flow/ continuity; it can be like a puzzle. In that case, I can often cheat the dialogue from one take even if I cannot use the picture exactly when and how I want to. Or I will cheat the continuity, which the editor Dede Allen famously advocated in order to prioritize the performances. And if all else fails, I'll abandon my attempts to use the select, but only after I've done everything possible to try to make it work.

There's a gorgeous reference to Bob Fosse's *All That Jazz* in *Marie Antoinette*. Could you talk me through that scene?

That's a great example of the way Sofia and I work together, and similar things have happened with us over the years. Sofia was in France filming, and I was putting together the rough cut in New York. We separately had the same idea about the music for a series of scenes portraying the court ritual of Marie Antoinette's "Morning Dressing Ceremony" at Versailles. The way those scenes were scripted and filmed made me think of the "It's showtime, folks!" sequences in Bob Fosse's *All That Jazz*, especially the Vivaldi music in those montages, which were iconically edited by Alan Heim.

I wasn't sure if I should make such a direct allusion to *All That Jazz* by using that music in my rough cut, even though Sofia and I had talked about our mutual love for the film a few years earlier. (*All That Jazz* is also the film that made me want to be an editor!)

But Sofia must have been thinking the same thing about her "Morning Dressing Ceremony" footage, because as I was editing it in NY she emailed me from France and suggested that I use that Vivaldi piece for those scenes! It was composed a few decades before the events in the film, so it also was plausible that the real Marie Antoinette would have heard it. But most of the music in *Marie Antoinette* is from the twentieth century so that was not essential, just a coincidence!

Perhaps more than any other director working today, Sofia is known for her integration of music into her films. What sort of challenges does that present from an editing point of view—are you presented with the footage and a song and asked to make it work?

I love the part of my work with Sofia which involves music! It's one of my favorite things to do in the editing room.

On all of her films, but particularly for *Lost in Translation* and *Marie Antoinette*, Sofia gives me a lot of songs to work with very early on—before the shooting starts, and as dailies are coming in. I love placing those songs with montages I've cut or cutting the montages to the music, or music-editing those songs to fit with the rough cuts as score, in addition to working with the actual score cues provided by Phoenix or other composers. The songs Sofia and her music supervisor Brian Reitzell gave me to work with on *Lost in Translation* were songs that she had listened to while writing the script, and during the other phases of production and preproduction, but when I received them I didn't know anything beyond that.

On the films we've done together more recently, I have really enjoyed working with Thomas Mars, the musician and lead singer of the band Phoenix, the band who composes for Sofia. Since Thomas lives in New York (all the other band members are elsewhere), he can come into the editing room easily. We "audition" various compositions or even early sketches of music cues for various scenes, and decide which ones are best for the places in the film that need music. Sometimes we discover new places where the music fits well even if it wasn't the original plan. Sometimes we narrow down to one of the two to three choices he and Sofia have made together, or adjust the timing, placement, and music-editing of specific choices they already made, or simply cut in things that have been decided upon by Sofia and Thomas or Phoenix, and don't require any further adjustments.

All of Sofia's films have a very particular rhythm to them—I'm particularly thinking of *Marie Antoinette* and *Somewhere*, then *The Beguiled* followed by *On the Rocks*. How much of that pace comes together in the edit suite?

The pace of *Somewhere* was largely determined by the way the shots were constructed. The shots, and the movie, were designed not to have a lot of cuts. Sofia wanted to show the lead character's boredom, and the rhythm of the movie was meant to bring the viewer into the rhythm of his life, so the audience would feel the pace of his lifestyle as well as his frame of mind.

Except for *Somewhere*, Sofia and I have never discussed the overall pacing for her films in advance, but we work on it as we go along. One overall pacing note that Sofia gave me for the rough cut of *The Beguiled* was to slow it down considerably. She thought that my rough cut had been more efficient than she had envisioned—she wanted to draw everything out and to show the pace of wartime life for the girls and women marooned at Miss Martha Farnsworth's Seminary. Usually editors and directors end up tightening the rough cut in the months after filming; rough cuts generally are the longest version of a film, so it was kind of a luxury to work on lengthening the rough cut. For an editor it's always a fine line between wanting to present a director with all the options as well as a film that moves along.

At a more granular level—the rhythm of the cuts from shot to shot as I construct the scenes and montages for the first time, like the montages in *Marie Antoinette*—I'm guided by my instinct as well as what the footage is, and what feels right for any given scene or section of the film. And that instinctive approach continues for both of us as we work together in the months after the shooting. In the course of our conversations in the editing room, the rhythm naturally works itself out as Sofia gives me notes. Sofia and I "hear" music and feel rhythm in the same way, so the scenes and montages have always turned out in their final incarnations without much specific discussion about their rhythm. We work on everything together as the editing progresses, and the rhythm evolves naturally as a result of Sofia's notes and our discussions about things like shot choice, performance, emotion, and story.

Bill Murray in *St. Vincent* (Theodore Melfi, 2014).

You've edited Bill Murray three times as part of Sofia's work. Given that timing is everything with comedy, and editing is also all about timing, could you talk a little about your experiences of working across *Lost in Translation*, *A Very Murray Christmas*, and *On the Rocks*?

I have been so fortunate to get to work with Bill Murray's footage on three of Sofia's films, plus I co-edited another film he starred in, *St. Vincent*. In my rough cuts I work hard to incorporate all of the nuances from his performances in the dailies, including any improvisational moments. I watch every single moment in his dailies, including the footage before Sofia calls "action" and after she calls "cut." I try to use as many of these moments as possible, in the best ways possible, while still integrating his work into the context of the scene as a whole. He also offers improvisations and inspired variations on his line readings off-camera to the actors who are on camera being filmed. I always use those moments, too, even if Bill isn't on camera—I find ways to work them in. I particularly loved the scene with the cop in *On the Rocks*, which had a lot of that. Rashida Jones (who played his daughter Laura) had hilarious exasperated reactions and improvisations, too.

There are always more of Bill's "gems," as I call them, than we can use, and when Sofia and I start working together after the shooting we often add or change things. Because I have spent so much time immersed in the raw dailies by the time Sofia finishes filming, I can show her selected moments I've gathered from her notes and my choices (which often overlap as I noted earlier), or we hunt for new moments or line readings. It's always so much fun to rewatch Bill's dailies with Sofia and enjoy what he did on set as we continue to build and refine the scenes. In *On the Rocks* we particularly loved Bill "appreciating the flowers," as Sofia put it, when Felix picked up Laura for her birthday celebration. It hadn't been in my rough cut because it took a while for Bill to walk around the table and work his magic, and I'd had nothing else to cut to in order to shorten the time it took to get to the funniest parts. But Sofia didn't mind letting that walk play out in order to make sure that we could include what Bill did with the flowers, and we cheated some audio of his "flower appreciation" from another part of the take, and it stayed in the film! ☁

Philippe Le Sourd

Accomplished cinematographer Philippe Le Sourd has worked with Ridley Scott and earned an Academy Award nomination in 2013 for his work with Wong Kar-wai on *The Grandmaster*. He served as Director of Photography on *The Beguiled* and *On the Rocks*, as well as the recording of Sofia Coppola's staging of *La Traviata* in 2016 and her short film for the New York City Ballet in 2021.

You and Sofia met through a fellow cinematographer, Harris Savides, is that right?

Yes. I knew Harris from a long time ago. I met him through my agent. He was an amazing cinematographer but also an amazing man. Very generous. Harris was always giving advice and recommendations to people, and when he started being sick he recommended me when he couldn't do a job. I was working with Wong Kar-wai on *The Grandmaster*, but Sofia had a commercial job for Dior just after the movie. A few years before, when Harris was in Paris and I was in Paris, we took a Polaroid picture together as a souvenir. At this time Harris was very sick; he couldn't remember my name but he remembered who I was from the picture. He said to Sofia, "This French guy, you should meet with this French guy—the guy from the picture!" He passed away a few weeks later.

It's so lovely that he remembered that picture. What's the first thing that you and Sofia discussed when you decided you were going to work together?

When I decide to work with a director I try to know exactly what they're doing and understand their personality. Of course, it's not until you work with them that you really understand, but you get a feeling when you meet someone, through the space and freedom they give to you. They could be very specific on camera equipment, camera movement, storyboards and everything. Sofia is not like that. Most of the time she wants things to be simple; she doesn't use sophisticated camera language. Whenever we start a project together, she sends me an old movie as a reference. Like a mood.

I read that François Truffaut's The Story of Adele H and Roman Polanski's Tess were influences on The Beguiled.

It was the beginning of Tess, when you see the girls coming together, dancing together, and the sunset. That was a reference for her: that mood and that spirit. I think it was more that she mixed the spirit and emotion of the scene as a reference, and also for the camera movement. In the first scene of Tess when you see this beautiful procession with the girl walking on the path in the countryside, we don't have that, but it was more a feeling of what the girls could be in The Beguiled. Sofia is a very resourceful and emotionally visual person. Even On the Rocks, she sent me an old movie from the fifties. I looked at it and said, "Hmm, I'm not sure I understand." It was far away from On the Rocks, it was more about the rhythm and the dialogue. For Sofia it was something like an expressionist impression for what she wanted to do.

Sofia has spoken a lot about screwball comedies and films like The Thin Man, which don't look anything like On the Rocks.

Because she has her own style, she doesn't copy anything. She doesn't say, "Oh, I want this camera movement from this movie, I want this light . . ." She's not interested in that. She's not a technical person. She cares more about emotion what the audience will feel. If you look at every movie she's done, they exist on their own but you can recognize that it's a Sofia Coppola movie. She's worked with a few different cinematographers, and we each have our own style, but in the end it's Sofia's movie.

Tess (Roman Polanski, 1979).

How do you keep that consistent Sofia mood across films as different as The Beguiled and On the Rocks?

It's the way she covers a scene, and how she goes through the emotions of a character. I would say she's a shy person, which is maybe not what you'd expect coming from an Italian family. Her emotions can be hidden almost. She's uncomfortable with too much emotion— you can see it when we shoot different scenes. For example, the scene in The Beguiled when Colin Farrell falls down the stairs and has to have his leg amputated, and the scene where

On the Rocks was filmed in New York City, which is a city that's been in so many movies. How did you go about shooting it in a way that felt fresh and interesting?

That was my main question, I would say. In a certain way, New York in *On the Rocks* is part of the story because of the way Sofia chose very iconic locations—probably because she wanted to show this traditional, old New York that has started to disappear. Century 21 has disappeared, I think they closed down because of the pandemic, which we all felt very sad about. So she wanted to capture that. As a foreigner, you look at someone like Andy Warhol and his work and you say, "Wow, how did this person in the seventies manage to capture the essence of New York?" And when you are in New York, it's a different city. There's a certain feeling about it that's very difficult to capture. New York was really integrated into the [*On the Rocks*] script, so I did a lot of research and sculpting by myself.

How did you shoot the car chase with Bill Murray? It's not the sort of scene you think of when you think of Sofia Coppola.

Sofia likes a challenge. The stunt in *The Beguiled*, for example, where Colin Farrell falls down the stairs, Sofia had never done a stunt like that before. She likes to set up challenges for herself in her movies. We looked at different car scenes together and I put together different references, so we had an idea of what we liked and what we didn't. In the end her brother Roman came to help and we storyboarded it. We also had New York to contend with, because you have to work with what the City of New York is willing to give you. "You want ten blocks? We're gonna give you four blocks." We shot it during the summer between 9 p.m. and 4 a.m. So it became a case of, "How many angles can we get in this amount of time?" Roman came up with the idea of using a biscuit rig, which is a Hollywood system where it feels like Bill is driving but somebody else is driving for him. For the tighter shots, we had three cameras locked to the car. It was certainly fun but very challenging to shoot on a car.

It sounds like it's very difficult to shoot in New York!

The best way would be handheld, no permit, because as soon as you ask for a permit suddenly you have restrictions. For *On the Rocks* I was looking at Agnès Varda's *Cléo from 5 to 7*. You can see her going around Paris and in the full shot she's in the middle of a crowd and you can see that they didn't have a permit. And the way she sees the city and discovers the city through the taxi, that was an inspiration. We had only one street block, so we were thinking, "How do we achieve the feeling of freedom?" That was challenging for sure. In London, the cars stop when you walk across the street, but in New York the people are all over the place, shouting "taxi!" crossing in the middle of the street, coming out of nowhere! It's very difficult to replicate that in a movie.

I wanted to ask about *The Beguiled* as well; the interiors are very reminiscent of *Barry Lyndon* and how Stanley Kubrick chose to shoot that film. I read an interview where you spoke about how candles actually would have been very scarce during the Civil War and they probably wouldn't have lit their whole house by candlelight because they couldn't afford it. Could you talk a little about the challenges of shooting that film?

It was a challenge because for starters we didn't have the same budget as *Barry Lyndon*—and I don't necessarily have the same talent! If you look at other period movies shot with candlelight, *Barry Lyndon* still has the best visual quality. I did a lot of tests—camera tests, film tests, lens tests—and we shot on film which is more difficult to shoot with than digital. I was thinking, "If Stanley Kubrick shot [*Barry Lyndon*] on film in the seventies, the sensitivity of the film stock was much much lower compared to what we had—I should be able to do it!" But it's also a dialogue with the director—you can do tests and all of that but you have to show the director and they have to agree with the direction you're going in. Sofia and I never had a disagreement about how to approach the movie because she gave me full trust.

Barry Lyndon (Stanley Kubrick, 1975).

The Beguiled was also shot in 1.66:1 ratio, which you don't see much anymore.

I know for a fact that Sofia doesn't like CinemaScope. She doesn't like to be too formal. At the same time, with the camera movement, with the coverage, she wants to tell a story with emotion without being over the top. CinemaScope in her head doesn't exist, because CinemaScope is a statement. I was thinking about 1.66:1 because I like the fact that when you shoot in a small location, and you put all these women together in a relatively small space, you can read their body language. Compared to 1.85:1, 1.66:1 catches more body language inside the frame. It's always about the hands and the body language.

Do you enjoy working with physical film stock in an industry where it is now quite a rarity?

I felt very lucky to be able to shoot on film. It's a completely different way of shooting: the rules; the way you organize. When you shoot on film, the time it takes to light a scene is completely different to digital. Sometimes you worry that you might have missed something, but you won't know until the next day. It's something mysterious and challenging—that's the beauty of film. Also, film has certain qualities: the skin tone, the depth of field. *The Beguiled* looks that way because we shot it on film. It would look completely different on digital. You can say, "Oh, but it's easier on digital to shoot with candlelight because there's more sensitivity," but shooting on film makes you challenge yourself, it makes you think differently. If I think back to the night scenes in *On the Rocks*, I did some tests between digital and film, and I found it was more interesting to keep shooting on film because the highlights—the darkness, the shadows—gave something different emotionally to the film. ☁

Nancy Steiner

Nancy Steiner is a legend of the costume design world, having worked with Todd Haynes, Yorgos Lanthimos, and David Lynch. She designed the costumes for *The Virgin Suicides* and *Lost In Translation*, and in the latter lent her (uncredited) voice to the role of Bob Harris's long-suffering wife Lydia.

You and Sofia met through the music video scene. What are your memories of that time?

Yeah, we were working out of the same production house, so I first met her in and around the office. I knew somebody she was going out with so we saw each other at social things, and when she started going out with Spike [Jonze], he was also working at the same production house. So we kind of became this little group of friends, going to dinners with them with Dayton/Faris, who are another directing team that I did *Little Miss Sunshine* with. They were friends of mine from a long, long time ago and so I worked with them doing videos for a long time, even in the late eighties and early nineties. We all just became friends and we would go and have dinner every few months at Musso and Frank's in Hollywood. Lance Acord, who was the DP on *Lost in Translation*, I knew before through my boyfriend; it was a smaller world back then. One night at Musso and Frank's Sofia said to me, "Oh my god, we just watched *Safe* and it's such a great movie and I can't believe you did the costumes. I've got a script, would you read it?" And I said, "Of course!" So that's how that came about.

Sofia is obviously so driven by music and the iconography of music videos—it's in the DNA of *The Virgin Suicides* and *Lost in Translation*. How much do you think your background working in music influenced your approach when it came to designing costumes in film?

Everything we do and how we grow up influences our taste and our aesthetic in a way. Music is hugely important to me. I grew up with music, my mom was a singer, but I'm not really sure how much the music videos I did influenced my work on those films. I approach each project on its own terms and whatever is in me I guess comes out in some way. For *The Virgin Suicides*, I was really just recreating my own childhood, because I grew up in the seventies, so I felt like I knew it like the back of my hand.

It just felt so natural to me, that movie. So it was less about the music videos and more just about my youth, recreating that era.

Were there already details about the costumes in the script?

I think the only thing that was really written in the script was that the youngest sister, Cecilia, was supposed to be wearing an old lace wedding dress and we decided that it would be from the thirties. Otherwise, it was really thinking about creating a vibe for each of the four Lisbon girls—Lux was the flirty, sexy one, so she wore crop-tops and had a more fitted style, then the other girls, one was a little more studious, one was a little more funky. . . . We tried to give them each their own personality in the clothes they wear throughout the film.

That really comes through even with something like the school uniforms—they all dress differently even within a more rigid environment.

Right, well, you know when you go to private school where you have to wear a uniform, everybody tries to personalize it, so it becomes their own thing and says something about who they are.

In the early stages of pre-production and production, what were the conversations between you and Sofia about?

It was more about backstory, the personalities of these girls and boys, and just trying to keep it real. She wanted it to be really anchored that way. That's the way I like to work, too. I'm very realistic. The parents, for example, are supposed to be very strict and . . . poor Kathleen [Turner] . . . what I put her in, it was just . . . she actually said,"These are the most awful clothes I've ever worn!" *[Laughs]* We wanted to make the parents look really stiff and rigid. And that's what polyester does—those polyester dresses from the seventies were just so awful-feeling, you know. I still don't understand how people wore some of that stuff.

I wanted to ask about your approach for the girls' prom dresses, because what they wear is so different from the prom dresses we usually associate with the seventies.

The story for me was that their mom made those dresses. She went to the fabric store and got one pattern and made four dresses from that pattern: one with puff sleeves; one with long sleeves; one with a bow; so it was like a unit. They were like a team, Team Lisbon! Finding that fabric was a godsend because it was the same floral pattern but four different colorways. Because Mrs. Lisbon wouldn't spend a lot of money on the fabric; maybe it was even on sale. So that was my whole philosophy behind those prom dresses.

They're almost like old-fashioned nightgowns, or wedding dresses—long, white, very femine gowns. There's a lot of symbolism in the costumes. The most obvious comparison for me is the John Everett Millais painting, *Ophelia*.

I think I even had that picture as a reference— not for the dresses but more as a mood. I just thought they would be floor-length, they would be covered up, and also those dresses were

SOFIA COPPOLA: FOREVER YOUNG

super fashionable at that time. I don't know if you know Gunne Sax, but they made these prairie dresses in that era. And then we found all these other references for the background, stuff that's a little more flashy, or a little more sexy, or a little more colorful. Mrs. Lisbon was making these dresses but she wasn't making them to be attractive, she was just making them to cover the girls.

On the opposite end of the scale you have Trip's suit . . .

Yeah, burgundy velvet. I brought that idea to Sofia and she loved it. I said, "He's gotta stand out, he's the stud," you know. He can't be in a polyester suit like everybody else. We didn't have much money [for the costumes] but that was an expense we had to have.

Were you surprised how much the fashion of *The Virgin Suicides* took on a life of its own? It's inspired Marc Jacobs and the whole aesthetic of the Daisy perfumes is kind of based around the film.

To be honest, I'm not particularly attuned to the whole fashion world. People tell me how iconic it is and how it's used as a reference in other movies. But no, I never even imagined that would happen. I think at the time it came out it just struck a chord with people in a way that we didn't expect. It was the same thing with *Lost in Translation*—I never imagined it would be so influential and so well received. When you work on a film, it's so hard to tell. Even now, the same thing happened with *Promising Young Woman*; I just had no idea.

In *Lost in Translation* the character of Charlotte is based partly on Sofia—did her own style come into play there?

Yeah, I think it definitely did. Sofia is so understated and kind of "classic" in that way, and I think we wanted Scarlett [Johansson] to also be like that. Scarlett was only seventeen, and I don't think she really knew anything about clothes back then. She didn't really have much style, let's put it that way. So I think she thought the clothes were really boring. *[Laughs]*

The early 2000s were a weird time for fashion. . . . The other fashion moment I love is when Bob is going to meet Charlotte and he's wearing that bright orange camouflage shirt, which he turns inside out. What's the story there?

Well, actually, that camouflage shirt was written into the script. That was Sofia's idea, like, he was just trying to be young and hip, and then he realized how stupid it was. I sourced that shirt from the States, I think. I got several sent over from an army surplus place because in Tokyo they didn't have a lot of clothing in Bill's size. Even getting a US size eight shoe for Scarlett was sometimes hard, because sizes are very small in Japan. I bought a shirt for myself that was like a men's large. Like, really? Way to make a girl feel good about herself! Yeah, it was difficult. But there was this one large and tall shop in a department store and that's where I got some of Bill's stuff. We got some Helmut Lang and we had Agnès B. . . . I think that's it. And Scarlett wore Lacoste: those wide-legged cream pants she wears.

I'm sure we're going to see people wearing very similar clothes in the next year or so. Y2K fashion is suddenly everywhere again.

It's so weird, every twenty-five years things come back. Everything's such a mishmash. It'll all come back and be recycled as something new.

When you're planning outfits, do you start by reading the script and then make mood boards? What's your method?

I'll read the script, of course. I like to talk to the director and try to get a bit of backstory on these people so that I can come up with an idea of how I think they would dress. Being a costume designer is like being a psychologist, because you're thinking about people's relationship with clothing. How much do they care about their clothes? I think about, "Would this person come home, get undressed and just leave their clothes on the floor, or would they hang them up?" We all buy clothes for a certain reason, maybe you're trying to disguise your body, or emphasize it. Some people don't really care that much. They'll just wear the same T-shirt and jeans, whatever. And then there are people who have to have the newest and the coolest. It's a mindset—it's how you feel about yourself. Some people want things, some people don't. Some people don't care if a pair of jeans are in fashion or not. They'll just wear whatever works for them. Me personally, I'm kind of like that. I've worked with a few directors that wear the same thing all the time; it frees up the mind to think about other things. I worked with Wim Wenders on a movie and he had three Issey Miyake suits and they were all falling apart. One at a time, each piece would come into my costumes/ custom department and we'd have to repair a pocket or a pant loop. But it just gave him this freedom. And that's David Lynch, too. Black suit, white shirt. It's classic, it works, so why change? ☁

Brian Reitzell

Brian Reitzell is a composer, musician, and music supervisor, who has worked on projects such as Bryan Fuller's *Hannibal*, Charlie Brooker's *Black Mirror*, and François Ozon's *Summer of '85*. He became friends with Sofia Coppola while drumming in the band Redd Kross, and has worked on four films with her: *The Virgin Suicides*, *Lost in Translation*, *Marie Antoinette*, and *The Bling Ring*.

Brian Reitzell's mixtapes from the production of *Lost in Translation*.

You and Sofia met when you were drumming with your band in Los Angeles. Did you first bond over music or movies?

I actually lived in her apartment for two weeks. She was doing press for *The Godfather Part III* and I had joined the band Redd Kross and she was dating the bass player and living with him. Their relationship didn't last that long, but I remained friends with her and her best friend Stephanie who is my wife. They were both nineteen, I was like twenty-three and we had lots of things in common. Before I moved here I was a chef in San Francisco and we used to cook dinners all the time and play records. This was before everything was streamable, so I had all these cool records, and we made good food and we just became good friends. I was still in the band when she asked me to work on *The Virgin Suicides*. She needed a music supervisor, but I don't think either of us really knew what a music supervisor was. It was only when we had a meeting with Mitchell Leib, who's head of music at Hollywood Records, that I understood. I thought I was the guy that just picked the music and gave Sofia some mixes, which is what I did back then. She needed seventies music because that's when the movie is set. Sofia is a little younger than me and I'm a little younger than her brother Roman, and his taste in music certainly rubbed off on Sofia—punk rock and new wave.

There are a few musical references in the book and some of those we put in the movie, but mostly we picked the music. That movie was very scene specific. So the Al Green track, that was completely in context, whereas the other movies I did with Sofia, *Lost in Translation* and *Marie Antoinette*, those were not made in the same way. With *The Virgin Suicides* we were finding our way, figuring out what to do, learning how to license and pay for music. Paul Thomas Anderson's movie *Boogie Nights* had come out around the same time. I worked with a music clearance person named Jill Meyers who did all of Sofia's movies with me. She'd tell me, "ELO is going for $80,000 a side for *Boogie Nights*." That's more than $150,000; our budget was half that for the entire movie. So we had to be really creative and figure out a way to get what Sofia needed. I think I was pretty good at that because I'd been in bands and I just thought that if we got to the artist, or if we showed them the movie, they would want their music used in this movie. In the end that's how it worked—but it was a long ride to get there.

Sofia was already interested in having Air score the movie, and I was introduced to those guys by Mike Mills, another would be film director who had done a music video for Air. When I met them they actually hired me to be in their band. So now here I was, going on tour with them while working as Sofia's music supervisor. Air had never scored a movie, Sofia had not done a feature film before, I had certainly not done a movie before, but we all grew up loving soundtracks and movies, so it was kind of natural. Sofia, kind of like her father, thought totally outside the box. She didn't want a film composer, she wanted that sound that Air had created on their *Premiers Symptômes* EP, which was before *Moon Safari* even. That's how much ahead of the curve Sofia was. Nobody knew who they were! I think she may have got that at Rough Trade in London.

Brian Reitzell's mixtapes from the production of *Marie Antoinette*.

Opera Mix no. 1

01. Aria from "Orphée et Eurydice" - Gluck (1774)
02. Air from "Iphigénie Aulide" (end of act 2) - Gluck (1773)
03. Aria from "Semele" - Handel (1774)
04. Aria from "Iphigénie en Tauride" - Gluck (1779)
05. Chœur from "Iphigénie Aulide" (finale) - Gluck (1773)
06. Aria from "Le Nozze di Figaro" - Mozart (1784)
07. Aria from "Paride ed Elena" - Gluck (1770)
08. Aria from "Semele" ("Endless Pleasure") - Handel (1744)
09. Aria from "Rodelinda" - Handel (1730's)
10. Aria from "Alexander Balus" - Handel (1748)

Marie Antoinette
Versaille Mix Master

The impact that *The Virgin Suicides* and *Lost in Translation* had on the way directors and musicians thought about scoring and soundtracking a film can still be felt today. And *Lost in Translation* fueled the shoegaze revival; Kevin Shields came out of the ether to work with you guys. He's someone who is notorious for being hard to track down. Elliott Smith was another mysterious figure. Do you think that you coming from that world was a factor in being able to convince these kinds of people that their work would be safe in your hands?

To this day Kevin is one of my best friends. He lives in Ireland but I was just facetiming him a little while ago. Everybody's different though. I try to be really respectful of the people that I approach to work with. In the case of Elliott Smith, that was Mike Mills's idea. I had met Elliott because I had worked with Beck and he was part of that crew. And we lived in the same neighbourhood so approaching him was pretty easy. He was the hardest guy to get anything done because he was just not in a good state. I mean, he died in the middle of us making that movie. The fact is I just respect people's work, I'm not pushy, and I learned that I could bring a musician in—whether it was Britt Daniel or Kevin Shields or Elliott Smith, or a whole band like Explosions in the Sky—and shield them from Hollywood. I could shield them from producers. Because the only bullshit involved here has to do with producers. Or if you happen to work with a director who's an asshole. I'm very careful about who I choose to work with because I don't wanna be pushed around and told what to do. Some musicians are really insecure about making their art fit with someone else's art. When I was working on *Marie Antoinette* I met Richard James [aka Aphex Twin] who is one of the most reclusive musicians around. He agreed to meet me in London one day, and the first thing he said to me was, "You're Brian? You don't look Hollywood. You look like you're European." You know, I played with Air for a while and I spent a lot of time in Europe. I think the fact that I wasn't a Hollywood guy, that may have played a role in it, too.

On *The Bling Ring* soundtrack you have Frank Ocean and Kanye West. I remember reading at the time that they were a little bit hesitant. How did you approach them about using those tracks?

Technically speaking that was the hardest movie to license. There's a song in the movie called "All of the Lights"—it's a Kanye song but it has like thirteen guest writers and each one is a huge star. Elton John, Alicia Keys, John Legend. . . . When you talk to Kanye he says "I'm not a songwriter." We knew that we wanted that song in the movie. He wasn't the easiest guy to communicate with but from day one he was very good to us. He told us about Frank Ocean. So I went to Frank and his managers were lovely people, but the label said Frank doesn't allow his music to be licensed for anything. This is before *Channel Orange* came out. Sofia and I had this song that we wanted to put in the movie for the end credits, and I invited Frank to a screening and he didn't come. He had a rocky show at Coachella. It was all happening. His career was maybe gonna take off or maybe not. So getting him into a screening room proved to be impossible. In the end Frank agreed to it and I believe that's the first time he ever agreed to license his music. We always try to license really good music.

The Jesus and Mary Chain.

The end of *Lost in Translation*, when the drums kick in on "Just Like Honey," that's gotta be up there.

That still gives me goosebumps. I had originally put that song in a different part of the movie but Sofia thought it was perfect for the end. That record has a lot of meaning to me. When I was younger my band opened for the Jesus and Mary Chain. The fact that that song would become not a hit again, but would do so much for that band, it's a beautiful thing. I didn't see it but Scarlett [Johansson] went and sang with them at Coachella. That just makes me really happy. When the Jesus and Mary Chain came out I was just a teenager, and to me they were the coolest guys in the world. The other thing that has always been important to me is I would never use a song that I thought had been used in another film. In *Lost in Translation* one of the songs we wanted to use in karaoke was "Angie" by the Rolling Stones, because our friend

Charlie Brown—the guy that sings "God Save the Queen"—used to always sing Angie. His pronunciation of Angie was like "algae," it was just the funniest yet most heartfelt karaoke song. At that time it was a big deal to license a Rolling Stones song, but because Sofia's so charming and I could get to the right people, we were able to make it work. For *Marie Antoinette* we finally had some money, so I was actually in France for most of it, as everyone was. Everybody was listening to these two mixes that I made, which was cool because I think everybody understood from the beginning that we weren't doing a Merchant-Ivory type period piece, we were doing something that had an atmosphere that was much more along the lines of Sofia's style.

There's so much music in *Marie Antoinette*, it's almost constant. You can imagine a teenage queen would listen to that soundtrack, and being a teenage girl she would stop a song halfway through and start something else. It's not only perfect song choices—the way it's mixed and matched throughout the film really captures the way teenage girls listen to music.

That's all Sofia for sure. I'm just giving her mixes, she's actually putting them in the movie. That movie though does have many layers to it because there's a lot of period music that's spot on. I recorded orchestras in France and here in the Bay Area. Then there's contemporary music like the Strokes and the Radio Dept., Windsor for the Derby, these indie bands that were almost unknown. When we did *Marie Antoinette* I went to Stockholm to meet with the Radio Dept., which is a band that I had discovered, but you couldn't buy their records in the US. What I would do is, I would always go record shopping when I went to different countries because the distribution is not like it is now. Now you can get anything, anytime, anywhere. Back then you had to physically go to different countries to buy records. In doing so, and meeting that band there, I got other records from bands that would later become pretty famous like The Knife. Sweden has been fueling pop music in the US, and probably in the UK, for a while now.

Robyn as well. I went to university in Germany and I remember her first album was everywhere.

And before Robyn there was a girl named Annie. They're both electronic-y, dance-y, or whatever. One thing I would say that's interesting working with Sofia is that you'll notice there's not a lot of female singers. Siouxsie Sioux was one that is a classic, but there's not a lot of female singer songwriters in her movies. I didn't work on *Somewhere* but the Gwen Stefani track very much came from Elle Fanning. Sofia is very good at the teenage girl mentality though. That permeates everything that she does. I hope that doesn't go away.

The main one that sticks out to me is "212" by Azealia Banks in *The Bling Ring*, which I seem to recall Sofia saying was Emma Watson's contribution.

That's not true! She may have put it in the movie because of Emma but the real credit for that song would come from the record company. Because I was dealing with hip-hop, I went straight to Interscope and said, "What emerging artists do you have?" So they turned me on to

goes into every single thing. I was talking with Sarah Flack about the *All That Jazz* Vivaldi sequence in *Marie Antoinette*—the effort that must have been exerted in bringing that together is crazy.

we wanted because what we were doing was Bob Fosse doing Vivaldi. We were playing it faster, we were doing it differently. The most stress I ever had on any of these movies was dealing with the French orchestra that was involved in *Marie Antoinette*. It's interesting because now I'm working on this period piece about House de Medici and the filmmakers love *Marie Antoinette* and that Vivaldi stuff and Sofia's idea to make it like Bob Fosse, to show the habits of the court. I watch shows now and it's like, they totally did that thing that Sofia did. That makes you feel old but it also makes you feel pretty proud. I think *Bridgerton* has classical covers of contemporary artists.

Yeah, Taylor Swift done with an orchestra.

Right, exactly. We did that in *Marie Antoinette* with the intro to "Hong Kong Garden." I tried using covers of New Order songs that were done by orchestras and I didn't really care for much of it, which is why we did our own piece. Sofia blasted that at the Opera Garnier in Paris when they were acting. That's probably the only time rock music has ever been played at the Opera Garnier in Paris.

You also worked with Daniel Lopatin (aka Oneohtrix Point Never) on *The Bling Ring* and he's gone on to do scores with the Safdie brothers. They very much remind me of Sofia in a way because they're out there doing their own thing.

I'll tell you something that's really funny. Dan did a couple of things with me. He and I were totally aligned. When I worked on *The Bling Ring* we were trying to get The Weeknd to sing a song for us. At the time he only had this mixtape out but Dan thought he'd be the perfect guy to sing on a song that we were gonna do. We contacted him and his manager said "No, he's too messed up. Now's a really bad time." Fast forward to today, Dan has been working with The Weeknd as his musical guy for the last couple of years—he even did the Super Bowl with him. That connection

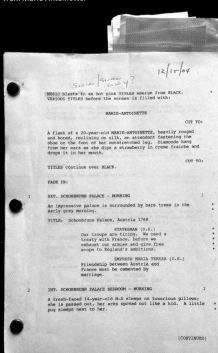

Brian Reitzell's shooting script from *Marie Antoinette*.

came up because of *The Bling Ring*. Dan's actually moving out here so I'm gonna get to spend more time with him. He's a wonderful guy.

I interviewed him for *Uncut Gems* and he was delightful, although he did say that doing that score has been very stressful.

He got put into a weird position. With *The Bling Ring*, honestly, he just came in over the course of two days and played on a couple of things. Though there is forty minutes of score in *The Bling Ring*. You wouldn't know because most of it is just atmosphere, but it's a very heavily scored movie. You'd have to literally watch it with the dialogue off to hear most of it.

I love "The Bling Ring Suite" . . .

We only had one track we could put on the record so we made a suite. I always do that, but when you do that you're killing yourself because you're only gonna get paid for one track when you're giving them three or four. Whatever works. The way we did *Lost in Translation* and *Marie Antoinette* was that Sofia made a little book and I made a mix CD—if you look at the book of *Lost in Translation* and you put on the CD, the movie's there. Even though there's no Scarlett Johansson or Bill Murray, the photographs that she collected and the music, it's all there. *Lost in Translation* only ever had two mix CDs, about twenty songs. They're almost all in the movie. And Sofia's photos, she would have [cinematographer] Lance [Acord] do those shots. It's amazing. I know a lot of people who work this way but with Sofia there's not ten thousand images, there's like twenty-five of them. Same with the music. It's just the right amount for what we needed to get across.

I think that's one of her strong suits, making that collage. There's something about her research in the beginning. I haven't worked with her for a while. We were about to work together before COVID happened. It was something that was gonna be shot in Italy, a commercial for Chanel or some company like that. I was excited to make another mix for Sofia. I haven't really done it since *The Bling Ring*. She knows where to find me though. Every once in a while I'll email her or she'll email me. Recently she told me she had just shown her daughter Romy *Marie Antoinette* and she was just saying how much Romy loved it; how great the music was and how proud Sofia was of the music. I think that's gotta be her best looking movie. I absolutely adore it. Milena [Canonero]'s costumes in that movie were just un-freaking-believable! That was a fun movie. Such a blast. ☁

L-R: Robert Smith, Sofia, and Brian Reitzell on the set of *Marie Antoinette*.

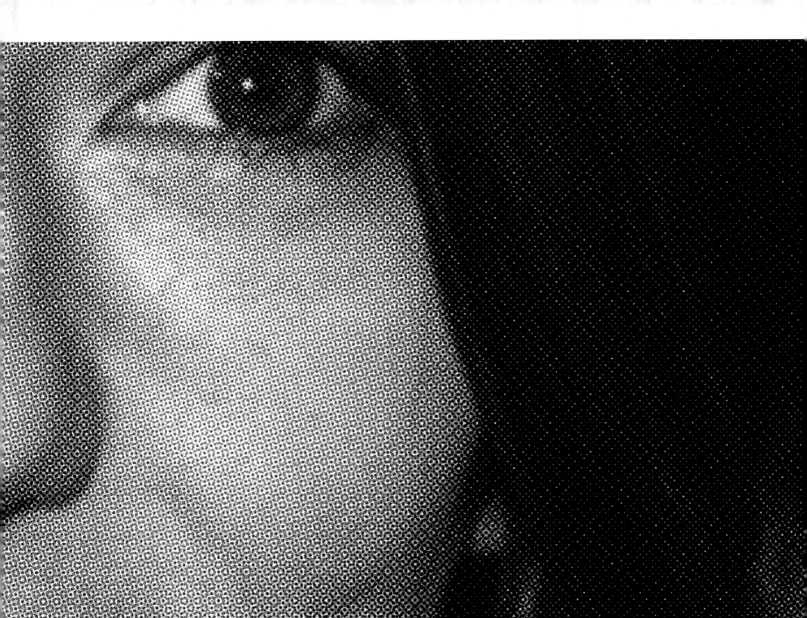

Afterword

"THE MORE YOU know who you are, and what you want, the less you let things upset you," Bob tells Charlotte in *Lost in Translation*, as she reflects on her doubts about her marriage and the existential dread of not knowing what to do with her life. This moment of tenderness is a quiet respite from the overwhelming world the pair exist in—not just the physical sensory overload of Tokyo, but the pressures of day-to-day life, where adulthood comes with the expectation that we all decide fairly sharpish who we are and what we want out of life.

I always believed that my life would be easier when I grew up. If I could just survive high school and fend off the desire to annihilate myself at any given opportunity, I would age out of anxiety and awkwardness, learn how to budget, find a good job, and somehow become a woman of the world, elegant and poised and wise. It didn't quite go like that, and the years since I left home have been a process of learning and unlearning, having my heart broken, clawing at my skin and standing on the proverbial edge, daring myself to jump. I could blame Hollywood for peddling the unrealistic expectation that closing the door on adolescence means an end to melancholy, but who doesn't want to dream—even in some small part—that brighter days are just around the corner?

Throughout the process of writing this book, I have thought long and hard about what brings me back to Sofia Coppola over and over again. I find myself listening to "Playground Love" on overcast afternoons; I daydream about the quiet hallways of the Chateau Marmont and the Tokyo Grand Hyatt. There's an obvious aesthetic attraction, and Sofia's work has influenced everything from a raft of recent television shows (including *Bridgerton*, *The Great*, and *Dickinson*) to

fashion designs from Anna Sui and Louis Vuitton. But beauty alone can't guarantee staying power. Of course, it helps that I discovered her films when I truly needed to feel connected to the world, but Sofia wasn't the only voice I turned to when I was younger, yet her presence is the most enduring in my life.

For me, it's the profound sense of truth about Sofia's work that resonates most of all. Amid the beautiful interiors and gorgeous gowns, she continually manages to capture something honest about the world around us, from the stifling loneliness of the teenage girl to the precarious nature of romantic relationships. She displays an interest in the idea of "work in progress," be it Charlotte's identity crisis or Bob's waning interest in the world around him. Though her characters might not always have the words to say how they feel, they do feel, and their joy, sadness, embarrassment, and anger are captured with an intimacy that forges a real relationship between audience and actor.

For all the beauty and opulence that features in her work, Sofia is a realist. Her films are rooted in emotion and connection, rendered with love and artistry. The scene in Sofia's work I think about most often comes at the close of *Somewhere*; almost a mirror image of its opening sequence. Johnny Marco, after dropping his daughter off at summer camp, leaves the Chateau Marmont and drives his car through the desert. Eventually, he pulls to the side of the road, gets out of his vehicle, and begins to walk away, an unreadable expression on his face. It's her most ambiguous ending (even more so than what Bill Murray whispered to Scarlett Johansson in *Lost in Translation*) but hints at the possibility of radical change, at the possibility that Johnny finally knows who he is, and what he wants. His mental disconnect

from the world around him is finally remedied by a physical disconnect: by taking control of his life. Sofia's protagonists are frequently unmoored from the world and the people around them. *Somewhere* strikes me as her happiest film for this very reason—it demonstrates a clear belief in the possibility of growth and change.

I've grown (and changed) so much since I watched *The Virgin Suicides* for the first time and fell in love with the worlds Sofia Coppola creates. I've made my peace with never quite looking like the beautiful protagonists of her films, or having the financial acumen to lounge around the suites at the Chateau Marmont or the Tokyo Grand Hyatt. These are the fantastical elements of her work for me, the magical, unreal settings and set-pieces. I appreciate them, but they aren't the heart of what makes Sofia's work special to me. For that, I look to the depiction of human loneliness and desire, her ability to say so much without a single word exchanged. I'm still a hopelessly fragile creature, and I'm not sure I entirely know who I am or what I want out of life, but I know when I find it, Sofia Coppola's films will have played no small part in getting me there. ☁

Sofia's director's chair, *Marie Antoinette*.
Palace of Versailles, 2005.

Production Details

Release Date	19 May 1999 Cannes Film Festival
	21 April 2000
Production Company	American Zoetrope
	Eternity Pictures
	Muse Productions
Cast	Kirsten Dunst
	Josh Hartnett
	James Woods
	Kathleen Turner
	A.J. Cook
	Hanna Hall
	Leslie Hayman
	Chelse Swain
Director	Sofia Coppola
Writer	Sofia Coppola Screenplay
	Jeffrey Eugenides Novel
Producers	Willi Bär Exec.
	Francis Ford Coppola
	Julie Costanzo
	Fred Fuchs Exec.
	Dan Halsted
	Chris Hanley
Composer	Air
Cinematography	Edward Lachman
Editing	Melissa Kent
	James Lyons
Costume Design	Nancy Steiner
Casting	John Buchan
	Robert McGee
	Howard Meltzer
	Linda Phillips-Palo
Production Design	Jasna Stefanovic

THE BEGUILED

Release Date	24 May 2017 Cannes Film Festival
	23 June 2017
Production Company	American Zoetrope
	FR Productions
Distributor	Focus Features
Cast	Nicole Kidman
	Kirsten Dunst
	Elle Fanning
	Colin Farrell
Director	Sofia Coppola
Writer	Sofia Coppola
	Thomas Cullinan Novel
Producers	Roman Coppola
	Sofia Coppola Produced by
	Youree Henley Produced by
	Robert Ortiz Exec.
	Fred Roos Exec.
	Anne Ross Exec.
Composer	Phoenix
Cinematography	Philippe Le Sourd
Editing	Sarah Flack
Costume Design	Stacey Battat
Casting	Courtney Bright
	Nicole Daniels
Production Design	Anne Ross

MARIE ANTOINETTE ♛

Release Date	24 May 2006 Cannes Film Festival
	13 October 2006
Production Company	Columbia Pictures Presents
	Pricel In association with
	Tohokushinsha Film
	Corporation In association with
	American Zoetrope Production
	Commission du Film France
	Commission du
	Film Île-de-France With the support of
Distributor	Columbia Pictures
Cast	Kirsten Dunst
	Jason Schwartzman
	Rip Torn
	Steve Coogan
	Asia Argento
	Marianne Faithfull
Writer & Director	Sofia Coppola
Producers	Sofia Coppola
	Francis Ford Coppola Exec.
	Ross Katz
	Paul Rassam Exec.
	Fred Roos Exec.
Composer	Dustin O'Halloran
Music Supervisor	Brian Reitzell
Cinematography	Lance Acord
Editing	Sarah Flack
Costume Design	Milena Canonero
Casting	Antoinette Boulat
	Karen Lindsay-Stewart
Production Design	K.K. Barrett

THE BLING RING ♦

Release Date	16 May 2013 Cannes Film Festival
	14 June 2013
Production Company	American Zoetrope
	FilmNation Entertainment
	NALA Films
	Pathé Distribution In association with
	StudioCanal In association with
	TOBIS Film In association with
	Tohokushinsha
	Film Corporation In association with
Distributor	A24
Cast	Emma Watson
	Israel Broussard
	Katie Chang
	Taissa Farmiga
	Leslie Bibb
Director	Sofia Coppola
Writer	Sofia Coppola
	Nancy Jo Sales
Producers	Francis Ford Coppola Exec.
	Roman Coppola
	Sofia Coppola
	Emilio Diez Barroso Exec.
	Youree Henley
	Darlene Caamano Loquet Exec.
	Paul Rassam Exec.
	Fred Roos Exec.
	Michael Zakin Exec.
Music Supervisor	Brian Reitzell
Cinematography	Christopher Blauvelt
	Harris Savides
Editing	Sarah Flack
Costume Design	Stacey Battat
Casting	Courtney Bright Courtney Sheinin
	Nicole Daniels
Production Design	Anne Ross

SOMEWHERE ★

Release Date	3 September 2010 Venice Film Festival
	22 December 2010
Production Company	Focus Features Presents
	Pathé Distribution In association with
	Medusa Film In association with
	Tohokushinsha
	Film Corporation In association with
	American Zoetrope
Distributor	Focus Features
Cast	Stephen Dorff
	Elle Fanning
	Chris Pontius
	Kristina Shannon
	Karissa Shannon
Writer & Director	Sofia Coppola
Producers	Michele Anzalone Exec.
	G. Mac Brown
	Francis Ford Coppola Exec.
	Roman Coppola
	Sofia Coppola
	Paul Rassam Exec.
	Fred Roos Exec.
	Roberta Senesi Exec.
Composer	Phoenix
Cinematography	Harris Savides
Editing	Sarah Flack
Costume Design	Stacey Battat
Casting	Courtney Bright
	Nicole Daniels
Production Design	Anne Ross

A VERY MURRAY CHRISTMAS ☰

Release Date	4 December 2015
Production Company	American Zoetrope
	South Beach Productions
	Departed Productions
	Jax Media
	Casey Patterson
	Entertainment
Distributor	Netflix
Cast	Bill Murray
	Paul Shaffer
	George Clooney
	Miley Cyrus
	Rashida Jones
	Jason Schwartzman
	Chris Rock
	Maya Rudolph
	Michael Cera
Director	Sofia Coppola
Writer	Sofia Coppola
	Mitch Glazer
	Bill Murray
Producers	Sarah Bowen Exec.
	Lilly Burns
	Roman Coppola Exec.
	Sofia Coppola Exec.
	Pauline Fischer Exec.
	Mitch Glazer Exec.
	Tony Hernandez Exec.
	Kelsie Kiley Exec.
	Bill Murray Exec.
	Ted Sarandos Exec.
	John Skidmore
	John Tanzer
Cinematography	John Tanzer
Editing	Sarah Flack
Costume Design	Stacey Battat
Casting	Jeffrey Lindgren
Production Design	Anne Ross

ON THE ROCKS ◉

Release Date	22 September 2020 NY Film Festival
	2 October 2020
Production Company	A24
	American Zoetrope
Distributor	A24
	Apple Original Films
Cast	Bill Murray
	Rashida Jones
	Marlon Wayans
	Jessica Henwick
	Jenny Slate
Writer & Director	Sofia Coppola
Producers	Roman Coppola Exec.
	Sofia Coppola Produced by / p.g.a.
	Mitch Glazer Exec.
	Youree Henley Produced by / p.g.a.
	Fred Roos Exec.
Composer	Phoenix
Cinematography	Philippe Le Sourd
Editing	Sarah Flack
Costume Design	Stacey Battat
Casting	Courtney Bright
	Nicole Daniels
	Allison Hall
Production Design	Anne Ross

LOST IN TRANSLATION ▯

Release Date	29 August 2003 Telluride Film Festival
	3 October 2003
Production Company	Focus Features Presents
	Tohokushinsha Film
	Corporation In association with
	American Zoetrope
	Elemental Films
Distributor	Focus Features
Cast	Bill Murray
	Scarlett Johansson
	Giovanni Ribisi
	Anna Faris
Writer & Director	Sofia Coppola
Producers	Francis Ford Coppola Exec.
	Sofia Coppola
	Ross Katz
	Fred Roos Exec.
Composer	Kevin Shields
Music Supervisor	Brian Reitzell
Cinematography	Lance Acord
Editing	Sarah Flack
Costume Design	Nancy Steiner
Production Design	K.K. Barrett
	Anne Ross

Acknowledgments

FROM THE AUTHOR

I'VE ALWAYS HEARD it takes a village to raise a child, and as this book is my baby, it seems only right to thank the many, many people that have helped bring her into the world. I owe my undying thanks to my editor and colleague, Adam Woodward, for sending countless emails on my behalf and whipping my copy into shape, as well as providing assurance I wasn't fucking everything up. Thanks also to Clive Wilson for believing in me long before we started work on this project, Marina Ashioti for her excellent transcription and bibliography work, and the infinitely talented Tertia Nash for her mind-blowing creativity and hard graft in designing this gorgeous book. Also at *Little White Lies*: huge thanks to David Jenkins for support both in writing this and in my general life, and for teaching me the correct use of an em-dash and ellipsis.

At Abrams, thanks to Meredith Clark for overseeing the project, and in Sofia Coppola's camp, thanks to Bumble Ward for supporting us from the start and connecting me to so many wonderful people. I'm particularly grateful to Jean-Benoît Dunckel, Kirsten Dunst, Sarah Flack, Philippe Le Sourd, Brian Reitzell, and Nancy Steiner for providing me with such amazing insight into working with Sofia—and to Brian and Philippe for digging out never-before-seen material from their archives for us to include. A special thanks also to artist Andrew Durham, who generously allowed us to feature some of his gorgeous set photography in the book. It has been my privilege to have had truly wonderful conversations with these artists and to glimpse into the extended creative family Sofia has created.

I extend my love and gratitude to my esteemed, patient, endlessly sweet colleagues Mark Asch, Charles Bramesco, Isaac Feldberg, and Madeline Whittle who gave up their time and energy to read portions of this book and provided detailed, thoughtful feedback. The best of their number, I feel truly blessed to call them my pals. A special shout out to my good friend Ella Kemp, who has given me feedback, cooked me dinner, and took the beautiful portrait of me for the back page. You're the Kirsten to my Sofia.

To other friends who have supported me along the way: the Sheffield Gals, the Bozo Bois, the TIFF group chat, Ingrid, Laura E, Sophie Mo, Sophie Monks Kaufman, and Beth. Your support and cheerleading made this a hell of a lot easier. Thanks × infinity.

And perhaps the biggest thanks of all: to my family, who have gamely indulged my love of movies for as long as I can remember despite having very little interest in the art form themselves. Grandma, who has been my archivist and biggest fan since I was writing parody movie scripts at the tender age of eight; Grandpa who introduced me to the computer which started it all. Jack and Elle, who are different from me in every way but graciously allow me to be the Cool Sibling. Mum, for keeping me alive long enough to realize I had something worth saying, and always at least pretending to be interested when I try to explain films to you. Also our horde of cats, but especially Margot, who contributed nothing in the way of feedback but everything in the way of morale-boosting.

Finally: thank you to Sofia Coppola, for making the films that I love so much, and for caring so deeply about the agony and the ecstasy of being a teenage girl. ❤

FROM THE EDITOR

IN THE SUMMER before she joined David Jenkins and I on the *Little White Lies* editorial team, Hannah Strong wrote a couple of articles for our website, including one entitled "What Sofia Coppola's films taught me about being a teenage girl." In it, she spoke with great insight, clarity and candour about her affinity with the Lisbon sisters, and how Coppola's unsugarcoated depiction of young womanhood resonated with her: "When I found Coppola, I found meaning in my misery." Hannah's writing possesses that rare quality of always feeling like an invitation rather than a one-way conversation, even when she's describing something as intimate and personal as being a teenage girl. I've learned more from her in the three years we've been working together than she probably realizes, and I'm immensely proud to call her my colleague and friend.

Huge thanks to two TCO legends: Tertia Nash, whose design skills are second only to her positivity and good humour; and Clive Wilson, a consummate pro who is as sagacious and sharp-minded as they come. Of all the books we've copublished, I think this one really raises the bar. A special mention must go to Eric Klopfer, Meredith Clark, and the whole Abrams family, with whom we've formed a close and fruitful creative bond over the past few years. Long may it continue. Thanks also to Alice Rohrwacher for providing such a beautiful foreword, and to her producer, Giulia Moretti, for connecting us. Lastly, thank you to Alex Wade, Bumble Ward, Megan Senior at Slate PR, Alexandra Amin at UTA, Nicki Bergman at ICM, Christine Russell at Evolution, Sophie Newman at Grand Musique Management, Marina Ashioti for tirelessly transcribing all the interviews, and Alex Comana for the ace translation job. ❤

Image Credits

Author Image	Ella Kemp
Cover Image	Creative Commons Postcard Sky by 'Playingwithbrushes'
Endpapers	Sophie Douala
Collage Artist	Alice Isaac
Icons	GT Alpina, Tertia Nash
Typefaces	Fortescue, Post Grotesk

Every effort has been made to identify copyright holders and obtain their permission for the use of copyrighted material. The publisher apologizes for any errors or omissions and would be grateful if notified of any corrections that should be incorporated in future reprints or editions of this book.

Index

Bibliography

Alexander, Ella. "Sofia Coppola Made Karl Lagerfeld's Coffee." *Vogue*, June 2013.

Atwood, Margaret. *Words: Selected Critical Prose, 1960-1982*. Toronto: Anansi, 2000.

Bachor, Kenneth. "A Very Murray Christmas Director Sofia Coppola: I Wanted To Do Something 'Joyful.'" *Time*, December 2015.

Bastién, Angelica Jade. "How *The Beguiled* Subtly Tackles Race Even When You Don't See It." *Vulture*, July 2017.

Bell, Keaton. "Sofia Coppola on Dressing Her Characters, Working With Her Husband, and Why We Need a Love Letter to New York Right Now." *Vogue*, October 2020.

Bland, Simon. "'I never expected people to connect with it so much' – Sofia Coppola on *Lost in Translation* at 15." *Little White Lies*, August 2018.

Bloom, Andrew. "*Groundhog Day* at 25: Bill Murray Finds Freedom While Trapped in a Nightmare." *Consequence*, February 2018.

Brubach, Holly. "The unashamedly feminine filmmaking of Sofia Coppola," *The Gentlewoman*, Spring & Summer 2017.

"Cool and the Gang," *Sight & Sound*, January 2003.

Cooper, Sarah and Ashley Young. "PopRally Exclusive: Sofia Coppola on Directing Phoenix's 'Chloroform' Video." *MoMa | INSIDE/OUT*, November 2013.

Coppola, Eleanor. "Making of 'The Virgin Suicides'" (1999). *The Virgin Suicides* Blu-Ray, 2018, Criterion Collection Edition.

Coppola, Eleanor. *Notes on a Life*. New York: Knopf Doubleday Publishing Group, 2008. p. 118, 173, 237.

Coppola, Eleanor. "The Making of 'Marie Antoinette'" (2007). *Marie Antoinette* DVD, 2007 Sony Pictures Home Entertainment.

Coppola, Sofia. "In redoing 'The Beguiled,' Sofia Coppola had to erase the camp but heighten the gender power struggle." *Los Angeles Times*, December 2017.

Coppola, Sofia. "Sofia Coppola on making *The Virgin Suicides*: 'When I saw the rough cut I thought: Oh no, what have I done?'" *Guardian*, January 2020.

Coppola, Sofia. "Sofia Coppola Responds to 'The Beguiled' Backlash — Exclusive." *IndieWire*, July 2017.

Coyle, Jake. "For 'The Beguiled,' Coppola turns again to Dunst and Fanning." *AP News*, May 2017.

Cullinan, Thomas. 2017. *The Beguiled*. 5th ed. London: Penguin Publishing Group. (First published 1966, Horizon Press, USA).

Cuttle, Jade. "Rereading: Dangerous Liaisons by Pierre Choderlos de Laclos review — the sex lives of the French aristocracy." *The Times*, November 2020.

Day, Kiku. "Totally lost in translation." *The Guardian*, January 2004.

De Graaf, John, Thomas Naylor, David Wann. *Affluenza: The All-Consuming Epidemic*. Oakland: Berrett-Koehler Publishers, 2001.

Ebert, Roger. *Pretty in Pink*. Roger Ebert, October 2006.

Ebiri, Bilge. "In Conversation: Francis Ford Coppola." *Vulture*, December 2020.

Ebiri, Bilge. "The Sofia Coppola Touch." *Village Voice*, June 2017.

FilmIsNow Movie Bloopers & Extras. "The Beguiled | On-set visit with Colin Farrell 'John McBurney.'" *YouTube*, June 2017.

Five Things With Lynn Hirschberg. 2020. Sofia Coppola. [online] Available at: https://open.spotify.com.

Fleming Jr, Mike. "Sofia Coppola To Helm 'The Little Mermaid.'" *Deadline*, March 2014.

Foo Fighters. "The Colour and the Shape: Dave Grohl's Guide to Every Song." *FooArchive*.

Fraser, Antonia. "Sofia's Choice." *Vanity Fair*, October 2006.

Freddie Mercury Interview, *NME*, February 11, 1974.

Fumudoh, Ziwe. "ZIWE INTERVIEWS ALEXIS HAINES (NEIERS) TRANSCRIPT." *Generation Ziwe*, July 2020.

"Funny Or Die - Sofia Coppola's Little Mermaid." *YouTube*, May 2014.

Gilchrist, Todd. "Interview: Sofia Coppola." *IGN*, May 2012

Ginsberg, Merle. "Launching Sofia," *W* magazine, January 1994.

Harada, Yasuhisa, Tomiuri Shinbun, quoted in "A Sampling of Japanese Comment on 'Lost in Translation.'" *UCLA Center for Chinese Studies*, June 11, 2004.

Hatcher-Mays, Meagan. "How Sofia Coppola Whitewashed The Bling Ring." *Jezebel*, June 2013.

Hattersley, Giles. "'We Didn't Know We Were Making A Period Movie': Behind The Scenes Of 'On The Rocks' With Sofia Coppola.'" *Vogue*, October 2020.

Herbert, Ian. "Libelled or a libertine? New research debunks Coppola view of Marie Antoinette." *Independent*, September 2011.

Hirschberg, Lynn. "The Coppola Smart Mob," *New York Times* magazine, August 2003.

Hohenadel, Kristin. "French Royalty as Seen by Hollywood Royalty." *New York Times*, September 2006.

Hughes, Howard. *Aim for the Heart: The Films of Clint Eastwood*. London and New York: I.B.Tauris & Co Ltd, 2009. p. 99.

Itzkoff, Dave. "How Francis Ford Coppola Got Pulled Back In to Make 'The Godfather, Coda.'" *New York Times*, December 2020.

Itzkoff, Dave. "Sofia Coppola's Muse? Bill Murray, of Course." *New York Times*, December 2015

"Jeffrey Eugenides's First Time," *Paris Review*, April 16, 2016.

Kael, Pauline. "Vanity, Vanities," *The New Yorker*, January 1991.

Kang, Inkoo. Lost In Translation Is An Insufferable, Racist Mess — Why Would We Expect The Beguiled To Be Any Different? MTV, June 2017.

Kaufman, Sophie Monks. "Sofia Coppola: 'I'm telling the same story but from the women's point of view.'" *Little White Lies*, May 2017.

Kohn, Eric. "Sofia Coppola on the Identity Crisis That Led Her to Make 'On the Rocks' with Bill Murray." *IndieWire*, October 2020.

Leon, Humberto. "Sofia Coppola 'Somewhere' Interview." *Anyonegirl*, December 2010.

Levy, Shawn. *The Castle on Sunset: Life, Death, Love, Art, and Scandal at Hollywood's Chateau Marmont*. London: Orion, 2019. p. 306, 307.

Lim, Dennis. "It's What She Knows: The Luxe Life." *New York Times*, December 2010.

Longworth, Karina. "Film director Sofia Coppola's journey to 'Somewhere.'" *SF Weekly*, December 2010.

Madison III, Ira. "Sofia Coppola's 'The Beguiled' Controversy and What We Expect From White Directors." *Daily Beast*, August 2020.

Marche, Stephen. "The Scene That Made Mike Nichols's Career." *Esquire*, November 2014.

McGilligan, Patrick. *Clint: The Life and Legend*. London: HarperCollins Publishers, 2000.

Miller, Julie. "How Miley Cyrus and George Clooney Saved Bill Murray's Netflix Special *A Very Murray Christmas*." *Vanity Fair*, December 2015.

Mojica, Frank. "Cinema Sounds: *Lost in Translation*." *Consequence*, May 2010.

Morrow, Fiona. "Sofia Coppola: Hollywood princess." *Independent*, January 2004.

Mottram, James. "Sofia Coppola: My feminist retelling of 'The Beguiled' may 'flip' the male fantasy – but it's no castration wish." *Independent*, July 2017.

Myers, Owen. "Jeffrey Eugenides' virgin suicides." *Dazed Digital*, August 2013.

Nelson, Steffie. "Coppola, Mars make music together." *Variety*, November 2010.

Nolfi, Joey. "Sofia Coppola says dad's spirit lives in Bill Murray's *On the Rocks* character." *Entertainment Weekly*, October 2020.

Nolfi, Joey. "Sofia Coppola: Studio was 'afraid' of girls watching *The Virgin Suicides*." *Entertainment Weekly*, April 2018.

O'Hagan, Sean. "Sofia Coppola." *Guardian*, October 2006.

Olsen, Mark. "How Sofia Coppola and Rashida Jones put their own family lives into 'On the Rocks.'" *Los Angeles Times*, September 2020.

Parker, Jerry. "Checking in Among the Stars," *Newsday*, August 1979.

Prince, Richard. "Sofia Coppola," *Interview* magazine, June 2013.

Rickey, Carrie. "Lost and Found," *DGA Quarterly* magazine, Spring 2013.

Rosenbaum, S.I. "When Every Day Is 'Groundhog Day.'" *Vulture*, April 2017.

Sales, Nancy Jo. "The Suspects Wore Louboutins," *Vanity Fair*, March 2010.

Sarris, Andrew. *You Ain't Heard Nothin' Yet: The American Talking Film, History & Memory, 1927–1949*. New York: Oxford University Press, 1998.

Satenstein, Liana. "Sofia Coppola and Zoe Cassavetes Look Back on Their Cult '90s It Girl Show." *Vogue*, May 2020.

Setoodeh, Ramin. "Kirsten Dunst and Sofia Coppola on Hollywood Sexism, Their Feminist 'Beguiled' Remake." *Variety*, May 2017.

Sollosi, Mary. "The Beguiled: Sofia Coppola on how she made the remake her own." *Entertainment Weekly*, June 2017.

Stern, Marlow. "Sofia Coppola Discusses 'Lost in Translation' on Its 10th Anniversary." *Daily Beast*, July 2017.

Stevens, Dana. "Queen Bees." *Slate*, October 2006.

Thompson, Anne. "Tokyo Story." *Filmmaker*, Fall 2003.

Travers, Ben. "Sofia Coppola on Directing 'The Fantasy Version' of Bill Murray in Netflix's 'A Very Murray Christmas.'" *IndieWire*, December 2015.

"Death in the family," *Guardian*, April 2000.

Somewhere: About The Production. Focus Features, August 2010.

Urbanek, Sydney. "Notes on Marie Antoinette, or: the MTV Sensibilities of Sofia Coppola." *Bright Wall/Dark Room*, February 2021.

The Virgin Suicides: Looking Back. Criterion Collection, 2018.

Wise, Damon. "How Stephen Dorff's journey down the dumper made him perfect for Sofia Coppola's new film." *Guardian*, December 2020.

Yule, Andrew. *Al Pacino: A Life on the Wire*. New York: Little Brown, 1991. p. 293.

FOR LITTLE WHITE LIES
Editor Adam Woodward
Art Director/Designer Tertia Nash
Head of Books Clive Wilson
Publisher Vince Medeiros

FOR ABRAMS
Editor Meredith Clark
Managing Editor Mike Richards
Design Manager Heesang Lee
Production Manager Denise LaCongo

ABOUT THE AUTHOR
Hannah Strong is a film critic and writer.
She is the Associate Editor at *Little White
Lies* magazine and has written about films
for the *BBC*, *Guardian*, *GQ*, *Vulture*, and
Dazed & Confused, among other publications.
Originally from Sheffield, she currently lives
in London with her cat, Margot.

—

Library of Congress Control Number: 2021946856

ISBN: 978-1-4197-5552-1
eISBN: 978-1-64700-363-0

Text copyright © 2022 Hannah Strong and Little White Lies
Illustrations copyright © 2022 TCO

Cover © 2022 Abrams

Printed and bound in the United States
10 9 8 7 6 5 4 3 2 1

Abrams books are available at special discounts when purchased in quantity for
premiums and promotions as well as fundraising or educational use. Special editions
can also be created to specification. For details, contact specialsales@abramsbooks.com
or the address below.

Abrams® is a registered trademark of Harry N. Abrams, Inc.

 **ABRAMS** The Art of Books
abramsbooks.com

195 Broadway
New York, NY 10007
abramsbooks.com